UNDERSTANDING OUR FELLOW PILGRIMS

Compiled by
**The Sub-Committee for Inter-Religious Dialogue
Goa Archdiocesan JKL 2000 Committee**

Edited by
Gregory Naik, S.J.

2000
Gujarat Sahitya Prakash
P. Box 70
Anand
Gujarat 388 001

ISBN   81-87886-10-2

Published by X. Diaz del Rio, S.J., Gujarat Sahitya Prakash,
                    P. Box 70, Anand, Gujarat 388 001, India.
Laser-set and printed by S. Abril, S.J., Anand Press,
                    P. Box 95, Gamdi, Anand 388 001, India.

UNDERSTANDING
OUR FELLOW PILGRIMS

We believe that...

In the past God spoke to our ancestors many times and in many ways through the prophets, but in these last days He has spoken through His Son. He is the one through whom God created the universe, the one whom God has chosen to possess all things at the end. He reflects the brightness of God's glory and is the exact likeness of God's own being, sustaining the universe with his powerful word. After achieving forgiveness for the sins of all human beings, he sat down in heaven at the right hand of God, the Supreme Power. (Hebrews, 1/1-3)

The sacred *Gäyatrï* Mahamantra:

AUM, Bhoor Bhuvah Swah!
Tat Savitur varennyam
bhargo devasya dhïmahi
dhiyo yo nah!

O Supreme Lord,
the Source of Existence, Intelligence and Bliss!
We meditate on the lovely light of the Sun;
May it stimulate our thoughts!

(RgVeda, III, lxii, 10)

A Note on A-U-M

A-U-M (sometimes written as OM) is a sound-symbol of the Indian tradition. It is equivalent to the Greek letters A (alpha) and Ù (omega) of the book of Revelations in the Bible. (Rev. 1/8) According to *Mändükya Upanishad*, "the syllable 'AUM' is the whole universe. Whatsoever has existed, whatsoever exists, and whatsoever shall exist hereafter, is AUM; and whatsoever transcends past, present, and future, that also is AUM." And according to *Prashna Upanishad*, the **A** stands for the Rigveda and comprises the world of men, the earth; the **U** stands for the Yajurveda and comprises the world of the moon, the atmosphere; and **M** stands for the Samaveda and refers to the Purusha, the Supreme Being. (See V, 1-7). Logically, therefore, it stands for the Supreme Being.

TABLE OF CONTENTS

Part III: Worship and Rituals

Part IV: Other Religions

Part V: Suggestions
Appendix:

FOREWORD

The mission of the Church in the world requires that she adopts a dialogal attitude: a Church of dialogue, that presents herself not only as someone who gives, but also as someone who receives, a Church that not only speaks and teaches, but also listens and learns; a dialogal Church that recognizes sincerely that she is not the exclusive depository of truth, that opens herself respectfully to the dignity and the autonomy of every human person, of every historical situation, of every cultural context, in order to discover the values which are present and to propose the evangelical Word.

The theological foundation of this dialogal approach is to be found in the "Christic" dimension of the entire creation and in the cosmic dimension of the Incarnation. It leads the Church to take the world as a serious partner in the dialogue of salvation.

This dialogal approach calls for a serene relation with persons, situations, and cultures. It is in the context of such a dialogal relation that the Church is called to proclaim the Word and to give a living testimony to it, thus allowing the Word to release its transforming power with regard to persons, situations, and cultures. This type of dialogue may well lead the Church into a process of discovery, in which she herself may discover something about the Gospel, which she did not know, a process in which both the partners in the dialogue may find themselves transformed.

Such a vision of a dialogal Church comes across quite strongly in the documents of Vatican II. In *Gaudiumet Spes*, the Council begins by expressing the solidarity and the respect of the Church for the whole human family, with which she wants to engage herself in conversation, as a partner in the dialogue, about the various problems that concern the entire mankind (cf. G.S., No.3). Towards the end of the same Pastoral Constitution, the Council indicates the link between the ecclesial mission and the dialogue: "By virtue of her mission to shed on the whole world the radiance of the Gospel message, and to unify under one Spirit all men of whatever nation, race or culture, the Church stands forth as a sign of that brotherliness which allows honest dialogue and invigorates it" (G.S., No.92).

The Vatican Council emphasized particularly the need for the Church to adopt a genuine dialogal attitude with regard to the followers of other religions; "The Catholic Church rejects nothing which is true and holy in these religions. She looks with sincere respect upon those ways of conduct and of life, those rules and teachings which, though differing in many particulars from what she holds and sets forth, nevertheless often reflect a ray of that Truth which enlightens all men. She therefore has this exhortation for her sons: prudently and lovingly, through dialogue and collaboration with the followers of other religions, and in witness of Christian faith and life, acknowledge, preserve, and promote the spiritual and moral goods found among these men, as well as the values in their society and culture" (N.A., No.2).

During his 1986 visit to India, Pope John Paul II underlined the importance of inter-religious dialogue in his address to the leaders of other Religions: "Dialogue between members of different religions increases and deepens mutual respect and paves the way for relationships that are crucial in solving the problems of human suffering. Dialogue that is respectful and open to the opinions of others can promote union and a commitment to this noble cause. Besides, the experience of dialogue gives a sense of solidarity and courage for overcoming barriers and difficulties in the task of nation building."

The dialogal attitude of the Church must lead her to engage herself in sincere inter-religious collaboration in various spheres of life, as Pope John Paul II highlighted explicitly during his speech, given in New Delhi in 1986, to the representatives of religious, cultural, social, economic and political life of India: "To work for the attainment and preservation of all human rights, including the basic right to worship God according to the dictates of an upright conscience and to profess that faith externally, must become ever more a subject of inter-religious collaboration at all levels. This interreligious collaboration must also be concerned with the struggle to eliminate hunger, poverty, ignorance, persecution, discrimination, and every form of enslavement of the human spirit. Religion is the mainspring of society's commitment to justice and interreligious collaboration must reaffirm this in practice".

The Post-Synodal Apostolic Exhortation of the Special Assembly for Asia of the Synod of Bishops, *Ecclesia in Asia*, dwells extensively on Interreligious Dialogue (No. 31). While speaking of the need for a dialogue of life and heart it offers a very relevant advice to all the disciples of Christ about the manner in which such a dialogue is to be promoted: "The followers of Christ must have the gentle and humble heart of their Master, never proud, never condescending as they meet their partners in dialogue (cf. Mt 1:29). Inter-religious relations are best developed in a context of openness to other believers, a willingness to listen and the desire to respect and understand others in their differences. For all this, love of others is indispensable. This should result in collaboration, harmony and mutual enrichment" (E.A., No.31).

It gives me special joy to present this book — Understanding our Fellow Pilgrims — which has been compiled by our JKJ 2000 Sub Committee for Inter-Religious Dialogue, through the painstaking efforts of its Convenor, Fr Gregory Naik, S.J. It is my earnest wish and prayer that this publication may contribute significantly to enhance such a meaningful dialogue of life and heart, enabling all of us, as co-pilgrims, to join hands in our common mission of building a better India and a better world in the New Millennium.

+ *Filipe Neri Ferrão*

(✝ Filipe Neri Ferrao)
Auxiliary Bishop of Goa and Daman

INTRODUCTION

Communal harmony is presently the greatest need of our country and a keen desire of so many interested in its welfare. There is, however, a great difference between "communal harmony" and "peaceful co-existence" as it exists in Goa and in many other parts of our country. For true communal harmony it is essential that members of one community come to know and appreciate what makes the members of another community what they are — in some ways different from themselves.

Here we are concerned mainly with inter-religious harmony, as we believe that such harmony is essential not only for the personal wellbeing of individuals and communities, but also for carrying out the common mission that we all have — Christians, Hindus, Moslems, etc.: to build a "better India".

The Mission of Christians

As followers of Jesus Christ we have a mission. The Goa Diocesan Pastoral Plan says that it is to contribute towards the building of the Kingdom of God. "The Kingdom of God" is a very rich and mysterious concept, but may be expressed, as it has been done in some Church documents, as the "New Society". In fact, the motto of the national celebration of Jezu Krist Jayanti 2000 is TOWARDS A NEW SOCIETY.

What we call "the Kingdom of God" seems to approximate the Hindu concept of "Ramarajya" or the "Golden Age" of some Hindu sects. Hence the task of establishing the "Kingdom of God", the "New Society" is not a monopoly of Christians. Pope John Paul II, in his encyclical letter *"Redemptoris Missio"*, asserts that "the Kingdom is the concern of everyone: individuals, society, and the world" (N.15); and so, as part of the celebration of the Great Jubilee 2000 in Goa, we are called upon "to work, in solidarity with others, for the establishment of a New Society, the Kingdom of God."

A Call to Dialogue

This is a mighty task: to build a New Society, a society where there is wholesome progress and a just distribution of its benefits among all, where there is honesty, justice, love and peace; and no single community can hope to achieve it unless all — Christians, Hindus, Moslems, Sikhs... — work hand in hand, and not just side by side. There is a long road to traverse and on it we are all fellow pilgrims.

Sitting side by side, as we do in a theatre or in a doctor's waiting-room, and even walking side by side, as we do on our way to school or office, may be easy, but not so joining hands. This requires that we come to know each other, and that we respect and accept each other with our differences. How much do we know the members of other religions? Not just their names, qualifications, and family background, but the principles and values they live by, and the customs and practices that mark the significant moments and stages of their lives.

We Catholics have come a long way since we thought as did St Francis Xavier and the people of his time, that all who were not baptised went to hell, or that Hindus worshipped devils in their temples. But do not some of us still think that all Hindus are idol worshippers, that their God is different from ours, that "prasad" is like Holy Communion, that the "tikka" on a woman's forehead is a purely religious symbol, that Hanuman was really a monkey that was divinised?... Ignorance leads to suspicion and prejudice, and prejudice to mutual contempt. And people harbouring suspicion, prejudices, and contempt, can never join hands for anything worthwhile, much less to usher in a New Society!

The remedy suggested by the Church is "inter-religious dialogue".

This means, first of all, reaching out to members of other religions in understanding, respect, love, and service; it means sharing joys and sorrows, concerns and endeavour; it means listening to their faith experiences and being ready to tell them ours; it means even occasionally lifting up our hands together to the one God, Father of us all, in praise and thanksgiving, repentance and supplication.

In some of its documents, the Church has spelt out four categories of inter-religious dialogue: dialogue of life (trying to relate to the non-Christians by visiting them, through social celebrations, etc.; dialogue of action (by joining hands in some service activity); dialogue of shared experience (by sharing experiences of how religion helps to cope with life problems, etc.); and dialogue of theological reflection (by experts from various religions sharing their theological insights and reflections.)

When Pope Paul VI came to Bombay in 1964 he declared in a speech to religious leaders: "Yours is a land of ancient culture, the cradle of great religions, the home of a nation that has sought God with a relentless desire in deep meditation and silence, and in hymns of fervent prayer." And he added, "We must come together with our hearts, in mutual understanding, esteem and love... In this mutual understanding and friendship, in this sacred communion, we must also begin to work together to build the common future of the human race."

More recently, when Pope John Paul II came to India in 1986, he announced at Delhi Airport: "My purpose of coming to India... my sincere interest in all the religions of India — [is] an interest marked by genuine respect, by attention to what we have in common, by a desire to promote inter-religious dialogue and fruitful collaboration with people of different faiths." And on the following day he told the bishops, "Inter-religious dialogue is a serious part of your apostolic ministry. The Lord calls you...to do everything possible to promote this dialogue according to the commitment of the Church... As ministers of the Gospel here in India, you have the task of expressing the Church's respect and esteem for all your brethren and for the spiritual, moral, and cultural values enshrined in their different religious traditions... The dialogue you are called to is one of courteous respect, meekness, and trust, from which all rivalry and polemics are excluded. It is a dialogue that springs from faith and is conducted in humble love."

Here is an invitation and a challenge for us, the Church of Jesus Christ in India, to walk hand in hand. We already admit that religion does not prevent us from visiting our sick Hindu neighbours, from caring for their children, from helping in time of need. We often do this already. On the foundation of this closeness, we need to build up our deep interest in their religions and in their social customs, attend not only their marriages but also their funerals, sit together to reflect on the common problems of the neighbourhood and be ready to undertake joint action. Then we shall be really walking not side by side but hand in hand.

This book is a humble contribution of the Goa Archdiocesan Committee for JEZU KRIST JOIONTI 2000 to enlighten the Catholics about the religious beliefs and practices that give meaning and strength to their "fellow pilgrims" to be what they are and to do what they do. Most of the material was prepared by the members of the Sub-Committee for Inter-Religious Dialogue and some of their friends. The material was published earlier in a series of booklets, and is now put together, after some revision, in one handy volume that could serve as a reference book.

In presenting the material we claim neither scholarship nor originality, because the writers themselves are not

xvi

scholars or experts, barring three or four whose names are mentioned at the beginning of their respective contributions. However, they are very interested in sharing with their fellow Christians, sometimes verbatim, what they have read in books available to them. A list of such books has been given at the end.

Here I would like to express my personal gratitude to the following who were members of the Sub-Committee and/or contributed one or two articles each: Frs Theodore Pereira OFM (Cap.), John Pereira SFX, Aleixo de Menezes, Cosme J. Costa SFX, Bismark Dias SSS, Noel Sheth SJ, Apolinaris Pinto SJ, Sr Alba PBVM, Mr Curcinho Pinho; also to Fr Almir de Souza and Fr Leonard Pegado, Chairman and Secretary respectively of the Committee for JEZU KRIST JOIONTI 2000. Finally, a word of sincere thanks to Ms Maureen Pereira who patiently typed innumerable pages of manuscripts both for the present book and for the earlier booklets.

It is our fond hope that a better knowledge of the religious beliefs, traditions, and customs, of our fellow pilgrims, the members of other religions, will help to enhance the good neighbourly relations that already exist among us and raise them to the level of genuine "communal harmony". Thus we shall be able to join hands in creating a better India and a better world for the future.

Gregory Naik, S.J.
Editor and Convenor of
the Sub-Committee for
Inter-Religious Dialogue

A Note on:

CULTURE, FAITH, AND RELIGION
— Theodore Pereira, OFM (Cap.)

At the origin of every religion, there is an ineffable God-experience of an individual or community, that evokes a faith-response. Though inexpressible by its very nature, the experience is too overwhelming to be kept secret. Therefore, the individual or the community that underwent the experience seeks to articulate it in ideas and symbols, and to communicate it through beliefs (creed), behaviours (code), and rituals (cult). Thus, the original faith experience evolves into "religion".

This articulation and communication of the original faith-experience takes place in a concrete cultural context of ideas and expressions, values and behaviours, that necessarily reflect the environment in which the individuals and communities exist — Indian, Chinese, Tibetan, Greek, Roman... That explains how the experiences of the one and same God even by Abraham, Moses, Isaiah and Jesus led to different expressions of religion. That also explains why God who has no physical body was presented as male and referred to as He in the Jewish patriarchal society, in which father (*abba*) was considered more caring and nurturing than a mother (cf. Isaiah 49,15), but as female in the Indian society where those characteristics are even now attributed to the mother and God is often referred to as Mata or Devi.

Considerations of such cultural differences are extremely important for the understanding of many of the differences that exist even among the major religions of the world and much more so for inter-religious dialogue. We begin then to realise that comparative religious experiences are often articulated and communicated through language, art, and ethics, that may be baffling to individuals and communities belonging to a totally different culture. Mutual respect and appreciation will be the fruit of such an exercise.

A Note on:

HOW HINDUISM CAME TO MEAN A RELIGION

'HINDU' in The New Oxford Illustrated Dictionary is defined as a person who practises 'Hinduism' which is defined as a 'religious and social system' characterized by 'belief in reincarnation, worship of several gods, and caste as basis of society'. This definition of 'Hindu' embodies the change that came about during the period of colonial rule.

In Alberuni's *Kitab al-Hind*, 'Hindus' stand vaguely equated with 'Indians'. About three centuries later, Amir Khusrau, in the early 14th century, equates 'Hindu' with Hindustan whose people are described as Hindustanis. However, these are classified as Muslims and Hindus. Therefore, his 'Hindu' stands equated with 'non-Muslim Indian'.

Though the criterion of this distinction is religion, the connotation of 'Hindu' is still that of a people (not a religion).

In the *Babur Nama* too, the Hindustanis are both Hindus and Muslims of Hindustan, which covers nearly the whole of the subcontinent. This remained the connotation of 'Hindu' in the *Ain-i-Akbari* of Abu al-Fazl.

Guru Nanak makes only a few references to Hindus in the entire range of his compositions which otherwise contain numerous references to what would be called Hinduism today; but his Hindus are also the non-Muslim peoples of Hindustan. The author of the *Dabistan-Mazahab* written in the 1640s, refers in fact to 'religions of the Hindus' (*adadin-i-hunud*) in the plural.

Even the European writers of the 18th century talk of the literature, mythology, arts and sciences of the Hindus, and equate them with the indigenous non-Muslim peoples of India.

2

The term 'Hinduism' began to be used by the Christian missionaries for the Brahmanical systems of religious belief and practice. They lumped together the Vaishnavas, the Shaivas, and the Shaktas. But they did not know how to categorise either the Buddhists, Jains, or the Sikhs.

Furthermore, the Christian missionaries denounced 'Hinduism' as a monolithic whole, imposing conceptual unity on a plural empirical reality. The defenders of indigenous faiths against this onslaught began to defend not Vaishnavism or Shaivism, or any other distinct system of Indian belief and practice, but 'Hinduism' in general.

It came to be assumed rather unquestioningly that there was a time in the history of the country when all its people subscribed to a single system or religious belief and practice, and that this system was 'Hinduism'. A secular topographical identity was thus transformed into religious identity, leading in due course to the conception of a monolithic Hindu community.

PART I
HINDU RELIGION

PART I

HINDU RELIGION

HINDUISM

As Understood by a Modern Hindu

Swami Agnivesh

(This is an extract from an article published in COMMUNALISM COMBAT (No. 36, Sept. 1997) under the title "What kind of a God will condemn a 'heathen' child to eternal Hell", written by Swami Agnivesh, an unconventional Swami, better known for his work among bonded labourers and other oppressed classes. It is reprinted here with the permission of the publishers.)

Spelling out the Hindu view of a multi-religious society is certainly not an easy task because within Hinduism there are innumerable paths, philosophies, sects, systems — some of them highly sectarian. Of them, some are open and tolerant, some highly philosophical, while others are plainly fanatical.

Dharma, meaning eternal righteousness, rule of law, ethical conduct, etc., flows from the lofty ideals and principles set in the Vedas. Hinduism has no founder or prophet but there are common grounds which most Hindus can accept.

One of them is that the purpose of religion is to take the individual through a gradual process to a higher and higher, or deeper and deeper awareness, ending finally in liberation of the soul from all bondage.

Religion should also create the necessary environment

7

to support such a lofty pursuit. We Hindus believe that the Creator is in everything there is and Her/His divinity is the innermost core of every man and woman. Through the illusory veil of ignorance about the self and our attachment to ego we are unable to realize our oneness with God.

Innumerable paths have been developed by our sages and yogis, but they can be generally divided into four major groups:

* *Bhakti Yoga*, the path of devotion;
* *Karma Yoga*, the path of selfless service;
* *Jñana Yoga*, the path of inquiring reflection; and,
* *Raj Yoga*, the royal path of meditation.

Each one of these specific ways to God has countless sub-divisions, cross-sections, and syntheses. Regrettably, not one individual follows any one of the yogas in its purest form. All paths will lead — as the Bhagavadgita, the most popular and revered scripture among Hindus says — eventually to the realization of God.

We have been enjoined that by ceaseless introspection, each of us should discern which is the path which is best suited to us at that moment or in that stage of development. The responsibility is placed on each of us to discern our *swadharma*. The task of the *guru* or teacher is to lead us to discern that *swadharma*. To facilitate this approach to the Divine Self within man, our ancient seers introduced the concept of *Varna Ashram Dharma*.

Varna, derived from the root *vri* — to choose. Varna generally gives each individual his/her place in society, with corresponding rights and duties. Varna cannot be passed onto the children. Our scriptures are clear that by our nature and by our specific activity or profession we belonged to a given varna.

The yardstick for judging one's varna is *guna* (abilities), *karma* (action) and *swabhava* (aptitude). In the scriptures it says: "At birth we are all *shudras*, but by our action and qualification we become twice-born."

Life was also divided into four major stages under the *ashram* system: the first part of one's life is to be devoted to study; the second to be lived as a householder, having a family, enjoying wealth and all the material and psychological properties (*dharma, artha, kāma*); the third stage is meant for retirement and reflection; and the fourth is to be lived in complete renunciation from all worldly desires and attachments, living a life of spiritual practice and service to God and humanity.

The much-maligned *Varna Ashram Dharma* is a revolutionary concept of socio-spiritual engineering. While the caste system is based on birth which breeds inequality and immobility, *varna* (derived from vri, to choose) negates any status, social or economic, based on birth. In fact, it militates against the very institution of private property and private ownership of means of production.

At the same time it discounts staticism. Its a beautiful concept but unfortunately has fallen into the hands of people who have given it a bad name. It is very difficult though not impossible, to retrieve and resurrect it. Everything in Hinduism, be it the question of how to rule the country or that of the Tantric sexual union, has ultimately only one final aim that: God or self-realization.

Hindus look at everything in terms of involution and evolution, an eternal coming and going represented by the Trinity of Matter, Soul, and God — *Traitavada*. Hinduism contains the widest spectrum of religious thoughts and practices, from the most primitive idol worship and sacrifices to the highest, and the most profound techniques of meditation.

Hindus are normally guided by a teacher whose sole duty is to lead the seeker to the divine God within him. Since we believe that all humans are on different evolutionary levels of spiritual awareness; we also accept the fact that there are different teachings, paths, techniques, methods, to reach the final goal.

As we believe in an evolutionary process of the soul (which is supposed to be identical with God), we move from lower to higher, in a cycle of numerous lives, taking birth according to our *karma*, or the sum total of our previous acts and deeds.

In each life we draw closer and closer to God to reach final liberation, which can be experienced, according to our sages, here and now, in this very life. In the close proximity of the individual soul (*Atman*) with the Universal Soul (*Paramatman*), we finally realize that we have always been with God, though having fallen to the illusion of separateness due to clinging to our ego and illusionary individuality.

Our scriptures say there is nothing but Brahman — God — who is all-pervasive, all-embracing and all-containing. The total surrender to this Ultimate Reality and living one's own *svadharma* (given duties) without the sense of "I am the doer" is the highest purpose of life.

All religions, rooted in Hindustan, be it Buddhism, Jainism or Sikhism, and a multitude of smaller sects, believe in the Law of Karma. This law has been distorted and even perverted to justify social, economic, and gender disparity/discrimination. The Law of Karma means that the soul or the individual re-incarnates on this earth till it finally dissolves in *Moksha* — liberation.

All spiritual schools coming out of the Indian soil believe that each individual must work out his own salvation, by continuous spiritual, mental, and physical purification till the grace of God is manifest.

For a Hindu it is unthinkable that there is only one true Saviour or one last Prophet and that whosoever does not

10

believe in his message or gospel will be condemned to eternal hell-fire. For us, the Grace of God is always present and we find it incomprehensible and philosophically unacceptable that an all-loving and all-powerful God condemns his own creation, his own children into an eternal abyss. We believe that God, the Self within us, seeks itself, or in classical Vedantic parlance, The Self seeks itself through the self.

A Hindu can accept the idea that there are innumerable paths and ways to God. He has no problems whatsoever in accepting different names for the Ultimate Reality, be it called Brahman, Allah, Tao, Jehovah, or whatever, since he knows that the Ultimate is beyond name and forms.

With such a religious outlook, it is transparently clear why a Hindu has no difficulty in entering into a dialogue with other religions, so long as they drop their exclusiveness in any system, since each one only represents a part and never the whole, which contains all. With such an all-embracing view it is easy to see why Hinduism has no missionary command.

As we can see from this short but necessary introduction, there are fundamental differences between prophetic religions and religions having their roots in Indian soil. We are facing a situation where some religions on one side have a missionary command and a moral obligation rescuing others from the world of Satan, and on the other side with religious systems which believe in pluralism and a multitude of approaches to God. In the East, religion is an inner process of Yoga and no book or holy revelation is taken as absolutely authoritative and above one's innermost experience.

"The scriptures lead beyond scriptures", declare the Upanishads. Though human in origin, an exposition of truth is to be accepted. If otherwise, even what is regarded as divine revelation is to be rejected. "Even a young boy's words are to be accepted if they are words of wisdom; else

11

reject them like straw, even if uttered by Brahma, the Creator", says Vashishta.

I have no intention to praise Hinduism in this article; I am fully aware that our shortcomings are too plentiful, particularly on the social level. I will gladly admit that we also have some Hindu fundamentalists who consider Sanatan Dharma as absolutely unique and above other systems of self inquiry and spiritual realization, but this view is not common.

The dreadful situation that India finds itself in is mainly due to a totally disinterested and alienated elite, due to a corrupted priestcraft and the consequential inferiority complex which is due to a thousands of years of exploitation and suppression.

In recent times, Hinduism has never had a real chance to reform itself and bring out the timeless universal ideals because the slightest genuine spiritual movement among the Hindus is immediately being branded by the minority communities as Hindu-chauvinism, Hindu backlash or fundamentalism. We are basically victims of our own tolerant philosophical outlook.

THE BASIC BELIEFS
OF HINDUISM

Original Hinduism, which is among the oldest of the world's religions, was based on the teachings of the Vedas, which Hindus believe were eternally with the Supreme Being and were at a particular time revealed to the sages. The original name of Hinduism was, therefore, "*Vaidika Dharma*" (the Vedic Rule of Conduct) or "*Sanatana Dharma*" (the Eternal Rule of Conduct). "Hindus" were the people residing in the Indus region. It was the British in the nineteenth century that gave to that word a religious connotation and called "Hindus" those who were neither Christians, nor Moslems, nor Parsees, nor Buddhists. (At one time, even Sikhs, Jains, and Tribals, were counted among the "Hindus".)

→ Genuine Hinduism is not merely the acceptance of certain academic abstractions or the performance of some rituals. It is an experience of reality, an <u>insight</u> into the nature of reality — a way of life (literal meaning of dharma).

a. God in Hinduism

Hinduism, unlike some other religions, has no well--defined doctrines, or a uniform way of worship, or one particular god whom all Hindus worship. In Hinduism each individual is free to follow his own pattern of worship, and choose his own god. Due to this doctrinal tolerance and individual freedom, in Hinduism we see different forms of creed, worship and gods. In principle, Hinduism welcomes all forms of belief and worship; one is not forced to select

13

any one particular god and leave the others aside. A Hindu, for example, may "believe" in Jesus, want to follow his teachings, but without ceasing to be a Hindu.

Some of the Hindu Sages, who seemed to have reached the mystical heights of union, describe God in an impersonal way. In the Upanishads, God is said to be someone we cannot describe because the human mind cannot comprehend or know God. They call this God *'Brahman'*, the beginning and the end of all that is. Everything that we see in this world is a manifestation of this divine reality. Thus, they attribute different names to their God or Brahman, viz.: "Brahman is without a second"; "The Supreme Brahman is *'nirguna'*" (free from all determinations or attributes); "Brahman is *Sat, Chit, Ananda*" (Reality, Intelligence, Bliss); "Brahman is the origin, the life, and the goal of all being", i.e., "the One wherefrom we spring, by whom we breathe, to whom we shall return".

This type of understanding of God is possible for the intellectuals and the spiritually attuned, who have reached the heights of mysticism. But the common people find it hard to relate to God in this way. So, they conceive God in a personal way, as *'Trimurti'*, for example. This personal way of understanding God makes them feel comfortable in their worship and devotion. Though each individual sees God in his/her own way, the various names and representations which appear strange to us who are unfamiliar with their culture, are only different descriptions or manifestations of the one Ultimate Divine Reality whom some call God, others Yahweh and others still Allah.

The *'Trimurti'* — Brahma, Vishnu, and Shiva — are considered by the educated to be different manifestations of Brahman. Ordinary Hindus, however, who worship either Vishnu or Shiva, as their "favourite God" (*Ishtadevata*), consider them as separate individuals, the other two being subordinate to their respective Ishtadevata. The third member of the Trimurti, Brahma, the personification of the

14

creative aspect of the impersonal Brahman, remains usually in the background and is rarely worshipped.

Hindus generally are not concerned about how many gods there are or how many one may worship, or what kind of dogma or creed one may follow. Rather they are concerned about the importance these gods hold in an individual's life, i.e., how they help an individual in his/her search for meaning in life. (See chapter Four of this section for more details.)

b. Relationship between God and Man

Hindus believe that God created the world of his own <u>free will</u>. There are different accounts of this creation in Hindu Scriptures. (See Rig Veda, X, 121; *Atharva Veda*, X, 2; *Brihadarannyaka Upanishad*, I, 2 and 4). Man is eternally dependent on God and, while living in this world, has to promote this relationship between God and himself. It is variously through Devotion (*Bhakti*), Knowledge (*Jñana*), or Action (*Karma*), that man gives himself completely to God. God in return showers his grace upon man as he surrenders himself to Him.

c. God-Experience

God-experience is a very important reality in the interaction between God and man. Such an experience cannot be "proved". One has to have faith. Hindu asceticism aims at facilitating God-experience, for it is only after having such a deep and intimate experience of God, that man begins to live as a true human person. This religious experience builds in man a complete trust and confidence in God and the God-experienced man remains calm and patient in all situations of life.

d. The World

Hinduism believes that the world has a beginning and a final end. God manifests the world and, in some way, God

15

is also not separate from the world. Hinduism holds the view that all the beings in this world and not only the human, are real manifestations of God. This world is not static. It is always proceeding towards a final end, after many cycles of re-creation, deterioration, and destruction. This teleological tendency will ultimately reach a state where the entire creation will be "spiritualised", i.e., become one with Brahman.

e. Karma

Hinduism believes in the doctrine of 'karma'. This means that the karmas (actions) performed by an individual in this life will determine his future. The theory of karma says that, instead of throwing the blame on others for what you are, you should consider yourself responsible for your present state. Our future state in life would be likewise dependent on the present actions we perform.

The law of karma comes into being (1) as a punishment for evil deeds committed in the past, and (2) as a means of correcting or reforming the individual. According to the law of karma people undergo rebirth when their actions are not in accordance with the scriptures.

f. Doctrine of Re-birth

The doctrine of re-birth is a corollary to the law of karma. The differences in dispositions found in one individual and another even at birth are due to their respective past karmas; and past karma implies past birth. Similarly, we notice that all our actions do not bear fruit in this life. Hence, there must be another birth for enjoying the residual karmas. As a person casts off worn-out garments to put on others that are new, so does the soul cast off worn-out bodies to enter into others that are new. Each soul has a series of births and deaths. This migration of the soul into a series of bodies is called 'samsara' or wheel of existence. It goes on till the cycle of karma is broken and the soul attains Final Release (Moksha)

16

in its realisation of God. Till then, the soul is subject to the law of births and deaths.

g. Scriptures

The *'Shruti'* and *'Smriti'* literature constitute the authoritative religious sources of Hinduism. Of these, **'Shruti'** holds the primary place and is authorless. 'Shruti' literally means 'what is heard; The great rishis of old are said to have 'heard' the eternal truths of religion and to have passed them on to others for their benefit. These records are called Vedas. There are four Vedas: the Rigveda, the Yajurveda, the Samaveda, and the Atharva Veda. Each Veda consists of three parts, namely: Samhita, Brahmana, Arannyaka, and Upanishad. Of these, the Upanishads are the most important since they are the philosophical-spiritual reflections of the ancient sages. They form the foundations of Hinduism. Next in importance to the *Shruti* is the *Smriti* literature. The corpus of **Smriti** literature derives its authority from the Shruti, because its objective is to expand and exemplify the principles of Veda. The Smriti literature consists of:

1) *Smritis* or codes of law
2) *Itihasas* or epics
3) *Puranas* or chronicles and legends
4) *Agamas* or manuals of worship
5) *Darsanas* or schools of philosophy
(See next Chapter for details)

h. Rituals

Hinduism lays great stress on the correct performance of rites *'Kriya'*. The Hindu rituals are of two kinds: Vedic and Agamic. The Vedic rituals are of the nature of sacrifices to cosmic gods. The Agamic rites are mainly connected with the worship of gods present in idols. The mantras (prayer formulas) are to be used in sacrifices. The section of the scriptures called 'Brahmanas' explains how they are to be

17

used. The whole body of scriptures dealing with the religious ceremonials and practices of Hinduism is referred to by the term "*Kalpa*" which means 'usage'. '*Kalpa-Sutra*' is the ritual text. According to the Brahmanas the ceremonial observances control the processes of nature and even the gods. The simple forms of ceremonial observances, such as the '*samskaras*', were codified in the text called '*Grihyasutras*'.

i. Basic Ends of Human Life

The four basic ends or goals (*purushartha*) of human life are: *artha* (wealth), *kama* (physical love), *dharma* (right conduct), and *moksha* (liberation).

The word '**dharma**' comes from the root *dhr*, which means 'to sustain', 'to support'. Thus duties, obligations, justice in general, rules of conduct, and guidelines for action come under 'dharma', as these are essential to the protection and perpetuation of both individuals and society. Thus, it is dharma which makes it possible for people to live and function harmoniously in their society by fulfilling themselves and at the same time contributing to the well--being of society at large. This is the reason why Hindus consider it unimaginable that a person should change his dharma! (It was unfortunate that this term was used by Christian missionaries for the English word "religion", which means something quite different!)

'**Artha**' refers to the economic and the political life of man. It covers job, wealth, and all other material means necessary for the maintenance of life. All means of livelihood are 'artha'. However, a person should not earn his living and acquire wealth in violation of dharma — for instance, by deceiving, stealing or killing.

'**Kama**' comes from the root which means "to desire". Desire seeks fulfilment and this brings about satisfaction or pleasure. So enjoyment and pleasure are deemed to be 'kama'. 'Kama' includes food, drink, sex, home, friendship, etc. Pleasure and enjoyment are not to be thought of as being

18

unworthy and sinful; on the contrary, they are one of the main aims of life. However, one should acquire 'kama' within the norms of 'dharma'.

The fourth aim of life is **'moksha'** which is a state of freedom from all *dukha* (pain, suffering). It is a spiritual realisation. Moksha is self-emancipation, the fulfilment of the spirit in us. This is what gives ultimate satisfaction. All other activities are directed to the realisation of this end.

j. Paths to Attain Moksha

The different paths to Moksha have been broadly distinguised into *'Jñana'* (knowledge), *'Bhakti'* (devotion), and *'Karma'* (service). These three are not exclusive, but emphasise dominant aspects.

Knowledge (*jñana*, in Greek *gnosis*) does not mean intellectual acumen or dialectical power. It is a realised experience gained through reflection and meditation. If we have true insight, right action will take care of itself. Truth cannot but act rightly.

The way of devotion (*bhakti*) is the most popular one. Sinners as well as saints, ignorant as well as learned, foolish as well as wise, find it easy to reach God through this method. Prayer and petition, fasting and sacrifice, communion and self-examination, are all included in the life of devotion. In its high flights, bhakti coincides with jñana, and both these issue in right karma or **virtuous life**.

k. Salvation According to Hinduism

Salvation is the ultimate goal of all that exists. It is the stage where everything goes back to its original state. Salvation presupposes release from bondage. A Released Soul (*Jivan Mukta*) works for the liberation of others. The whole universe will reach its final goal when every individual has realised the divine within.

3

HINDU SCRIPTURES

The sacred language of Hinduism is Sanskrit. It was in this language that most of the Hindu scriptures were written. These sacred writings may be divided into two categories: the "revealed" (shruti) and the "handed-down" tradition (smriti).

The main "revealed" books are the four Vedas, with later "additions" to each of Brahmanas and Ärannyakas and Upanishads. Pious Hindus believe that the Vedas were from all eternity in Brahman and where revealed at a particular time to the holy men of old. Variously, the composition of all these books is attributed to the mythical sage Vyasa, a feat impossible to any one person! In the larger collection of the "tradition" (smriti), the veracity of whose teachings is subject to the authority of the revelation (shruti), are the two epics, Mahabarata and Ramayana, the 18 Puranas, the Dharma Shastras, the Smartha Sutras, the 6 Vedangas, and the Niti Shastras. There are also the six philosophical treatises, the Darshanas, which are neither shruti nor smriti.

Although the canon of Hindu Scriptures is vast, it is generally agreed that only a relatively small portion of it is of abiding interest and importance. This portion, the latest in time and hence called "Vedanta" (end of the Vedas), refers to the speculative treatises in prose and verse known as the Upanishads. To these has to be added the Bhagvadgita which falls outside the canon but has from the earliest times been held to rank equally with them in authority.

I. THE SHRUTI LITERATURE

A. The Vedas

The four Vedas, in particular the *samhitas* ('collection' of hymns, chants, etc.), are considered by the Hindus as eternal, indestructible, infallible. They are "greater" than the gods! When gods perish in the great cataclysm the Vedas will survive. They are coeternal with the Supreme Being, above the ravages of time.

1. **The Rig Veda** contains the earliest Indian literature in the form of hymns to the great Vedic deities like Indra (Sun), Varuna, Maruts, etc. Some of these hymns were composed more than 5,000 years ago and handed down orally. It also contains hymns in praise of nature, its beauty, grandeur, majesty, and mystery. Very interesting is a hymn to the Man (*Purusha*) in Book X, ch.90 who reminds us of the "Suffering Servant" of Isaiah (ch. 53) and from whose sacrificial death arose the entire creation. Also interesting is the description of the "void" that existed before Creation. (Book X, ch. 129. Compare it with Genesis 1 and 2). Please note that unlike the Holy Bible, the Hindu Scriptures do not subscribe to the doctrine of "creation ex nihilo" (out of nothing).

2. The **Yajur Veda** and the **Sama Veda** have almost the same hymns as in the Rig Veda, but arranged in particular ways for recitation during the rituals.

3. The **Atharva Veda** was of so much later origin that it is not even mentioned in the ancient literature. It contains a mixture of sublime wisdom (e.g., creation of man: BkX, ch.2) and beautiful poetry (cosmological hymns to *Prāna*, the Breath of Life, and to *Vākya*, the Word) with witchcraft and silly charms for exorcising evil spirits.

B. The Brahmanas

The Brahmanas are ritualistic precepts attached to the hymns of the Vedas. By this time sacrifices (*yajñas*) had become very elaborate as they represented, and in a sense they were, the creative process. Were the sacrifice to cease, the world itself would come to an end! But in between the Brahmanas also contain interesting stories, which provided plots for later epic stories, and shrewd observations even of a scientific nature. Thus the Rig Veda has two Brahmanas, Aitareya and Kaushitaka; the Yajur Veda another two, Taittiriya and Sata-patha; the Sama Veda has eight, the best known among them being Panch Vimsa, the Tandya, and the Shad Vimsa; and finally the Atharva Veda has only one, Go-patha.

C. The Arannyakas

The Arannyakas are the books of the Forest-dwellers (*vanaprasthas*) who had renounced the ritualistic sacrifices in favour of meditation (*tapas*). In these books we find an allegorical and symbolical explanation of the sacrifice, which enables the hermit to perform mentally his sacrificial duties.

D. The Upanishads

The explanations of the Arannyakas did not satisfy the more intellectually inclined. Hence there arose the Upanishads containing mystical and philosophical doctrines. Their main aim is to investigate the nature of reality and their main conclusion is that in both the universe at large and in the individual human being there is a ground of Pure Being that is impervious to change. To realise this Being in oneself means salvation. Once this is done, re-birth and re-death are done away with, and man realizes himself as at least participating in Eternal Being. Even when he comes to a knowledge of God as being transcendent as well as immanent, he does not interpret this realisation as "union" with God. The immanent God is everything, the transcendent largely irrelevant. This is the position as we find it at the end of the Upanishadic period, and it is from here that the Bhagvadgita takes on. Thus the Upanishads are

22

the mainstay of the later philosophical systems of Shankaracharya, Ramanuja, etc.

The Upanishads are called Vedänta, the end portions of the Vedas, and the philosophy taught in the Upanishads is also called Vedänta. While the whole of the earlier portion of the Vedas is supposed to preach karma or action, this last portion containing the Upanishads is supposed to deal mainly with jñana or knowledge. The ten principal upanishads are attached to the different Vedas as follows:

Rg—Veda = Aitareya
Yajur—Veda = Isha, Katha, Tattirïya and Brahadärannyaka
Sama—Veda = Kena and Chändogya
Atharva—Veda = Munnddaka, Männddükya and Prashna.

(There is an interesting passage in Brihadärannyaka Upanishad [Bk.V, ch.5] that reminds us of our Christian doctrine of the Holy Trinity: "Fullness beyond, fullness here: fullness from fullness doth proceed. From fullness take away: fullness yet remains.")

II. THE SMRITI LITERATURE

A. The Epics

The two great Indian epics are the Mahabharata and the Ramayana. Of these the Mahabharata is the more ancient, but it deals with a later epoch than that of the Ramayana.

1. The incidents narrated in the Mahabharata are said to have taken place during the Dwapara Yuga, the third age of the Hindu cycle. The original was a small work which treated of a war of succession between the Kauravas and their cousins, the Pandavas. The Kauravas were the persecuted heroes and the Pandavas the murderous villains. This work was, however, re-written by some partisans of the Pandavas, who then exchanged their respective role.

23

The main story of the present Mahabharata is the war between two branches of the Kaurava family — the Kauravas proper, that is, on the one hand, the 100 sons of Dhritarashtra led by their eldest brother, Duryodhna, and on the other, their cousins, the Pandavas or the sons of Pandu, led by their eldest brother, Yudhishthira. Yudhishthira had been cheated out of his kingdom in a game of dice to which he had been challenged. He lost and was thereby condemned to cede his share of the kingdom to Duryodhna while he and his four brothers had to go into exile for 13 years, the last of which they had to spend in concealment. All this they did, but when Yudhishthira asked for his kingdom back, Duryodhna bluntly refused. Yudhishthira, who was by nature a pacifist, and had an instinctive loathing for war, reduced his demands to a mere five villages; still Duryodhna refused. As a final gesture Yudhishthira sent his friend Krishna, son of Vasudeva, on an embassy in which Krishna was to make a final bid for peace. Duryodhna then, knowing full well that Krishna was God, rejected for the last time Yudhishthira's offer, thereby defying God himself. Yudhishthira, having gone to the utmost limit to avoid war, now reluctantly gives in and the scene is now set for a battle that was to prove ferociously destructive. There is, however, a last-minute hitch: Arjuna's nerve fails him!... Here, in Book VI, chapters 25-42, comes the **Bhagavadgita** which eventually became an inspiring book by itself.

As it presently stands, the Mahabharata is the longest single poem in the world, with about 100,000 stanzas. Besides the main story, the work contains many digressions which deal with statecraft, the art and science of war, philosophy, rules of conduct of the four castes, etc. Side by side with these profound subjects are fairy tales, mythical geography and history, and idle passages which teach nothing! In fact the whole of Hindu tradition is supposed to be contained in this work, which is called the "fifth Veda" and also attributed to the sage Vyasa. It is believed that the sage dictated it to Ganesh, who then wrote it down. These beliefs demonstrate the sanctity of the work among the Hindus.

The original book is of great antiquity, the present compilation however is not older than the 4th century A.D., and some parts even later.

2. The **Ramayana** is a smaller work than the Mahabharata, and consists of 24,000 couplets. It is attributed to Valmiki, a sage greatly venerated by the Hindus. The date of the Ramayana is uncertain, but the spirit of the whole work indicates that it is of much later origin than the Mahabharata, though treating of a more ancient age, the second (Threta Yuga) of the Hindu cycle.

The book deals with the fortunes of Rama, prince of Ayodhya, who is considered by the Hindus the 7th incarnation of Vishnu. For details about this hero and the epic and the cult that developed around him see the article on the festival of Ramanavami (Ch. one of Part II).

3. The **Bhagavadgita** (the Divine Song), or simply **Gita**, can be said to be the cream of Hindu philosophy. It is a poem of about 700 verses, found in Book VI of the Mahabharata, put in the form of a dialogue between two principal characters of that epic, Arjuna and Krishna. The poem so brims with the spirit of Hinduism that every school of philosophy and every sect believe that it teaches their particular doctrines. It even inspired Gandhiji and Tilak to launch into political life.

The object of the Gita is to elucidate a highly complex moral situation, and incidentally it surveys briefly the whole field of philosophical thought. Arjuna, one of the heroes of the Mahabharata, stands in the battle-field, bow in hand, awaiting the signal for action. Suddenly he becomes troubled by fears and despondency. Of what use, he asks himself, is a kingdom to him if it be won at the cost of so many lives? Besides, would he be justified in killing those men, many of them his seniors in age and enjoying the reputation of being

25

venerable, for any gain whatever? Arjuna is overcome by these and similar thoughts and the bow drops from his hand. Now Krishna, his charioteer, comes to his aid and infuses courage into him by revealing the Gita.

First and foremost, the Gita teaches a philosophy of action (karma yoga). The correct type of action which ennobles a man is duty done with no thought of personal gain. For example, the soldier's duty in the battle-field is to fight his foes, and not to question the wisdom of war! The Gita also upholds the doctrine of *bhakti* to a personal God, and the teaching that whenever dharma fails and adharma (evil conduct) begins to predominate in the world, God incarnates himself for the destruction of the adharma. The Gita breathes the spirit of universal toleration, and reiterates the orthodox view that every form of religious worship, even if it is apparently crude, is in effect a stepping stone towards a higher form, and hence should be respected. "Whoever with true devotion worships any deity, in him I deepen that devotion; and through it he fulfills his desire." "Those who devotedly worship other gods, they also worship me though only imperfectly." The different forms of worship are compared to different roads that lead to the same destination.

In brief, the aim of the Gita is to teach the social nature of man and to show that it is not in lonely forests that a man should seek salvation but in the midst of life. To live in this world, to do the duty allotted to one by birth and special circumstances, without fear of consequences or love of gain, without the bonds of love or hatred marring one's vision, is the object of life. "Only a literary and religious genius of the highest order could endow mankind with a work so redolent with the fragrance of God's Spirit itself," wrote Fr R. de Smet SJ. (pg. 197)

B. The Puranas

These are 18 in number and all of them are believed to

have been written by Vyasa! Their object is to convey to the ignorant and the dull, the teachings of the Vedas. They are, therefore, meant for popular piety. Each Purana is supposed to treat of five subjects (*lakshanas*): (1) the creation of the universe, (2) its destruction, (3) principal gods and patriarchs, (4) Manvantaras or the reigns of the Manus (the 14 world teachers), and (5) the history of the two great races (Solar and Lunar) of Indo-Aryan kings. The Puranas are metrical compositions, with occasional passages in prose.

The 18 Puranas are grouped into three, each group exalting one of the members of the Hindu trimurthi. The six Puranas that relate to Brahma are: Brahma, Brahmananda, Brahma-vayvarta, Markandeya, Bhavishya, and Vamana. Those related to Vishnu are: Vishnu, Bhagavata, Naradiya, Garuda, Padma, and Varaha. Finally those related to **Shiva** are: Shiva, Linga, Skanda, Agni, Matsya, and Kurma. Of these, the Vishnu Purana is the most interesting and complete, and the Bhagavata Purana, which exalts Krishna, is the most recent and also most influential in promoting the Bhakti spirituality in Hinduism. It shares with the Bhagavadgita a unique position in the devotional literature of India.

What Puranas are to the others, the **Tantras** are to the *Shaktas*. (See chapter Five for a description of Shaktas.) They are little-known works, but they too, like the Puranas, treat of five subjects: the creation of the universe, its destruction, worship of the gods, attainments of super-human faculties, and the modes of union with the Supreme Spirit. Besides, the following subjects are also treated in the various Tantras: praise of Female Energy (shakti) and spells for bringing people into subjection, for making them enamoured, for unsettling their minds, for fattening, for destroying sight, for producing dumbness, etc.

The principal Tantras are: Rudrayamala, Kalika, Mahanirvana, Kularnava, Shyama-rahasya, Sharadatilaka, Mantra-mahobodhi, Uddisa, Kamada, and Kamakhya.

C. Dharma Shastras

The Dharma Shastras are the collection of the various law books which regulate political, religious, and social lives. They are believed to have been given by the ancient sages — 47 of them, according to some! Manu is the best known of them. Some of the others are: Yagnavalkya, Atri, Vishnu, Harita, Usanas, Angiras, Apastambha, Yama, Brihaspati, Parasara, Samvarta, Katyanaya, Daksha, Vyasa, Likhita, Sankha, Gautama, Shatatapa, and Vashishta.

D. Smartha Sutras

There are two categories of Smartha Sutras: the *Grihaya Sutras* or aphorisms connected with domestic rites, and *Samayacharika Sutras* or aphorisms relating to "conventional practices". These are more ancient than the Dharma Shastras and are quoted by some of them. They are generally attached to the Vedas, and the best known of them are: Asvalayana's Grihya Sutra attached to the Rig Veda, Gobhila's Sutra attached to Sama Veda and the Sutras of Paraskara, Baudhayana, Apastambha, and Bharadwaja, attached to Yajur Veda.

The Sutras order in great detail each and every act of a person, from the time he gets up from bed till he goes to sleep, and give elaborate instructions for the performance of rituals and ceremonies. While the Smartha Sutras still remain the final authority in most of the ceremonies performed by the Hindus, the details vary according to localities.

E. The Vedangas

Vedanga means the limb of the Veda. The Vedangas include works on grammar and metre, subjects that are essential for the correct reading and understanding of the sacred books. The Vedangas are six: Kalpa (ceremonial), Siksha (phonetic directory), Chandas (metre), Nirukta (exposition), Vyakarana (grammar), and Jyotisha (astronomy).

Each Veda has its own Sutras of various types. Among the Siksha Sutras is the grammar of Panini which even now is the last word on Sanskrit grammar.

F. The Niti Shastras

There are two types of *Niti Shastras*: first, the Niti Shastras proper, that are the regular moral teachings of ancient masters strung together in verse, as a complete guide for conduct; and the other, are the numerous fables and stories about animals, found in Hindu literature, which are designed to drive home a moral.

The better known in the first category are the Nitisara of Kamandaki drawn by the author from Chanakya, the Sayings of Bartrihari, Vridha-Chanakya or Rajniti Shastras, and Sarn-gadhara-paddhati. Belonging to the second category are the *Jataka* tales of the Buddhists in which the Blessed One, during his various incarnations, appears as a wise animal, bird, or insect. These probably provided a model for the Panchatantra and Hitopadesa of Hindu authors. The object of these fables, according to some of the writers, was to teach the foolish sons of a king some wisdom, as they would read no books and listen to the preaching of no wise man.

The Indian fables were borrowed by the Greeks and the Arabs. The wise Aesop is believed to have learnt his fables from Indians. Even now the charming beast fables of ancient India are found to have a perennial appeal to all men, especially in their young age, and Kipling in his Jungle Book, has copied with advantage ancient Indian sages. The Panchatantra never loses its moral and didactic character and the beasts ably represent the human kingdom with its various types. The fox is always wise, and the crow cunning; the stork is a hypocrite, and the donkey a fool; the monkey is meddlesome and the lion brave.

29

4

GODS AND GODDESSES

Before we begin to speak about specific gods and
goddesses, we need to clarify what we or the Hindus mean
by "god". It is an English term used to translate <u>deva</u> or
<u>devata</u>. The immediate question is whether deva corresponds
fully to the English term "God" as understood by Christians.

In popular parlance it would seem that "god" and "deva"
are interchangeable. However, "deva" does not always refer
to the "Supreme Being", and there can be only one such
being, as the superlative implies. This Supreme Being is
referred to among Christians as "God", "the Almighty", "the
Eternal", etc. Jesus called him the "Father". Jews speak of
Him as "Yahveh" and the Muslims as "Allah".

Hindus too accept one Supreme Being, for whom they
have different names. The term "deva", however, seems to
refer to some supernatural beings somewhere between mere
mortals and the Supreme Being. During the Vedic times, like
in the early years of Judaism, the concept of one universal
Supreme Being seems to have been weak. Like the Jews of
old, different Hindu individuals or groups considered the
particular deity they worshipped as Supreme, whilst
conceding that others had their own Supreme gods.

I.   VEDIC GODS

From the reading of the Vedas it is impossible to identify
all the gods that were worshipped by the Aryans and to
determine whether the various names that are mentioned
are actually different individuals or different names of one
or another individual.

It would appear that the Aryans came to our sub-continent with a pantheon that was common to their counterparts who travelled westward. They worshipped *Dyaus* (also called "*Dyauspitar*", heavenly father), just as the Greeks worshipped Zeus or Jupiter. They also worshipped *Prithvi* (Earth) and eventually some beings in the atmosphere, *Antariksa*. A particular verse in the Rig Veda mentions thirty-three deities, whilst another declares that "three hundred, three thousand, thirty-nine gods have worshipped Agni."

Later on in the Upanishads, when **Brahman** emerges as the Supreme Being, there is an attempt to bring some order in this multiplicity of gods. Sage Yajñavalkya was once asked "How many gods are there?" Quoting a current hymn to the All-gods he stated that there were "three hundred and three and three thousand and three" (=3,306). The enquirer was not fully satisfied. "Yes, but how many gods are there really?" "Thirty three", he suggested. But on further questioning, he kept on reducing the number first to six, then to three, two, one and half, and finally to one. If so, what about those "three hundred and three and three thousand and three", the enquirer wanted to know. "Those are only their attributes of majesty (*mahiman*)," said the sage. (See Brihadārannyaka Upanishad, III, ix, 1)

The thirty-three "gods" of the Vedas were categorised by Yājñavalkya thus: There were the eight Vasus (fire, earth, wind, atmosphere, sun, sky, moon, and stars). They are called "*Vasus*" (wealth) because all wealth is entrusted to them. Then, there were the eleven Rudras (the ten breaths in man, plus the self). When they depart from the mortal body, they make people weep (*rud*) and hence they are called "*Rudras*". Finally, there are the twelve Adityas (the twelve months), that carry off (*ädä*) everything, though going on (*yanti*) themselves. Hence they are called "Adityas". The remaining two are Indra (thunder) and Prajapati (the sacrifice). The sage insisted, however, that God is one, Brahman, the breath of

31

life, the beyond (*tya*). (See "Brihadārannyaka Upanishad", Bk. III, ch.9, 1-9. There are other texts that categorise the gods differently. For example, Book I, chapter 4, 11-15 of the same Upanishad describ how the other gods originated from Brahman.)

From among all these gods, three emerged as pre-eminent during the Vedic period: Agni, Indra, and Surya. Agni (god of fire), was eulogised as the Supreme God, creator, sustainer, and the all-pervading cosmic spirit. He acted as the mediator between men and gods by carrying the human offerings to the gods. He was sometimes identified with Rudra, the god who howls and roars. Rudra is depicted as armed with terrible weapons, but is always benevolent and merciful toward humanity and protects it against enemies. He is an excellent physician and cures all diseases of humanity. He is described as the father of the Maruts, the warlike storm gods. Indra, god of storms, of lightning and thunder, was also considered the war-lord and a symbol of royal power. He is related to Indrani, Parjanya, Vayu, and the Maruts. Surya (god of light), who manifested himself at times as Varuna, the deity who upholds the physical and moral order of the universe, and is the personification of the sky, and is associated with clouds and waters, as Pushan and as Mitra.

II. THE SUPREME GOD OF THE UPANISHADS

BRAHMAN was the name given by the sages of the Upanishads to the Supreme Being, and all the Upanishads attempt to understand his nature. He was the *Vishwakarman*, Maker of All (Rg. Ved X,81), the *Prajapati*, Lord of Creatures, and the *Hiranyagarbha*, the Golden Embryo (Rg.Ved X,121) from whom all creation evolved (Rg. Ved X,129) and who formed the *Purusha*, the Primal Man (Atharva Ved X, 2). Quoting the Rg. Veda, a later Upanishad (Brihadārannyaka) says:

Such is a Brahman's eternal majesty:
By works he grows no greater, grows no less.
Seek out the track of it! For knowing Him,
By no evil work wilt thou be defiled. (IV,ch.4,No.23)

Brahman, according to the Upanishads, is the Absolute, beyond all multiplicity, change, division, or relation. He is the one reality which is the ground and principle of all beings. Bhagavadgita describes Brahman as "beginningless", and, though it cautions "call it not Being, call it not Not-Being", yet attempts to describe Him:

"In the world all things encompassing, changeless It abides. Devoid of all the senses, It yet sheds light on all their qualities; from all detached, yet supporting all; free from Nature's constituents, It yet experiences them; within all beings, yet without them; unmoved, It moves in very truth; so subtle It is you cannot comprehend It; far off It stands, and yet how near It is; undivided, in beings It abides seeming divided: This is that which should be known, — the One who upholds, devours, and generates all beings. Light of lights, 'Beyond the darkness' It is called; true knowledge, what should be known, accessible to knowledge, abiding in the heart of all. (BHAGVAD GITA, XIII, 14-18).

Nothing can really be predicated of Brahman, because all "qualifications" or "attributions" would go counter to the very absoluteness and unicity of the Supreme Reality. Brahman cannot be known by who he is because that would be limiting. To know Brahman correctly one must first resort to negation, the *"neti neti"* (not this, not that) method advocated by the Upanishads.

III. THE EPIC AND THE PURANIC GODS AND GODDESSES

As we enter the Epic and the Puranic periods, by which time the Aryans had come into contact with and conquered many local kingdoms, we find that Hinduism absorbs many deities of these conquered people into their own pantheon. It was, then, in an attempt to control the process, that the Brahmins tried to popularise the idea of Trimurti: one god with three different aspects respectively of creator, preserver, and destroyer.

Popular religiosity, however, took a different course. Ordinary people kept on accepting the gods of the conquered people as different individuals. Then the Brahmins tried to solve the impasse by identifying these with the minor Vedic gods, or by presenting them as their emanations or incarnations. Thus the pre-Aryan god Shiva of South India was identified with Rudra, and the Vedic Vishnu acquired a totally new identity in the Puranas. Soon these two gods began to compete in pre-eminence with Brahma. He was eventually relegated to the background and Shiva and Vishnu, in their various emanations and incarnations, emerged as the main gods of Hinduism. Their "divine power" (Shakti) was also personified as a female consort, and her worship often eclipsed that of the respective god.

The Vedic and the Upanishadic gods were an impersonal reality, now during the Epic and Puranic eras, the "gods", including Brahma himself, began to be represented with human qualities and shortcomings and as entering into a personal relationship with the humans.

A. THE TRIMURTI

1. Brahma

The Brahma of the Epics and the Puranas is quite different from the Brahman of the Upanishads. There he was the Supreme Being, here he becomes subservient either to Shiva or to Vishnu.

The icon of Brahma has four heads. Originally he was supposed to have had five. The Matsya Purana describes their origin. From his own immaculate substance, Brahma formed a female called variously Satarupa, Savitri, Sarasvati,

Gayatri, or Brahmani. On seeing his own beautiful handiwork, Brahma fell in love with her; "How beautiful she is!" he exclaimed. The woman tried to escape his gaze by turning first to his right, then to the left, then behind and finally to the sky, and each time a new head issued from his body. Unable to escape his gaze, Brahma proposed to her that they should consort and produce all kinds of animated beings: men, *suras* (gods), and *asuras* (demons). The woman agreed... Various other Puranas, like the Padma Purana, describe how Brahma lost one head — punishment from Vishnu or Shiva for some wrong behaviour!

In pictures Brahma is represented as a red man, dressed in white, and riding upon a goose. The four heads of Brahma are shown facing the four quarters. They are supposed to represent the four Vedas, the four Yugas (epochs), and the four Varnas (castes). The eyes are closed in meditation and the faces sport a beard. Sometimes he is represented as having two arms, in one carrying a staff and in the other the begging bowl of the brahmins; at other times, there are six arms holding *akshamala* (rosary), *kurcha* (brush), *shruk* (ladle), *shruva* (spoon), *kamandalu* (water-pot), and *pustaka* (book). The rosary represents time; the water-pot represents the waters from which all creation has sprung; the brush, ladle, and spoon, represent the sacrifices which are part and parcel of human existence; and the book represents knowledge.

At present Brahma is not frequently worshipped by Hindus. Having completed his work as Creator, there is nothing more he can do! The Skanda Purana claims that this neglect of worship among Hindus was a curse put on Brahma for some falsehood. As a matter of fact, there is only one temple dedicated exclusively to Brahma and it is found in Pushkar, Rajasthan.

2. Vishnu

Vishnu is responsible for sustenance, protection, and maintenance, of the created universe. The word *Vishnu* is said to be derived from the root vish (to enter) and means one who pervades, one who has entered into everything. He is the inner cause and power by which things exist.

Vishnu is commonly known as Narayana, which means one who is the abode of all human beings and one who has made his abode in human hearts. Vishnu is also described as *Nilameshghashyama*, the infinite empty space in the sky which is deep-blue in colour and depicts the all-pervading cosmic power. In the *Padma Purana* Shiva is represented as admitting Vishnu's superiority over himself. But no Shaivite will accept that!

In pictures Vishnu is represented as a black man with four arms. He rides upon the bird Garuda and is dressed in yellow robes. He is depicted wearing a necklace with the famous gem Kaustuba. He is also wearing a garland of gems or flowers, Vaijayanti. The four arms represent the four quarters which are under his absolute power. The arms are shown holding respectively a *shankha* (conch), *chakra* (discus), *gadä* (mace), and *padma* (lotus). The conch represents the five elements; the discus represents the cosmic mind; the mace stands for the cosmic intellect; and the lotus points to the evolving world.

The Avataras (incarnations) of Vishnu are many, though ten are normally considered the most important. Of these ten, nine have already been accomplished; one, the *Kalki*, is still to come.

➢ *Matsya* (fish)
➢ *Kurma* (tortoise)
➢ *Varäha* (boar)
➢ *Narasimha* (man-lion)
➢ *Vämana* (dwarf)
➢ *Parashurama* (Rama with axe)
➢ *Sri Rama*
➢ *Sri Krishna*

➢ *Balarama* (the elder brother of Krishna)
➢ *Kalki* (yet to come at the end of the Kali Yuga to destroy evil and re-establish Kritā Yuga, the Era of Purity).

According to certain scholars, some of these Avataras are of an entirely cosmic character; others, however, are probably based on historical events, the leading personage of which was gradually endowed with divine attributes, until he was regarded as the incarnation of the deity himself. Thus, according to some, even Buddha is considered as an avatar of Vishnu.

Among the many names of Vishnu, the following are most commonly known: Hari (the saviour), Madhusudana and Kaitabhajit (the destroyer respectively of the demons Madhu and Kaitabha), Vaikunthanath (the lord of paradise), Keshava (the one with excellent hair), Madhava (made of honey), Swayambhu (self-existent), Pitamvara (wearing yellow garments), Jannardana (making people worship), Vishamvara (protector of the world), Ananta (endless), Damodara (bound with a rope), Mukunda (deliverer), Purusha (the man or the spirit), Purushottama (the supreme man or spirit), Yajneshwara (the lord of sacrifice.)

In some places Vishnu is worshipped as Jaganatha, Panduranga, Vitthala or Vithoba, Ranganatha, Varadaraja, Venkatesha, Srinivasa or Balaji or Vishvakshena.

3. Shiva

Shiva is responsible for the dissolution and reformation of the universe. Literally, Shiva means one in whom the universe sleeps after the destruction and before the next cycle of creation. Hence, Shiva is not only responsible for the destruction but prepares the ground for the next cycle of creation.

Shiva is pictured as a very handsome youth of white complexion. His limbs are besmeared with ashes and are strong and smooth. He has three eyes, with one on the forehead, between the regular two eyes. He has four arms: two are holding *trishula* (trident) and *damaru* (drum), while the other two are manifesting *mudras* (postures) namely *abhaya* (protection-giving) and *varada* (boon-giving). He has a crown of long matted hair from which flows the river Ganga. He wears a crescent moon as a diadem. His body is covered with tiger skin and elephant skin. Serpents ornament his body as necklace, girdle, sacred thread, and arm-bracelets. He wears a garland of skulls around his neck.

This picture of Shiva is very symbolic. According to some scholars, the white colour manifests his abode in the snow-covered Himalayas, as well as the light that dispells the darkness. The eyes represent the Sun, source of light, the Moon, source of life and the Fire, source of heat. The third eye also manifests omniscience. Since the tiger and the elephant are ferocious and powerful animals that destroy anything that comes in their way, the wearing of their skin represents his mastery over desire and animal impulses. The garland of skulls represents the appearance and disappearance of human generations. The Ganga stands for the purifying and redeeming power. The crescent moon shows that Shiva has control over time. The snakes manifest that Shiva has mastery over time, energy, and death.

Parvati is the consort of Shiva, and Ganesha and Kumara are their sons. He is associated with animals: Nandi, the vehicle bull; Bhrngi, the Rshi with three legs and three arms; the mouse of Ganesha and the peacock of Kumara. Although his abode is in the mountains, he is found roaming the burial grounds and cremation sites.

Panchanana are the five aspects or faces of Shiva: Ishana faces the zenith and is the highest aspect and is also called Sadashiva; Tatpurusha faces the east and stands for power that rules the air, the forces of darkness and the obscuration on spiritual life; *Aghora* faces the south and stands for the power that absorbs and renovates the universe; *Vamadeva* faces the north and is responsible for preservation; and *Sadyajata* faces west and represents the power that creates.

Shiva is the great master of dance. He dances every evening in order to relieve the sufferings of creatures and entertain the gods. One hundred and eight modes of dancing are attributed to him, of which **Nataraja** is the most famous. The dance of Shiva indicates a continuous process of creation, preservation, and destruction. Shiva is master of Yoga and spiritual sciences.

As a universal teacher, he is called *Dakshinamurti*; in the heart of the Linga, he is called *Lingodhbavamurti*; as a naked beggar, he is called *Bhikshanantamurti*; as half-Shiva and half--Vishnu, he is called *Haryardhamurti*; and as half-man and half-woman, he is called *Ardhanarishvara*.

Shivalinga is the emblem of Shiva which is venerated by his devotees. Literally, linga means a sign or symbol. Hence, shivalinga is the symbol of the great God of the Universe. It is often also considered a phallic symbol. The shivalinga may be *chala* (movable) or *achala* (immovable). The Chala-linga is kept temporarily in the home-shrine and then dispensed with after worship. It is made of clay or dough and is worn on the body as Ishtalinga. The Achala-lingas are those that are installed in the temples. Their lower part represents Brahma, the creator, and is called *Brahmabhaga*; the middle part represents Vishnu and is called *Vishnubhaga*. These two parts are immersed in the pedestal. The visible part is called *Rudrabhaga* and worship is offered to it. Hence it is also called *Pujabhaga*. It has certain lines drawn on it called *Brahmasutra*.

B.   THE GODDESSES

Hinduism has identified **shaktis**, the power or energy of the gods as distinct female deities. Thus, each member of the Trimurti has his respective Shakti as his divine consort. Sarasvati is the consort of Brahma; Lakshmi of Vishnu, and Parvati of Shiva. Each of these appear under innumerable names, each with its own mythology. There are besides other goddesses who are sometimes considered as independent deities, or as incarnations of the above three or as personifications of some aspect of Shakti.

1. The Triad

a. Saraswati

Saraswati is the consort of Brahma and the mother of the entire creation. Literally, her name means the "flowing one". She is connected with fertility and purification and represents power and intelligence. She is the personification of all knowledge. She is pictured as extraordinarily beautiful and graceful; she is clad in a spotless white apparel and is seated on a lotus seat. She has four hands and holds a *vina* (lute); *aksamala* (rosary); and *pustaka* (book). Sometimes she is shown with five faces and eight hands holding *pasa* (noose), *ankusa* (goad), *padma* (lotus), *trishula* (trident), *sankha* (conch), *chakra* (discus); her vehicle is the Hamsa, swan, or peacock.

The image is symbolic. The spotless white apparel represents her power and intelligence required for creation; the book manifests her as the goddess of learning; the Vina shows her as the mistress of the fine arts; the rosary manifests the need of all spiritual sciences or Yoga. The book in the left hand and the rosary in the right hand manifest that spiritual sciences are more important than secular sciences. The Swan shows her as the consort of Brahma; while the Peacock stands for the world in all its glory, over which she has control.

The other names of Saraswati are Sarada (giver of essence), Vagishvari (mistress of speech), Brahmi (wife of Brahma), Mahavidya (knowledge supreme).

b. Lakshmi

Lakshimi is the consort of Vishnu and the goddess of

fortune. She is usually depicted as an enchanting beautiful woman standing on a lotus and holding a lotus in each of her two hands. She is adorned with a lotus garland. On either side, she has an elephant emptying pitchers of water over her. She is described in various colours like dark, pink, yellow, and white. Sometimes she is shown with four hands, two holding the lotuses while the other two manifesting the symbols of the *abhaya* and *varada* mudras.

The image is symbolic. When her colour is dark, she is depicted as the consort of Vishnu, the dark god; in yellow, she is the source of all wealth; in white, she is the purest form of nature from which the universe developed; in pink, she reflects her compassion for creatures as a mother. Her four hands signify the power to grant *purusharthas* (goals of human life), namely, *dharma* (righteousness); *artha* (wealth); *kama* (pleasures of the flesh) and *moksha* (beatitude). The lotuses represent the world and creatures in various stages of evolution. The owl is portrayed as the carrier vehicle of Laksmi. The owl is said to be the bird of wisdom and Laksmi is the mistress of spiritual wisdom.

Some of the common names of Lakshmi are: Sri, Padma or Kamala, Rukmini, Haripriya (beloved of Hari), Jaladhija (occean-born), Chanchala (the fickle one) and Lokamata (mother of the world).

c. Parvati

Parvati, the consort of Shiva, is the goddess of power. She is worshipped under innumerable names and is generally referred to as *"Mata"*. Among her many names are: Uma, Ambika, Haimavati, Gauri, Girija, Daksayani, Mrdani, Rudrani, Sarvani, Aparna. Parvati has two aspects, namely, mild and terrible. As mild, she is known as Parvati or Uma and is pictured with two hands, the right holding a blue lotus and the left hanging loose. In this aspect, she is usually shown with Shiva. As terrible, she is known as *Rudra*.

41

Parvati is said to have seven emanations or aspects called *Saptamatrkas* or Seven Little Mothers: Brahmi or Brahmani represents the primordial energy and the origin of all creation; *Maheshwari* is the power which gives individuality to the created beings; Kumari is the ever-youthful deity; Vaishnavi brings symmetry, beauty, organisation and order in the universe; Varahi is the all-consuming power of assimilation and enjoyment; Aindri or Indrani symbolises the terrible power that destroys all that opposes the cosmic law; Chamunda is the force of concentrated awareness and the power of spiritual awakening in the heart.

2. Other Goddesses

a. Durga

Durga means the one who is difficult to approach or to know, because she is the personification of the totality of the powers of the gods. However, being the mother of the universe, she is also the personification of tender love. Durga is pictured as having four or eight or ten or even eighteen hands. Usually she has three eyes. The hair is combed as a crown. She is dressed in red clothes and adorned with several ornaments. In her hands she usually holds a conch, discus, trident, bow, arrow, sword, dagger, shield, rosary, winecup, and a bell. She is either standing on a lotus or a buffalo's head, or riding a lion.

Symbolically, the lion, being the mightiest of the animal kingdom, represents the greed for lust and food, and is being subdued by the goddess who has the totality of powers; the many hands manifest her as the mother of the universe who embraces everything; her three eyes signify her omniscience; the red clothes manifest her as one who is difficult to approach; the various objects in her hand signify her victory over evil.

Some of the aspects of Durga are personified as Sailaputri, Kusmanda, Katyayani, Kshemankari, Harasidhih, Vanadurga, Vindyavasini, and Jayadurga.

b. Kali

The name of this goddess is derived from *kala* (time) and hence she is the goddess of time. Kali is pictured with a cremation or burial-ground or a war-field as the background. She stands in a challenging posture over the 'dead' body of Shiva. She is deep-blue in colour. She is completely naked except for an apron of human heads. She also wears a garland of human heads or skulls. Her hair is completely dishevelled. She has three eyes and four hands. In the two upper hands she holds a severed, bleeding, human head and a sword; and the lower hands are in the abhaya and varada mudras. Her face is red and her tongue is protruding.

The image is symbolic. The severed head and the sword indicate that destruction of evil has taken place. The nakedness represents her unveiled divinity. She is also called Digambara, the one clad in space, having the whole space as her dress. The deep-blue colour represents her as the state where time, space, and creation, have ceased to exist. The hands represent her capacity to work. The dishevelled hair speaks of her absolute freedom. The garland of heads manifests that the whole process of creation has been withdrawn and now stands in the state of destruction. The abhaya mudra depicts her motherliness towards the dear stricken children and the varada mudra depicts her desire to grant boons. After the destruction, she begins to dance in joy at which the frightened gods ask Shiva to stop her. Shiva, being unable, also lies among the corpses, when suddenly she steps on him. Realising what she has done, she puts out her tongue in shame!

Kali is not only the goddess of destruction, but also of the eternal night of limitless peace and joy which follow the transcending of time. Hence, she is the *Maharatri*.

c. Lalita

Lalita is the personification of Shakti's beauty. She is

depicted as an extraordinarily beautiful woman, slightly red in colour. She has four hands holding respectively a bow of sugarcane, arrows, a gourd (*ankusa*), and a noose (*pasa*). Her left foot rests on a pedestal made of diamonds. The image is symbolic. The sugarcane bow represents the mind through which we experience all joy. The arrows are the five subtle elements, namely *akasa* (ether), *vayu* (air), *agni* (fire), *apas* (water) and *prithvi* (earth). Since the sense organs are products of these subtle elements, that are shot by the mind towards sense objects, the bow and the arrow in her hands signify her power to energise and control our minds and sense organs. The noose is for binding, and the gourd is the anger which hurts. Should we forget the goddess, she will "bind" us with the noose and pierce us with her anger!

CONCLUSION

Every morning pious Hindus begin their prayer with a salutation to various gods and goddesses that make up the Hindu pantheon. They believe, however, that although God, the Absolute, is nameless and formless, it is for the human convenience that He is invested with many names and forms. As Catholics do for the Blessed Virgin Mary, Hindus have given the one Supreme Being many names and forms, according to their spiritual needs and different degrees of understanding. These "gods" and "goddesses", even though at times they seem to have an individuality of their own and become the objects of a worshipping relation, remain the creations of man's religious imagination. Each person is free to worship the Supreme Being under a particular aspect, which in turn is personified as a "god" or a "goddess". "Just as the water which falls from the sky goes to the sea, so do the salutations offered to the various gods reach Brahman alone," say the Hindu Scriptures.

A Hindu worships the Divine Spirit also in places and things in which nature displays itself as most beautiful and

44

excellent, e.g., a huge tree, a big mountain, a majestic river, a fine animal, etc., When a Hindu worships these or the different deities, it is to that Divine Spirit that he really offers worship.

5

SCHOOLS OF THEOLOGY

Hinduism today presents itself as a sum total of various religious trends that characterise different Hindu communities. Shaivism, Vaishnavism, and Shaktism, are the three mainline sects or religious "philosophies", which are followed by most of the Hindus, the first being most popular and widespread in various forms and sub-sects. These sects find a focus in the mythological deities, respectively in Shiva, Vishnu, or Shakti or Devi.

I.   SHAIVISM

Shiva, the most popular deity in Hinduism, is known by countless other names — according to some, 1,008 in the Sanskrit language alone! His cult is very ancient and flourished especially in Kashmir and in Tamil Nadu. Temples dedicated to him under various names are found in Kashmir (Amarnath), the Himalayas (Kedarnath), Benares (Vishvanath), near Calcutta (Tarkeshwar), Orissa (Bhuvaneshwar), Kathiawar (Somnath), Kanjivaram (Kailasnath), Tanjore (Vrihdishwar), Chidabaram (Natraj), etc.

He is considered to be both the god of destruction and the god of regeneration (perhaps an attempt to explain both the good and the evil in the world by monotheism), and his most popular form of worship is the lingam (a rather vague representation of the male organ of reproduction). He is, in a special manner, the great god of the mountains (Himalayas): inaccessible, transcendent, absorbed in sublime contemplation. He can be both terrifying and gracious: he dances either as the Natraj, in the sheer joy of creation, or as the god of destruction, in the mad frenzy of the Tannddva.

Shaivism consists in the exaltation of Shiva to the position of a Supreme Being, exempt from the law of ultimate absorption into the Universal Spirit. Shaivism also means exclusive devotion to a personal god who, unlike the absolute and impersonal Brahman, possesses a body through which he thinks, feels, and acts. The Shaivas are generally distinguished by a horizontal tilak mark on the forehead, and rosaries of rudraksha berries.

A. The Origin and Development of Shaivism

The origins of Shaivism are obscure. There seems to be ample evidence that it was pre-Aryan and hence, probably, Dravidian. Even the word "Shiva" may be a Sanskrit adaptation of the Dravidian *shivan* (red). In fact, certain Vedic passages speak contemptuously of the people who worship *shishna* (lingam). But eventually, rather than oppose, the Aryans preferred to absorb Shaivism into their own religious culture. This they did by identifying Shiva with the Vedic Rudra, as one may notice in Shvetāshvatara Upanishad, III.

This Upanishad presents what we now call Shaivism as a monotheistic religion, a way to attain "liberation". This liberation (*mumukshu*) is effected through the illumination of the intellect (*buddhi*) by the "One God, the Blessed Lord" (*Bhagvat*), when self (*atman*) becomes eager for Him and seeks refuge (*sharana*) in Him. The austerity (*tapas*) of the atman, which detaches him from worldly desires, is met by divine grace (*prasad*) which turns the tapas into the highest devotion (*bhakti*). He is now a self (*atman*) fixed on the Supreme (*Mahatman*)

There was a steady rise of Shaivism to supremacy and a corresponding decline of Buddhism and Jainism in the 7th-8th century A.D., under the influence of the great philosopher Shankara Acharya and the intolerant rule of

Sashanka. It was this ruler who burnt and destroyed the Bodhi tree at Gaya, as Hiuan-Tsangh, the Buddhist pilgrim from China, narrates with horror.

Shankaracharya, the wandering scholar from Kerala, interpreted the Hindu Scriptures to teach the oneness (*advaita*) of all creation with Brahman, the creative source of all things, whom he perceived as pure thought, formless, and without attributes. Only by understanding that God alone is real can each individual soul be united to God after death. Because all things exist through God and in God, after death each soul returns to be part of God.

As Shiva rose to eminence as the supreme God and became the object of speculation and meditation, this led to the formation of various sub-sects within Shaivism itself: some intending to follow Shaivism in its more refined form, others tending towards various degrees of aberration of doctrines and ascetical practices.

B. The Shaiva Sects

From the theological point of view, Shaivas are divided into four groups: Samanya Shaivas, Mishra Shaivas, Shudha Shaivas, and Vira Shaivas. The members of the first two groups worship both Shiva and Vishnu, whilst the other two worship Shiva alone.

1. The Lingayats

Powerful among the Vira Shaivas are the Lingayats who wear the lingam on their persons and are very numerous in Karnataka. As a community they were founded by a leader named Basavesvara (1125-?) who taught the suppression of all caste distinctions and the uselessness of all Brahmanical rites. Initially people of all castes and even "outcastes" could join the movement, but eventually the upper-class members succeeded in keeping out the latter. The Lingayats bury their dead in a sitting position, rather than burn them on the pyre. They are also strict vegetarians.

2. The Shaiva Siddhanta

The Shaiva Siddhanta is the theology of monotheistic religion, which developed outside the Brahmanic circles both in Tamil and in Sanskrit. Like all philosophies of religion, the Shaiva Siddhanta seeks to determine the relation of God to souls and to the world. According to Shaiva Siddhanta, there are three eternal and real substances: *Pati, Pasu, and Pasa*. The Pati (the Lord Shiva) helps Pasu (the soul) who is chained by Pasa (the shackle) of *annava* (ignorance), *karma* (merits and demerits of its actions), and *maya* (empirical reality), to be released of these bonds through the three paths of *karya* (service), *kriya* (worship) and *yoga* (meditation). All these should be animated by *bhakti* or loving devotion to Shiva. Thus freed by Shiva's grace, the soul rises to live eternally in the conscious and full enjoyment of Shiva's presence.

The membership of the sect is through a progressive initiation into three grades: samayi, nirvana, and sadhaka. Accomplished ascetics leave the matth and retire into more secluded ashrams, for a more contemplative life. Through mental purifications, yoga postures, breath control (*pranayama*), and steady contemplation (*dharana*), they reach the purest light of Brahman-Shiva: *samadhi*, a peaceful and intense awareness. In this supreme state of contemplation, the mind is fixed on Shiva in immediate, steady, spiritual attentiveness.

3. The Pashupatas

The Pashupatas (adorers of Pashupati or Rudra-Shiva) are yogis who try to attain union with the divinity by means of violent practices. According to the Pashupata doctrine, there are five things, the knowledge of which is needed for man to attain his last end. They are:

(a) *Karya*, the effect or the outcome of knowledge (*vidya*), the organs of knowledge (*kala*) and the individual soul (*pashu*);

(b) *Karanna*, the cause, identified with *pati* (the Lord);

(c) *Yoga*, the union of pasu and pati;

(d) *Vidhi*, the injunction, which consists in certain *vratas* (vows), e.g., to besmear one's body with ashes, to sleep on a bed of ashes, to worship Shiva by means of laughter, song, dance, prostration, and prayer); and in certain *dvaras* (lit. doors), eg. snoring, trembling, limping, mimicking a lover, acting and talking incoherently;

(e) *Duhkhanta*, the end of misery by the acquisition of superhuman powers, and the total destruction of misery.

The Pashupata scheme, therefore, is a method of intense asceticism in which divine grace has no place.

4. The Kapalikas and Kalamukhas

The *Kapalikas* (skull-bearers) and *Kalamukhas* (black-faces) form a group of worshippers of Shiva, whose tenets and practices are gruesome and repulsive. They are called *Mahavratis* (observers of the great vow) and the greatness of their vow consists in its extraordinary and aweful nature, such as eating food placed in a human skull, and besmearing their body with the ashes of human corpses. They are addicted to the worship of the female principle, which at times tends to degenerate into licentious orgies. More recent are the *Gorakhnathis* or *Kanphata-yogins*, the yogis with split ears, who form a school of Hatha Yoga and are found chiefly in North India.

5. Other Sects

The Sittar Shaivas of the South profess a pure monotheism, and their religious literature is comparable to that of the Hebrews, in its passionate belief in the unity of God and in its hatred of idolatry. Because of their monotheistic leanings and repudiation of the doctrine of transmigration of souls and of idolatry, it is even believed that the sect was founded through Muslim and Christian influence.

The Shaivism in the North, however, tends to be identified with the various sects of wandering ascetics. The practices of some of them emphasise the need for torturing the flesh in order to elevate the soul. The Bahikathas, for instance, tear their bodies with knives and daggers. The Khanphatas slit the ears of their recruits as the initiation ceremony. The Aghoris feed on carrion and excreta. The Kapalikas use a human skull for a drinking bowl. The Akashamukhins go about looking at the sky without turning their faces, and the Urdhavabahus keep their hands always lifted up. There are various other sects of these ascetics who select forms of self-torture which appeal to them most, without referring to sacred texts or traditions, whilst many other nameless sects organise themselves into gangs to terrorise the countryside in the name of Shiva.

In brief

Thus wrote R. de Smet S.J., a professor of Indian philosophy at the Papal Athenaeum, Pune: "As a system of religious thought, as an expression of faith and life in God, Shaivism is by far the best that India possesses. Judged by its intrinsic merits Shaivism represents the high-water mark of India's deeply religious intuition and life, for this religion favours a piety based on a conception of God and his relationship to the world, which stands nearer to Christianity than does any other system."

II.   VAISHNAVISM

Vaishnavism is a theistic religion in which **Vishnu** is the object of worship and devotion as the Supreme God. Whereas Shiva, the destroyer and the regenerator, is the god of the mountains, Vishnu, the protector and preserver of the world, is the god of the seas and the plains. More peaceful than Shiva, less awe-inspiring and transcendent, more anthropomorphic and essentially propitious, Vishnu inspires loving adoration. He is worshipped mainly in one of his two *avatars* (incarnations): Rama and Krishna. It would, however, seem that Vishnu is the combination of the various deities that were worshipped by different groups of people before Hinduism, as we know it now, came into existence. Most of those deities are now considered either incarnations or emanations or variations of Vishnu!

A. The Origin and the Development of Vaishnavism

The Vedas have little to say about Vishnu as a deity. Originally, the word referred to the activity of the Sun that encircles the earth majestically yet caringly. It was only in the later Vedic period that this activity was personified and called Vishnu. There is, for example, a hymn to Vishnu in Rig Veda (Book I, ch. 154) where it is said that "like a dread beast he wanders where he will, haunting the mountains; in his three wide paces all worlds and beings dwell."

In the Brahmanas, where considerable importance is given to the offering of sacrifices, Vishnu becomes the personification of sacrifices and the virtues implied in the them. Vishnu keeps a low profile in the Upanishads which are rather abstract philosophical treaties.

It was in the Epics (Mahabharata and Ramayana) that the monotheistic trend is given importance and Shiva and Vishnu are considered Supreme Gods. Here the Vedic Vishnu becomes identified with the epic Krishna and the Bhagavata religion begins to be known as Vaishnava dharma.

Finally, in the Puranas, Vishnu emerges as the only Supreme God to whom all others are subordinate. This, then, gave rise to an extensive literature on Vaishnavism by Alvaras (sometimes compared with Christian saints) and Acharyas, that has been collected in the Pancharatra Samhitas. It may be noted that Vishnu is also identified with

Narayana, a cosmic god of uncertain origin, represented as lying on the coils of the serpent Shesha or Ananta, floating on the primeval waters, the resting place of the world.

It was Ramanuja (1037-1137) who formulated the Vishistadvaita philosophy and also systematized Vaishnavism and propagated it throughout the country.

B. The Doctrine of Vaishnavism

The Vaishnavites hold the view that there exists an Absolute Self, called Vishnu, who is infinitely intelligent, powerful, and loving, and with whom we can have personal communion. This Absolute Self created the world out of his two "modes": *purusha* (subtle spirit) and *prakriti* (subtle matter). These "subtle" elements were eternally existing in the Self. The Self, therefore, is the unmanifested cause of the world, and Souls and Matter are related to Him "as attributes are related to a substance, as parts to a whole, or as a body is related to its soul."

The Vaishnavites believe that human Souls are the "modes" of the Supreme Being. They possess their own spontaneity and choice, but often times these Souls lose sight of their divine nature and identify themselves with the body. This is the origin of wrong thoughts, as well as actions, which force the Souls to the bondage of material bodies. The best means to attain liberation are: true knowledge, tender devotion, and perfect surrender to God, and the favour or grace of God himself. Intense and constant remembrance of God bring the liberative knowledge of God. But more effective is bhakti or loving devotion, through which the Soul becomes more and more conscious of its relation to God and surrenders itself completely and intimately to Him. Thus every vestige of self-love is removed from the Soul.

Now the Soul is ready to enter blissfully into God, to become one with Him, without becoming identical. The Soul is said to enter Vishnu's world (*vishnuloka*), the *vaikuntha*. As a denizen of the highest heaven, it will behold that form of God to which it has been attached in its earthly existence!

C. Sects in Vaishnavism

As in Shaivism, there are various sects among the Vaishnavites which differ from each other in various areas and in various degrees.

1. The Ramanuja Sect

As mentioned above, it was Ramanuja who gave a concrete shape to Vaishnavism in his *vishishta advaita* philosophy, but not all Vaishnavites follow his doctrines in their entirety. **Ramanuja** (1050-1137) was a South Indian Brahmin who originally accepted the advaita vedanta (pure transcendentalism) of Shankaracharya, himself a Shaivite, but was soon won over by the Vaishnavites of the Shrirangam Matth (Trichy). He is the first theologian of the Vaishnavites and became one of its leading promoters in the South. He spent most of his life near San Thome, Mylapore, where he was born, and near other Christian centres.

According to Ramanuja, there are three reals: God, Soul, and Matter. These are not, however, independent reals but interdependent. The Soul is the controlling factor of the body or Matter, and God controls both. Without God neither Soul nor Matter has any existence, except as a conception. The three are in fact inseparable and form a complex whole. Hence **Vishishta Advaita** is neither dualism nor pluralism, but monism with a qualification.

The object of life, according to Vishishta Advaita, is not realisation, but deliverance. The liberated soul does not lose its individuality, but finds God and is released from the cycle of births and deaths. To attain this state, *Karmayoga* (right activity) and *Jñanayoga* (knowledge) form the preliminary disciplines. But it is not enough to know and to act; to find God one should seek Him as a fond child seeks his mother, or as a fond lover seeks his lady. *Bhakti* (loving devotion), therefore, is essential for salvation. God is conceived of as completely personal. He is looked upon as having pity for erring man, and as actuated by a desire to show mercy to him. Benevolence, indeed, is one of his essential features.

The Vishishta-advaitin believes in something greater than bhakti: for him the highest activity, the highest knowledge, the highest devotion is *parapatti*, complete self-surrender to God. A person who surrenders his body, mind, and soul to God, with absolute faith in Him, is freed, through divine grace, from all the bonds of karma. In this highest expression of devotion, there is no place for caste, creed, or colour. Even the most abandoned dalit may be saved through divine grace, if he has the faith and the will to surrender himself completely to God.

The doctrine has a close resemblance to Christian theology, and its belief in divine grace is characteristically Christian; but the differences are too many and too deep to warrant genuine community.

The appeal of a personal God, however, to whom man can pray, do homage, and ask for forgiveness, is universal and hence Vishishta Advaita spread rapidly throughout India. It was carried all over India by a host of Vaishnavites, such as Ramananda, Chaitanya, Thukaram, Tulsidas, Mira Bai, and many others. The extraordinary appeal of the doctrine did not fail to attract the attention of Shaivas, and efforts were made, especially in South India, to exalt Shiva also to the position of a god of mercy and grace. But the attempt was only partially successful, and Shiva remains to this day the lean, irascible god of ascetics.

2. The Madhava Sect

Madhava (1199-1278 or 1238-1317) was born near Udupi in South Kanara and died there as the head of an order of Vaishnava ascetics founded by him. Initially, he too had been a disciple of Shankaracharya and his *advaita vedanta*. But soon he broke away from his master to evolve a theological system of his own. There are many Sarasvats in Goa who follow his teachings and who are called Madhavas.

Madhava's teachings are not fundamentally different from those of Ramanuja. Regarding the relationship between God, souls, and the world, he teaches the famous five-fold difference between (a) God and souls, (b) God and world, (c) soul and souls, (d) souls and world, (e) each object of the world and all other objects. The differences are such that there is absolutely no room for a really intrinsic community in being, such as we Christians affirm between the Creator and creatures. This, of course, is a very simplistic way of putting it!

Fr de Smet, whom we have quoted earlier, insists that the similarities between Madhava's writings and Christian philosophy are very superficial. "Madhava, however, is to be praised for his very religious view of the universe. It is, indeed, by abdicating all claim to selfish independence and by willingly abandoning our soul into the merciful hands of God that we shall save it."

3. The Rama Sect

Members of this sect consider Rama, the hero of the Ramayana, as an incarnation of Vishnu and the highest God. This deification of heroes that arose as a reaction to the cold and highly intellectual deities presented by the Upanishads, continued over centuries. Thus not only mythical heroes but even historical gurus like Ramanuja, Ramananda, Anandathirta, Banava, Chaitanya, Vallabhacharya, etc., have been divinised by the members of the sects that developed around them.

The Ramaite movement was spread in the North by **Ramananda**, a brahmin from Allahabad, the fifth successor of Ramanuja. Because of his laxity in observing caste laws, he was disliked by the other members of the sect. So he left the ashram and travelled to Benares where he founded his own sect. The chief doctrines of this sect are: God is personal; Rama is the true incarnation of Vishnu; the human soul is distinct from God; salvation is obtained by means of bhakti or loving devotion to Rama; and the gurus of the sect are also minor incarnations of Vishnu.

Tulsi Das (1532-1623), from whom came the Hindi edition of Ramayana, that was the basis of the TV serial by that name, gave further impetus to the movement. His interpretation of the epic is more spiritual, with many passages that come very near to Christian thought.

Another "Sant Kavi" who contributed to the development and spread of the movement was **Ramadas** (1608-1681), the spiritual teacher of Shivaji.

4. The Krishna Sect

Although Krishna was known and even deified from ancient times, Krishna's new cult was spread in North India soon after 1400, when the "bhakti" movement was becoming popular. Gifted religious poets like Vidyapati, Chandidas, and Mirabai; and, in Maharashtra, Dnyaneshwar, Namdev, Eknath, and above all Tukaram; and religious teachers like the Telugu Vallabhacharya (1479-1531) and the Bengali Chaitanya (1485-1540) raised Krishna worship to a level of high spirituality. The last of these was a religious leader endowed with an intense emotional temper, who could win success by a tempest of devotion towards Krishna. His prema-bhakti is still popular in Bengal. But when this emotional dimension began to be promoted by some lesser poets of doubtful character, who interpreted the "loving devotion" in the language of human passion, Krishna's worship became an erotic religion.

As a reaction to this aberration, the "Neo-Krishnaism" was started in Bengal. It tried to explain allegorically and mystically the much-abused Krishna cult and even to show parallels between Krishna and Christ, between Gita and the Bible. Thus Bankim Chandra Chatterjee (1838-1894), author of Vande Mataram and the first B.A. of the Calcutta University, wrote the Krishna Charitra; and Shishir Kumar Gose wrote the Lord Gauranga (1897). There was even a book called the Imitation of Krishna, like the Christian classic "Imitation of Christ" by Thomas à Kempis.

In the writings of these men, as well as of poet-laureate Rabindranath Tagore and philosopher-president S. Radhakrishnan, the dominant beliefs are very much Christian and in full harmony with the modern thought. There is no karma, no re-births, no inaction, no pessimism, no world-weariness; but instead the perception that nature is the revelation of God, the joy of meeting Him in the sun and in the rain, the dignity and worth of human toil, deliverance won only by going down where God is, namely, among the poorest and the lowliest.

III. SHAKTISM

There are individuals and sects among Hindus who worship Shakti, considered to be consort of Shiva, as the Supreme Deity, even higher than Shiva himself. They are called "Shaktas". Mother-cults were widespread before the Aryans and there was a variety of mother-goddesses among the non-Aryans. The Aryans connected them with various gods, as their consorts or manifestations of their power (shakti). Hence, although considered by many as consort of Shiva, Shakti could also be considered as a generic term for all the feminine manifestations of divine power: wisdom, benevolence, and even vindictiveness. And so Shakti herself is portrayed variously as Devi, Parvati, Kali, Bhawani, Durga, Amba or Ambika, Uma, Gauri, etc.

These representations or "incarnations" of Shakti portray mainly two of her aspects: that of the divine mother (e.g., Durga), and that of the goddess of terror (e.g., Kali). The mother aspect is common in the home worship, whereas the public worship and the worship of secret societies is usually devoted to the aspect of terror, with mysterious and terrifying practices and rituals like blood sacrifices, self--mutilation, etc.

Many of the great philosophers and holy men either worshipped Shakti (e.g., Ramakrishna Paramahansa) or had leanings towards Shaktism (e.g., Shankaracharya and Vivekananda).

The Shaktas are divided into two sects: The *Dakshinamargis* (the right-handers), who worship openly and are more numerous, and the *Vamamargis* (the left-handers), who are a secret society and whose form of worship is kept secret from all others. They strive to achieve salvation by means of the five M's: *Madhya* (liquor), *Matsya* (fish), *Mansa* (meat), *Mudra* (corn), and *Maithuna* (sex).

The sacred texts of the Vamamargis are the **Tantras** which are also normally kept <u>secret</u>. The principal Tantras are: Rudrayamala, Kalika, Mahanirvana, Kularnava, Shyamarahasya, Saradatilaka, Mantra-mahobodhi, Uddisa, Kamada, and Kamakhya. These texts treat of creation and destruction of the universe, divine worship, attainment of superhuman faculties, and modes of union with the Supreme Spirit. They also deal with topics like praise of female energy; worship of the female emblem with the five M's; ways of worshipping Kali; methods of breathing in certain rites; spells for bringing people into subjection, for making them fall in love, for unsettling their minds, or for bringing on them various evils, as well as for preventing such evils; language of birds, beasts, etc.

HINDU COMMUNITIES AND ORGANISATIONS

Hinduism, as we have seen, is a very complex phenomenon, whether you look at it from the social or religious point of view. In either of them there are divisions and sub-divisions, each group having its own family deities and religious heads, and often following divergent beliefs and practices.

According to Hindu tradition, at the beginning there was the Brahman or the Purusha (Person). From his face sprang the Brahmins, the Kshatryas from his arms, the Vaishyas from his thighs, and the Sudras from his feet. A more rational explanation is that this division evolved over some centuries and was based on functions performed: priesthood and the pursuit of knowledge indicating the Brahmins; wars and governance, the Kshatryas; trade and agriculture, the Vaishyas; and crafts and menial work, the Sudras.

These main castes, however, have their different sub-castes, which follow different religious trends. Similarly, the two major sects: Vaishnavism and Shaivism are practised differently in different caste groups, as well as in different regions of the country.

Hindus in Goa have four categories of "devatas" to consider: *grama devatas* (village deities), *kula devatas* (family deities), *ishtta devatas* (personal deities), and *vastu* or *griha devatas* (house deities, chosen at the house blessing). The *grama devata* of entire Gomantaka was Mhalsa devi, with her temple at Mardol (originally at Verna). She is considered to be the incarnation of both Lakshmi and Parvati, and hence is worshipped by both the Shaivite and the Vaishnavite sects. The other popular grama devtas are: Shantadurga, Santer, Bhumika, Vettal, Mauli, Rohini, Bhagawati, Durga, and Rawalnath. The popular *kula devtas* in Goa are: Mahalakshmi, Mangesh or Mangirish, Naguesh, Ramnath, etc. The worship of Vettal (kula devata of the Ranes), to whom the temple at Sanquelim is dedicated, is of a very old origin in Goa.

Given this complex situation, it is impossible to describe fully or even merely to enumerate the various Hindu sects, communities or organisations in the country. According to some anthropologists, there are 2,378 castes and sub-castes among the Hindus. Instead, we shall deal briefly with some of the groups that exist in and around Goa.

The main groups found among the Hindu Brahmins in Goa are: the Gouda Saraswats (divided into Madhavas and Smartas), the Karhadas, with the two sub-castes: Padye brahmins and Bhatta Prabhu Brahmins, some Chitapavan Brahmins and a few brahmins of Dravidian origin called Daivajnya Brahmins, Habbu Brahmins, etc., who are Shaivites and follow the religious leadership of Swami Adya Shankaracharya of Shringeri (Karnataka) and worship at the Mallikarjun Temple at Shristhal, near Chaudi on the Canacona-Karwar road.

Besides Brahmins, there are the Maratthas (some of whom claim to be Kshatryas), Bhandaris, Vannis, and Kunnbis (Gaudas). There are also artisans e.g., Sutars (carpenters), Sonars (goldsmiths), Lohars (blacksmiths), Cansars (coppersmiths), etc.; actors (like the Kolavants); herdsmen (like the Gonvllis), fishermen (Kharvis), and the Backward Classes like the Mahars and Chambars.

I. HINDU COMMUNITIES

A. BRAHMIN COMMUNITIES

1. The Saraswat Brahmins

As the name "*Saraswat*" suggests, the legendary origin of the community is Aryan, from the valley of the river Saraswati in Kashmir. Possibly they migrated from Kashmir, first, to Goud (Bengal) and from there (about the 12th century) to Goa. According to another legend, they are the descendants of the ten of his relatives whom Parashurama invited from Trihotra or Tirhut in North India to preside over a yagna at Ponda, and to whom he then gifted 96 villages (hence Shahnavi, Shenvi, or Shenoy Brahmins).

On arrival in Goa, the Gouda Saraswats built beautiful temples dedicated to their favourite deities: Mangesh, Mahalakshmi, Shantadurga, and Ramnath. A Saraswat couple visiting their *kula devata* (family deity), for the first time after their marriage, are "re-married" in the presence of the deity.

Originally, most of the Saraswats followed the Rig Veda, but among themselves they differed according to the *dharmasutra* (ritual) that they followed. Some who follow the ritual of Ashvalayana are called "Ashvalayans"; those following Hirannyakeshi are called "Hirannyakeshis"; and still others who follow the Krishna Yajurvedic ritual of Apastamba are called "Apastambas".

In the thirteenth century, some Saraswats came under the influence of Madhava (1238-1317). He had established a centre in Udupi in order to propound the Dvaita Philosophy. This philosophy postulates a transcendent and supreme God (paramätma), distinct from the universe, that is made up of chit (spirit) and achit (matter). Those who followed Madhava and became Vaishnavites are called Madhava Saraswats or Bhagwats, as they also follow the Bhagwat Purana.

62

Sometimes they are also called *ubhe* brahmin, because of the vertical lines drawn on their bodies. The majority of the Saraswats, however, are Smarta Saraswats who are Shaivites and follow the Advaita Philosophy of Shankaracharya. These are also called addve brahmins, on account of the horizontal lines.

Though each group owes allegiance to a different matth, they have no reluctance to worship at each other's temples. The chief matth of the Madhava Saraswats is the Gokarn Partagal Jeevottam Matth in Poinguinim, Canacona taluka, on the Canacona-Karwar road. It has temples dedicated to Ramdev and Vir Vetthal, the latter being the *"upasya devata"* of the Swami of Partagal, which he carries along wherever he goes. The Matth has branch monasteries elsewhere in Goa (Bicholim, Rivona) and in some other places in India (Bhatkal, Pandharpur, Gokarn, Ankola, Honavar, Venkatapur, Baroda, etc.). Also popular among these Saraswats is the Kasi Matth at Bandora, west of Ponda.

The family deities of the Smarta Saraswats are Mangesh, Shantadurga, Mahalakshimi, etc., who have their respective temples in various parts of Goa. Their chief matth, however, is the Shri Gouda Padacharya Matth, which is situated in Queula or Kavale, about 2.5 km west of Ponda. The matth was originally at Kushasthali (Quelossim) until it was damaged by the Portuguese in 1567. The present matth was constructed in 1925. It contains tombs of six swamis (who are not cremated, but buried with full honours) and, like the Partagal matth, also conducts Sanskrit and Veda classes.

When Goa was conquered by the Portuguese, many Saraswat families migrated southwards, up to Cochin and Travancore, for fear of being forced to accept Christianity. At the beginning of the present century, however, those residing in Karnataka began to migrate to larger cities, especially Bombay, so that few Saraswats still remain in villages. In fact, they are mostly an urban phenomenon.

Almost all Saraswats are educated, well placed, economically well-off and modern in outlook. There have been well-known artists, writers, industrialists, and business--men among them. They are said to be the first people in India to plan and execute a scheme for a cooperative housing project and they have operated many other cooperative activities. Liberal in their outlook, many young Saraswat Brahmins have married outside their religion and caste, uphold gender equality, accept re-marriage of widows, etc.

2. The Chitpavan Brahmins

Originally from the town of Chiplun (hence also called Chipluns). The town was once known as Chitpolan, hence these Brahmins are also known as Chitpols. In the Ratnagiri District, they began to be called Konkannasthas in about 1715, when their casteman Peshwa Balaji Vishvanath rose to importance in the Marattha kingdom. Their legendary origin, due perhaps to their fair complexion, has been attributed to some shipwrecked foreigners, cast ashore by the sea that washed the foot of the Sahyadri hills. Parashurama is believed to have purified and revived their corpses, taught them to perform religious rituals, which he himself could not perform (because he had been defiled by the slaughter of the Kshatryas) and, as a reward for their services, gave them a tract of land north of Ratnagiri.

Though originally farmers, the highly intelligent Chitpavan Brahmins soon launched into other professions and migrated to various parts of the Deccan, especially to Pune, where they founded the Ferguson College. Eminent social and political reformers like D.K. Karve, M.G. Ranade, G.K. Gokhale, B.G. Tilak, and S.M. Paranjpe, belonged to this community, so did also the notorious Nathuram Vinayak Godse, who murdered the Father of the Nation!

3. The Karhada Brahmins

These Brahmins originally lived in the southern part of

64

modern Maharashtra, between Konkan and Desh, in a province then called Karathak, comprising Satara, Sangli, and Kolhapur, with Karad as capital. Hence the name of Karhada Brahmins.

The Karhads are Shaivites and worshippers of Devi under different titles. Thus the Karhads of Kolhapur worship Ambabai and those of Goa worship Mhalsa or Shantadurga or Vijayadurga. Among them too there are Smartas and Madhavas or Bhagwats (Vaishnavites). In Goa they are divided into two sub-castes: Pandye Brahmins and Bhatt Prabhu Brahmins.

4. The Deshastha Brahmins

"Desha" is the name given to the territory of the valleys of the Krishna and the Godavari, and the Deccan Plateau. Hence this community is spread over the states of Maharashtra (especially in Kolhapur), Karnataka, and Andhra.

The Deshasthas, of whom there is a sprinkling in Goa, are very much of a Vedic group, some following the Rig Veda and others the Yajur Veda. Rigvedis are divided into Smartas and Vaishnavites, whilst among the Yajurvedis there are followers of Shukla (white) Yajurveda and of Krishna (black) Yajurveda. There are also the Madhyandins who are another sub-division of Yajurvedi Deshasthas and have their own two sections, Vajasaneyas and Kannvas. The family gods of the Deshasthas are Ambabai of Kolhapur, Bannshankari of Badami; Gajanana, Jogeshwari, Jotiba of Vadi-Ratnagiri (Kolhapur Dt), Khandoba of Jejuri (Pune Dt), Rama, Shiva, and Vishnu.

The Deshasthas are physically sturdy, of a relatively dark complexion, usually intelligent, courteous, and hospitable. Many of the well-known "saints" of Maharashtra, e.g., Dhyaneshvar and Eknath, belong to this community. Ramdasa too was a Deshastha. There have also been many

Sanskrit scholars and mathematicians who belonged to this community.

Some of the surnames of Deshastha Brahmins indicate traditionally-held administrative offices, e.g., Kulkarni, Deshpande, Patil, and Deshmukh; others, physical and mental characteristics: Hirve, Buddhisagar. Many adopt the name of the ancestral village by adding "kar", e.g., Madgaokar, Navelkar, Junnarkar, etc.

B. THE OTHER COMMUNITIES

The non-Brahmins may differ from the Brahmins in their social customs, but they are more or less close to them in the practice of religion, except that their worship is much simpler than the Vedic brahmin worship. The religious faith of the Hindu farmers and labourers, however, is a curious mixture of animism and Hinduism. They worship all the brahmanic gods and goddesses, but they have their own objects of worship, chief among whom are are: Bhairav and Bhavani (wife of Shiva, also known as Phirangai, Tukai, etc.), both considered as village guardians. The others whom they worship are: Bhairoba who lives outside the village in the form of an unhewn stone; Jakhai, Janai, Jokhai, Kalkai, Mettisai, Mukai, and Navlai (all local 'mothers', unkindly forms of Bhavani and capable of much mischief unless propitiated); Sattvai, the goddess of pregnant women and of smallpox; Khandoba, the sword-father, protector of the countryside; Maruti (Hanuman) a kindly god, saviour of those into whom evil spirits have entered; Mhasoba or Mhashkoba, the most feared evil spirit who lives in an unhewn stone coated with *shindur* (red-lead), and is worshipped with a promise of sacrifice of a goat or a fowl in order to cast evil spells on one's enemies; Vaghoba who also lives in an unhewn stone and, if worshipped, protects the village herds from tiger attacks; and Vettal, the leader of demons and evil spirits and also the patron of wrestlers and athletes. Like Mhaskhoba, he too can be persuaded, with a promise of a goat or a fowl sacrifice, to drive out evil spirits.

The Gaudas

A special mention may be made of Gaudas (also called kunbis, velips, gaonkars). They are the adivasis of Goa, belonging to the Munda section of the Astroid race, and have features similar to those of Santhals in North India. Many explanations are given to the origin of the name "gauda": they came in pre-historic times from some South-East Asian country called Gauda Desh; they spoke a now-extinct language called "gauda", the word being a corruption of "ganv", etc.

There are three main categories of Gaudas in Goa: Christian Gaudas, Hindu Gaudas, and Nav Hindu Gaudas who were re-converted to Hinduism around 1928. Even a few decades ago they had their own cultural peculiarities in dress and life-style. In 1940, for example, the Portuguese had to forbid the ladies to appear in public without cholis. Now they are being absorbed in the general culture of Goa. We rarely see nowadays their menfolk in their traditional "langottis" (loin cloths), but they do have still their peculiar folk dances like jagor, dhalo, and fugddi.

The Gaudas consider themselves to be descendants of the puranic king Bali, whom the Hindu Gaudas worship, together with Bhima (one of the Pandavas). Many of them worship at Mallikarjun temple in Canacona. The Goud Gaudas of Chimbel also worship Mahalsa, Kamakshi, Betal, Shivaikar, Folkar, Shantadurga, Mahadev, Boma, Kamaleshwar, Nagueshi, and Lohanai. The Nav Hindu Gaudas, on the other hand, worship Ravalnath, Mallikarjuna, Betal, Mahadev, Kamakshi, Nava Durga, Mahalakshimi, Chamundi, and Shantadurga.

The important holidays of the Gaudas are the Ganesh Chaturthi, Tulsi Vivaha, and Bali Pratipada. On this last feastday, the cattle are decorated, worshipped, and fed on *pole*. There is special worship on this day in the temple dedicated to Devaki-Krishna at Marcela.

II. HINDU RELIGIOUS ORGANISATIONS

When the more educated Hindus came into contact with the Western philosophies and the Christian religion in the 18th and the 19th centuries, some of them opened their eyes to the obsolete beliefs and customs of Hinduism and started a process of religious reform and revival.

1. The Brahmo Samaj

Ram Mohan Roy (1774-1833) was a Bengalee Brahmin who belonged to the Vaishnavite sect. He was much influenced by the monotheism among Muslims and Christians and started to write against idolatry and even in favour of Christ's doctrines: "The consequence of my long and uninterrupted researches into religious truth has been that I have found the doctrines of Christ more conducive to moral principles, and better adapted to the use of rational beings, than any other which have come to my knowledge."

His study of the Bible, as well as of the Vedas and Upanishads, led him to the conclusion that monism and polytheism are untenable in the light of history and the principles of reason, and that the religion of ancient Hindus was not monism and polytheism but monotheism. He conceived the idea of restoring the Hindu faith to its original purity. With this object in view, he founded the Brahmo Samaj in 1828. His Hall of Worship had no images, statues, or pictures. Only prayers and hymns that affirm One God were selected. Members offered worship as a group, something new in Hinduism. The various social reforms introduced by the British at that time were made possible because of the activities of persons like Raja Ram Mohan Roy.

The person, however, who put the Samaj on a firm

foundation was **Devandranath Tagore**, the father of the great poet. He too believed that Hinduism had to be reformed, not by borrowing from Christianity, but by returning to genuine Vedas and Upanishads. For this purpose he established a vedic school to train Brahmo missionaries and to check the spread of Christianity.

Another great reformer to join the Samaj was **Keshab Chandra Sen**. His admiration and appreciation of Christ and Christian principles were both sincere and great. He thought of a Christian India, industrialised and socially emancipated:

Christ has been my study for a quarter of a century. That God-Man — they say half-God and half-man — walks daily all over this vast peninsula, from Himalayas to Cape Comorin, enlightening and sanctifying its teeming millions. He is a mighty reality in Indian history. He is to us a living and moving spirit. We see him and commune with him. He permeates society as a vital force, and imbues our daily life, and is mixed with our thoughts, speculations, and pursuits. (Lectures in India, p. 330).

On another occasion he preached:

It is Christ who rules British India, and not the British Government England has sent out a tremendous moral force in the life and character of that mighty prophet to conquer and hold this vast empire. None but Jesus ever deserved this bright, this precious diadem, India, and Jesus shall have it. Christ comes to us as an Asiatic in race and as a Hindu in faith, as a kinsman, and as a brother... Christ is a true yogi, and will surely help us to realise our national ideal of yogi... In accepting him, therefore, you accept the fulfilment of your national Scriptures and prophets. (Sermon delivered at Calcutta in 1879.)

Under Sen's leadership the Samaj made such great progress that gradually it cut itself adrift from Hindu rites and customs and adopted many Christian ideals. Such radical reforms, however, were resented by Devandranath Tagore and there followed a split in the organisation: Adi

Brahma Samaj (representing the orthodox party of Tagore) and the Brahma Samaj of Keshab Chandra Sen.

Offshoots of the Brahmo Samaj were the more liberal Prarthana Samaj of Bombay (1867), the Poona Prarthana Samaj (1870), and the Servants of India Society. There were others also who castigated their Hindu religion for its polytheism and social aberrations. The "Tatva Bodhini Patrika", under the editorship of Akhay Kumar Datta and Ishvara Chandra Vidyasagar, became their mouthpiece where they attacked the belief in the infallibility and authority of the Vedas, that was being promoted by another group of staunch Hindus.

2. The Arya Samaj

One such staunch and militant traditionalist was the Gujarati Brahmin **Dayananda Saraswati** (1824-1883) from Kathiawar. He wanted that Hinduism (as well as India) be purified and reformed, and that foreign religions, like Islam and Christianity, be extirpated from the country. He spearheaded the "Back to the Vedas" movement, and for this some called him "the Luther of Hinduism." Like Luther, he too appealed from the authority of the Brahminical Church and of Tradition (smriti) to Revelation (shruti) as recorded in the Vedas. His other important watchword was "India for Indians". Hence the organisation, the Arya Samaj, that he founded, promoted both religious and political ends.

Like Raja Rammohan Roy, **Swami Dayananda** too opposed idol worship, animal sacrifice, child marriage and sat'ti, and introduced forms of worship similar to those of the Protestants. He also developed an anti-foreign and anti--Islam-Christian policy, and instituted "purification rites" for the re-conversion of Christians and Muslims to Hinduism. How the fear of Christianity played a role in the militant character of the Arya Samaj was expressed by Lajpat Rai, a historian of the sect: "The greater the activities of the Christian missionaries to convert India to Christianity, the

70

greater the chance of the Arya Samaj to work, to struggle and to thrive... It has two militant churches to counteract, viz., Islam and Christianity. Any increase in the activities of the latter is its chance and from its past history we may safely conclude that it is not likely to miss it."

Eventually, the Arya Samaj split into two branches: one (the Anarkali party) more progressive and open to western learning and institutions, and the other (the Wachowali party) more conservative, adhering more strictly to the Vedas which are supposed to contain all that the ancient and modern sciences can provide.

3. The Ramakrishna Mission

Shri Ramakrishna Paramahansa (1836-1886) was a simple and poor man by worldly standards, but a man of great detachment, with a warm heart, and deeply united with God. By the sincerity of his life and the depth of his knowledge about spiritual matters, he had influenced many, even from among the intelligentsia of Calcutta.

One of his disciples was Narendranath Datta, a young truth-seeker, later called Swami Vivekananda. Born in 1863 in an educated middle-class family of Calcutta, Narendranath attended Christian colleges there. After passing through various religious and economic crises, he became a devoted disciple of Shri Ramakrishna and travelled throughout the country meeting and mixing with various sorts of people of every religion and social class. In 1893 he attended the newly-started Parliament of Religions in Chicago, where he made a powerful speech that brought him admirers from all over America. He entertained great hopes of converting the West to Hinduism. With that intention and in order to propagate the religious ideas of his guru, he founded the Ramakrishna Mission (1897) on his return to India. He, however, died young in 1902 at the age of 40.

71

As a Jesuit missionary in Calcutta, Fr P. Fallon, wrote many years ago, Swami Vivekananda did much to turn the minds of Hindus towards social service and humanitarian work; he tried to infuse into Vedanta a positive and dynamic ethics; he gave back to many Hindus a sense of pride in their own religious tradition. His central idea was the affirmation of man's essential divinity which he found in the Upanishads read in the light of the late advaitins. He translated it into a thousand formulas which emphasized man's natural greatness, strength, and dignity. He wished Hinduism to be dynamic; religion and spirituality had to come out into the open to manifest themselves in deeds of service and social uplift. Jñana-yoga and bhakti-yoga were valueless if not accompanied by karma-yoga, that is, selfless work — social, educational, national.

For many educated Hindus, the type of Hinduism preached by Swami Vivekananda and propagated by the members of the Ramakrishna Mission provides a religion that is consonant with the modern era.

4. The Brahma Kumaris

a. Origins

The Prajapita Brahma Kumaris is a modern Hindu religious congregation of consecrated women committed to live according to the teachings of God Shiv-Baba, the Supreme Father of all, as revealed through his corporeal medium, the *Prajapita Brahma Baba*. It is also their mission to transmit that doctrine to all who would care to listen.

The members of the organisation tell us how it started:

A famous diamond merchant known as **Dada Lekh Raj** (1876-1969) had, in the late fifties of his life, been feeling a deep, divine urge for spending more time on and devoting more attention to the rediscovery of the self, understanding of the mystery of the world and realisation of the true nature of the Supreme Being. Though he had, since his childhood, been deeply religious-minded and had grown to be of strong character and charitable disposition, yet it was during this period of life that he felt the pangs of separation from the Divine.

In 1936-37, when he was around sixty, he had an irresistible yearning for a union with the Divine and he felt a strong pull from on High. It was during that phase of life that he saw many divine visions. He had a vision of the Incorporeal Supreme Soul — "the Supreme Father God-Shiva". One of the visions he saw was that a value-based society, characterised by love, peace, harmony, health, happiness, and law and order, will become an emerging reality during the early decades of the next century. He had a divine call to be an embodiment of virtues, to set an example of divinity, to inspire others by his practical life and to create other human instruments like himself to spread education in values, meditation, and holistic knowledge, so that the Golden Age might dawn again. He also saw a vision of a great catastrophic end of the present order of utter moral degradation and the descent of man to barbarity.

He now had a divine call to free himself and be a human medium of the Divine so that God might speak and manifest His knowledge through him. He was inspired to share God's wisdom with others. It was in response to this call that the institution *"Prajapita Brahma Kumaris Ishwariya Vishwa Vidyalaya"* in its nucleus form, was formally founded in the year 1937 to re-establish moral, human, and spiritual values. He renounced his flourishing diamond business in Calcutta and returned to his native place, Hyderabad, Sind (now in Pakistan), where he formed a Trust, consisting of mothers and sisters only, and placed all his movable and immovable properties in their hands to run the Institution. Thus, he gave high honour to women and they have, since then, been in the vanguard and been flag-bearers of a revolution in moral and spiritual values.

In course of time, Dada Lekh Raj came to be known as Brahma or *Prajapita Brahma* and those who were morally re-born or spiritually regenerated through oracles of God-Shiva through Brahma, were known as Brahma Kumaris and Brahma Kumars, and the institution that he founded to impart divine knowledge came to be known as Prajapita Brahma Kumaris Ishwariya Vishwa-Vidyalaya. Started as a family gathering (satsang) in 1936, it became a family institution in 1937 for education in Values, World-view, and Meditation, run mostly by women.

In 1951, after the Partition, Brahma Baba and his followers shifted to Mt Abu (Rajasthan), where the present international headquarters are at "Shantivan". It is a 60-acre sprawling complex, with lush green parks, lotus meditation hall, 15,000-seater Diamond Hall, etc. Here too they have the Prajapati Brahma-kumaris Ishwariya Vishwa Vidyalaya, whose main thrust is still to promote human, moral, ethical, social, and spiritual values in people's personal, professional, and public life thereby empowering and enabling them to realise peace, poise, progress, and harmony in self and society. Its first Administrative Head was Brahma Kumari Jagadamba Saraswati revered as World Mother and its present Administrative Head is Dr Dadi Prakashmani.

The Institution has now grown into a gigantic tree with more than 4,500 branches, spread over India and more than 70 other countries. There are three centres in Goa: Panjim, Margao, and Vasco. Brahma Baba left his mortal body on 18th January 1969, leaving others to continue his work.

b. Basic Teachings

The Brahma Kumaris have their own interpretation of world history, their cosmology, and their theology. Since its creation, they say, the world has passed through various Ages, each lasting 1,250 years. It started with the Golden Age under the sovereignty of Shri Lakshmi and Shri Narayana, when the people were pure and holy like them. Then change began to set in and slow degeneration through the Silver Age (of Sita and Rama), the Copper Age of sinfulness coupled with penance and worship; and finally the present Iron Age (Kaliyuga). Now, towards the end of the Iron Age, God Father-Shiva has descended in Prajapita Brahma Baba who is to lead humanity back to the Golden Age, thus completing the full circle.

The Brahma Kumaris have no prescribed scriptures, no particular guru (though they believe that God Shiva revealed himself through their Founder), and no external worship. They believe in the Fatherhood of God and Brotherhood of man. They believe that with the right type of approach and effort, the human community can usher in the dawn of the Golden Age within a very short time. Their principles include vegetarianism, celibacy, and abstinence from liquor and tobacco. According to their belief, Sahaj Rajyoga (the yoga of the intellect, meditation) is the means of realisation of God and of empowerment of self. For the purpose of promoting this yoga, the Brahma Kumaris have established the Rajyoga Education and Research Foundation with thirteen wings covering disciplines like Medicine, Science and Engineering, Law, Business and Industry, Administration, Education, Rural Development, Youth, Women, etc.

PART II

HINDU FESTIVALS

PART II

HINDU FESTIVALS

INTRODUCTION

T. Pereira, OFM (Cap.)

1. Festivals in Human Life

Festivals have always formed part and parcel of the socio-religious lives of people everywhere. This is because they are intimately connected with the basic finitude of human beings, their longing for liberation, and the infinite goodness, power, and will of God to save.

Whenever man found himself in moments of crises, owing to the threatening seasonal and cosmic changes; or to a host of uncertainties accompanying the important stages of life such as birth, adolescence, marriage, and death; or owing to human selfishness, greed, and ignorance, that occasioned wars, destruction, violence, fanaticism, pestilence and disease, he cried out to God for help. And, when through the intervention of the deity he was delivered from the impending disaster, he and the whole community gathered together to joyfully praise and thank God in word and deed, in sacrifice and libation, music and dancing, eating and drinking. These unforgettable experiences of divine intervention were so deeply embedded in the hearts and minds of the people that one and all would come together at fixed times every year to commemorate and celebrate God's salvific action.

The value of festivals can be gauged from this that through them communities came together to re-discover their identity, to re-emphasise those values and relationships that gave meaning to their lives and cemented the bonds of love and devotion between God and his people.

The festivals also bring people together and strengthen the bonds of union among them. Undoubtedly, differences of religion and culture can and often do undermine the unitive value of festivals, but most festivals have also social elements that make it possible for neighbours, belonging to different cultures and religions, to hold certain joint celebrations leading to the strengthening of the bonds of union.

Festivals are integrated in the people's calendars. Whilst Christians follow the Gregorian calendar, thus called because it was introduced by Pope Gregory XIII in 1582, Hindus have their own. These two calendars do not fully correspond with each other in the reckoning of days and months, because, whereas the Gregorian calendar is based on the solar movement, the Hindu calendar follows the phases in the moon.

The following are the months of the Hindu calendar, with approximately corresponding months of the Gregorian:

Chaitra (Mar.-Apr.)
Vaishāka (Apr.-May)
Jyaistha (May-Jun)
Asādha (Jun-Jul.)
Shrāvana (Jul.-Aug.)
Bhādrapada (Aug.-Sep.)
Ashvina (Sep.-Oct.)
Kārtika (Oct.-Nov.)
Mārgashirsa (Nov.-Dec.)
Pausha (Dec.-Jan.)
Māgha (Jan.-Feb.)
Phālguna (Feb.-Mar.)

The main Hindu festivals, some of which are celebrated only by certain sections of the Hindus, are distributed in the course of the year as follows. We shall, however, describe in these pages only those that are celebrated in Goa and along the West coast.

Chaitra:

    Gudhi Padhva
    Rama Navmi
    Mahavir Jayanti

Hanuman Jayanti

Vaishāka:

Budha Jayanti

Asādha:

Mahaekadashi

Shrāvana:

Nag Panchmi
Gokul/Janama Ashtami
(Krishna Jayanti)
Narali Purnima;
Rakshbandan

Bhādrapada:

Ganesh Chaturthi
Vaman Dvadashi

Ashvina:

Navratra
Dasrah
Divali (Laxmi Puja, Balipratipada, Bhau beej

Kārtika:

Tulsi Vivah

Māgha:

Makar Sankrant
Vasant Panchmi
Mahashivaratra

Phālguna:

Holi

2. History, Legends, and Myths

Underlying every festival are elements of history, legend,

81

and myth, because festivals do not celebrate merely a past event, but also a present human reality. Whilst **history** is a record of past events, based on sufficient evidence, **legends** are traditional stories, popularly regarded as historical, but for which there is no sufficient historical evidence. A **myth**, however, is difficult to define. It is a symbolic way of speaking of realities that are beyond space-time. Myths are stories of events that supposedly happened long ago and whose actors were divine or semi-divine beings. Through a language that is dramatic and action-centred, symbolic and evocative of several levels of meaning, the stories are narrated to groups of people as providing a meaning to some aspect of their identity. In this way, the myths have the function of holding the community together. This unifying function of the myth is experienced specially through a celebration, because through the celebration the community becomes conscious of its joint possession. (See *Major Hindu Festivals: A Christian Appreciation* by Subash Anand [St Paul Publication, 1991] pp.10-15.)

Although, whilst speaking of the various Hindu festivals, it is not essential to differentiate the historical from the mythical elements, it is important to keep on reminding ourselves that what we Christians call "God" and the Hindus call "*deva*" are **not** one and the same thing. "God" for us is a Supreme and Transcendent Reality. Many Hindus would call It "*Ishwar*" or "*Parameshwar*". "*Devas*", on the other hand, are spiritual but lower beings. Some compare them to our "angels", both good and bad (devils), with Indra corresponding to Michael and Narakasur to Lucifer. Others consider *devas* as forces in nature: good (devas) or bad (*asuras*). Still others think that they are really phenomena, powers, values, aspirations, and even projections of man in his search for the divine. Indeed, as Pope Paul VI asserted to the Hindus in Bombay during his visit to India in 1964:

> *Yours is a land of ancient culture, the cradle of great religions, the home of a nation that has sought God with a relentless*

desire, in deep meditation and silence, and in hymns of fervent prayer. Rarely has this longing for God been expressed with words so full of the spirit of Advent as in the words written in your sacred books many centuries before Christ:

From the unreal lead me to the real;
From darkness lead me to light;
From death lead me to immortality.

Asatô mä sad gamaya,
Tamasô mä jyotir gamaya,
Mrtyor mä amrtam gamaya.

(Brihadärannyaka Upanishad I.3,28)

CHAITRA — 1ST DAY
OF THE MONTH

GUDHI PADVA

Gudhi Padva is the New Year's Day, the first day (*shuddha pratipada*) of the first month of the Saka or Salivahan calendar (Chaitra) and is celebrated mostly in Maharashtra and Goa, because Salivahan is supposed to have ruled in Maharashtra. It is a day to thank God for his many blessings in the previous year, and to make a new beginning, to renew the resolution to aim higher in one's life and work. This is beautifully symbolised by the *Gudhi*, the pole that is erected on this occasion in front of the house. *Padva* is a variation of the word *pratipada*, the first day of a lunar month. A new cloth is tied on the gudhi, a metal vessel is put onto it and a garland of sweets is hung on it to signify the goal of one's struggle. The pole is usually lubricated with oil to remind one of the difficulties that one meets in aiming high. Any daring youngster who succeeds in climbing the *gudhi* gets the sweets as his prize!

This social event was eventually sacralised in the liturgical tradition of Hinduism. Gudhi Padva was made to commemorate the victory of Rama over Vali, a South Indian King. Rama and Lakshman in their search of Sita reached the Vanara (monkey) kingdom in the South. They met Sugreeva who with his minister Hanuman, was hiding in the forest for fear of Vali, his brother king. Vali had been challenged by a demon named Maayaavi.Vali and the demon fought inside a cave. After waiting outside the cave a long time, since Vali was not coming out, Sugreeva thought he was dead. He covered the mouth of the cave with a big stone and returned to Kishkindha, the capital, to occupy his brother's vacant throne, and also to take as his wife Vali's queen Tara. But then Vali appeared and became furious against his brother for what he had done. While Vali and Sugreeva were engaged in a fight, and Sugreeva was on the point of defeat, Rama, hiding behind a tree, shot an arrow at Vali, who fell mortally wounded.

As he lay dying, Vali reproached Rama and he was shocked at his perfidious behaviour. "Rama," he said, "you are the son of Emperor Dasaratha. Born of a noble race and famous by your own exploits, how did you bring yourself to do this deed? The world is full of praises for your valour and virtue. And yet, while I was absorbed in a battle with another, you came unseen and, from behind, shot a fatal arrow at me. How false and undeserved is your reputation for manly virtue, for truth and forbearance! What will the world think of you now? What harm have I ever done to you? Did I come out to fight with you? You have killed me like an assassin concealing yourself behind the trees. For a royal prince to kill an innocent person in this way is grievous sin. You are unworthy for kingship. The goddess Earth will never consent to take you for a bridegroom. My greatest sorrow is that I am killed by a base and sinful wretch... All who are born must die. This is the law. I do not therefore grieve for my death. Still, your sin is great in killing me in this treacherous manner."

How do the devotees of Rama defend his behaviour? C. Rajagopalachari, the first Governor-General of Independent India, and from whose book RAMAYANA the above passage is taken, writes: "In Valmiki's work Rama is portrayed as a great and unique man, not as an incarnation of God. True, in some chapters there are references to him as an avatar of God, but in the body of the narrative the Rama pictured by sage Valmiki is not God himself, but a great prince endowed with divine powers." But Rajaji continues: "If we keep in mind that when God takes a lower and limited form by His own ordinance, limitations follow and we should not be confused thereby... What I think is that an avatar is an avatar, and among the sorrows that the Lord and His consort had to endure in their earthly incarnation, this liability to have their actions weighed on the earthly scales is a part."

Perhaps not everybody will be satisfied with Rajaji's argument. In the Bible too we have similar problems, as when David committed adultery (2 Sam. 11), or Jacob lied to his father and obtained from him the blessing that was meant for his brother Esau (cf. Genesis 27,24). Here the Jerusalem Bible in a footnote offers an explanation parallel to Rajaji's: "The morality is immature, but the lie reported here mysteriously serves God's purpose: the free divine choice preferred Jacob to Esau."

Swami Shilananda writes in his book A RAINBOW OF FEASTS: "To celebrate Gudhi Padva in a truly religious manner, the cause of rejoicing must be found not merely in the victory of Rama over Vali, but in the victory of good over evil, in whatever form, or nation or time it may occur. Every man experiences in his heart the struggle between good and evil, and it is here that something practical and concrete can be done to show that we are honestly on the side of justice. Once things have been set right at home, one can try to co-operate in promoting justice elsewhere. It is dangerous to launch on social reforms if evil is not first overcome in one's own heart."

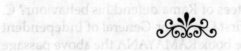

CHAITRA — 9TH DAY
OF THE MONTH

RAMA NAVAMI

On the ninth day of the Chaitra month, some time in the month of April, is celebrated the festival of Rama Navami, in honour of the legendary hero, now divinised, Ramachandra.

1. The Hero

Once upon a time, between the 8th and 7th centuries B.C., there was a prince of the royal house of Ayodhya (U.P.) and his name was Rama. Due to the cunning of his step-mother, Rama was banished for a time to the forests. He went into exile and his wife Sita and his brother Lakshmana gladly went with him. While they were living in the forest an aboriginal chieftain kidnapped Sita. Rama rescued his faithful Sita, but only after many adventures and only with the help of friendly aboriginal tribes. Then the time came for his exile to end and for him to return to his kingdom. He returned to Ayodhya, was crowned, and reigned successfully for many years.

2. The Myth

Over the years a myth developed around Ramachandra who was probably a historical figure. According to it, Lord Vishnu took the seventh avatar, and Sri Rama was born to rid the world of Ravana who was creating havoc. Lord Brahma had granted so many boons to Ravana in the past, that he had become almost invincible and extremely arrogant. He was destroying *dharma* both on earth and in *devlok* (the heavens) without a single thought for the future. The devtas ran to Lord Brahma. Brahmaji told them that he was well aware of the atrocities committed by Ravana, but he himself could do nothing about it; he had to depend on a human being for it because, due to some boon granted to him, Ravana could not be killed by any god or devta.

In his arrogance Ravana had forgotten to safeguard himself against a human being, for he believed that no man on earth could kill him. Hence, a human being stronger than Ravana had to be born to get rid of that evil force. At that very moment Lord Vishnu arrived on his vahan (vehicle), the Garud, and Brahma asked him to take avatar, as all the human beings on earth and the devtas in heaven were in utter misery because of the atrocities of the rakshasa. Vishnu agreed and Rama was born as the son of Dasaratha, King of Ayodhya and his consort Kaushalya, in the Threta Yuga (the Second Age of the Hindu cycle).

The prince was virtuous, brave and kind. As Dasaratha was growing old, he decided to crown Rama ruler of the kingdom, and to live a retired life. On the eve of the coronation day, Kaikeyi, the youngest wife of Dasaratha and step-mother of Rama, asked the King for a favour, and before knowing its nature he promised to grant her whatever she would ask. Kaikeyi now wanted the King to cancel all preparations for Rama's coronation, to install her son Bharata as king, in place of Rama, and send this prince into exile to the forests of Deccan for 14 years. Neither threats nor entreaties could deter Kaikeyi, and the miserable old King had to accede to her requests. Rama was exiled. His young wife, Sita, and half-brother Lakshmana, followed him.

When these things were taking place in Ayodhya, Bharata, Kaikeyi's son, was away on a visit to his uncle's kingdom. On hearing of Rama's exile, he hurried back to Ayodhya, but before reaching this city, Dasaratha, his father, had died of grief. Bharata, like Lakshmana, was much attached to Rama and had no desire to usurp his throne. He reviled his mother for her selfishness and cruelty, and set out in search of Rama. He met this prince in the forests of Dandaka wearing the garb of a hermit and living on jungle fare. The meeting of the brothers is described with much pathos and tenderness. But all the coaxing and pleading of Bharata could not deter Rama from the promise he had given his father, and he had to order his weeping half--brother back to Ayodhya to rule the kingdom as his regent.

Meanwhile Ravana, the demon-king of Lanka came to hear of the extraordinary beauty of Sita and abducted her. He took her away in his aerial chariot, Pushpaka,and interned her in his impregnable castle. Rama and Lakshmana were out in the forest when this happened and they set out on a search for Sita. After long wanderings in the forests of the Deccan, they found out the whereabouts of Sita with the help of the "bear" and "monkey" tribes that inhabited the hills. Under Rama's leadership, an army of redoubtable monkeys was raised, who built a bridge across the gulf and stormed Lanka. After many bitter and bloody battles, the ten-headed Ravana was slain and Sita reclaimed. The termination of the battle coincided with the end of the 14 years' exile, and Rama, Sita, and Lakshmana, returned to Ayodhya with many of the monkey chiefs. Of these, Hanuman was considered the most loyal and brave, and he is worshipped by the Hindus as a god.

There are undoubtedly in this Epic situations in which the behaviour of Rama may appear as scandalous, like when he killed Vali treacherously. Some explanation of such behaviour is given by C. Rajagopalachari, the first Governor--General of Independent India, in his book RAMAYANA: "In Valmiki's work Rama is portrayed as a great and unique man, not as an incarnation of God. True, in some chapters there are references to him as an avatar of God, but in the body of the narrative the Rama pictured by sage Valmiki is not

God himself, but a great prince endowed with divine powers." But Rajaji continues: "If we keep in mind that when God takes a lower and limited form by His own ordinance, limitations follow and we should not be confused thereby... What I think is that an avatar is an avatar, and among the sorrows that the Lord and His consort had to endure in their earthly incarnation, this liability to have their actions weighed on the earthly scales is a part."

3. The Epic

The bards of the court of Ayodhya made the adventures and heroism of Rama and the myths that had developed around him the matter of their ballads. They were already in circulatiion by the 4th cent. B.C. It must have been at about this period that Valmiki, the first of India's poets, conceived of the ambitious design of embodying the various stories about Rama into one long poem, with 24,000 couplets, which is called Ramayana, or the Wanderings of Rama.

Much later, after Rama had been divinised from about the 1st cent. A.D., variations of the original Ramayana began to appear in the vernacular languages. Thus the Tamil *Kamban Ramayana* was published in the 12th cent. *Ramacharita* and *Adhyatma Ramayana*, both in Malayalam, appeared respectively in the 14th and 16th centuries. Tulsidas's Hindi *Ramacharitamanas* came out in the 15th cent., and Eknath's *Bhavarth Ramayana* in Marathi appeared in the 16th cent.

Of all these, Tulsidas's Ramacharitamanas (the Holy Lake of Rama's Acts) became the most popular, especially in North India, where its moral and religious influence on millions of Hindus remains profound. More recently, it was the basis for the TV serial RAMAYANA. When this serial appeared, however, there were complaints from certain quarters that this particular version of the Ramayana was chosen in order to uphold the supremacy of the North Indian Brahmins!

Tulsidas's purpose was to propose the devotion to Rama as "the royal road to salvation". For this purpose he re-wrote Valmiki's story that had come to him through the 14th-cent. version "Adhyatma Ramayana" in Sanskrit. He left out the first and the last books of the original and modified some episodes that he found incongruous with his purpose. For example, in III. 46, he makes Rama describe the virtues of his devout servants (*dasya bhakta*): (1) They display no pride or self-conceit or arrogance, (2) nor even dream of setting foot upon the path of vice; (3) they are ever singing, or listening to, his sporting acts; (4) and are unselfishly devoted to the good of others (*para-hita*).

4. The Festival

Among the Vaishnavites, the festival begins on the first day of the month of Chaitra and continues till the ninth (hence Rama Navami). Rama is said to have been born on this day at noon. The birthday of Rama is celebrated in all important Vaishnavite temples. When the sun reaches the meridian, the priest publicly exhibits a coconut, puts it in a cradle and announces the birth of the god. The main features of the festival are: organizing gatherings and regaling them with stories of the exploits of Sri Rama, the hero who conquered Lanka and destroyed the demon-king Ravana. Religious dances and plays depicting episodes from Rama's life are also organized. These dances and plays are known as Rama Lila (playfulness of Rama), and are particularly popular in U.P., where the ancient kingdom of Ayodhya, the birth place of Rama was situated .

5. A Reflection

The legend of Rama gives witness to man's longing to have God-with-us (Immanuel), not merely as some distant and impersonal Supreme Being. However, there are substantial differences between the Hindu avatar and the Christian concept of Incarnation. For one, whereas in the avatar a divine being "appears" as an animal or a human being, in Incarnation God becomes fully man, without ceasing to be God.

Further, in the "Bhagavad Gita" Lord Krishna asserts: "Whenever the law of righteousness withers away and lawlessness arises, then do I generate myself (on earth). For the protection of the good, for the **destruction of evil-doers** (*emphasis added*), for the setting up of the law of righteousness do I come into being age after age" (4: 7-8). Jesus on the other hand claimed that he came not to destroy evildoers, but to destroy sin and save sinners, by himself dying for their sake.

All the same, there are in the story of the Ramayana many lessons to learn that are related to the Kingdom of God (Hindus call it "*Ramarajya*"): fraternal love, espousal fidelity, sense of justice, patriotism, and trust in God.

92

SHRAVANA — 5TH DAY OF THE MONTH

NAG PANCHAMI

The month of Shravana (corresponding to July-August of the solar calendar) witnesses the celebration of a number of festivals among which the most important perhaps is that of *Nagpanchami*. This festival is kept on the 5th of the bright half of *Shravana*, although in Bengal and in South India "*Manasadevi*" (the queen of snakes) is worshipped on the 5th of the dark half of *Shravana*[1]. As the name itself indicates, this feast revolves around veneration or worship of serpents, either as symbols of the divinity, or in themselves as objects of fear, awe, or reverence.

1. Origin of the Feast

It is really very difficult to lay one's finger with certitude on the precise origin of this feast, because of its widespread observance, its varied ritual practices, and the many reasons connected with human situations, experiences, customs, and folklore, underlying the rites. Certain, however, it is that serpent-worship goes back to the very early beginnings of the human race and that it finds a place of importance in the cultic life of peoples of practically every time and place.[2] (See Holy Bible: Num 21.8; Rev 12.9)

According to P. V. Kane, a renowned Indologist, the Rig Veda contains no reference to snake-worship. On the contrary the Vedic god Indra is said to be the killer of '*ahi*' (a serpent). In the *Asvalayana Grhyasutra*, the *Paraskara*

Grhyasutra and some of the other *grhyasutras*, a rite called '*sarpabali*' (offering to serpents) is mentioned as being performed on the full-moon day of Shravana. The Mahabharata and the Puranas abound in stories about *nagas*. It is not exactly clear, however, what is the difference between '*sarpa*' and '*naga*'. Kane opines that '*sarpa*' refers to all creeping things, while '*naga*' indicates 'the cobra'.[3]

Be that as it may, and coming to the probable reasons for serpent-worship, we find that, as in many cases having to do with cult, these are connected with ambivalence and with the nature and the environmental situations of the reptiles themselves. Because of these attendant circumstances, serpents have almost universally been held in reverence or fear, attraction or repugnance, love or hatred.

The fact that serpents are mostly to be found in or near water, in marshes and river deltas, in places where the vegetation is wild, luxuriant, and dense, as also in abandoned wells, may have led people to readily view them as symbols of life and fertility. Several peoples also believe them to be guardians of houses and temples, and bearers of good fortune, health, and prosperity. This is why to injure or to kill a snake is believed to be inauspicious and fraught with danger. If one were to add to this the consideration that serpents live in or near trees with hanging roots (such as banyan trees) and that they seem to mysteriously rejuvenate themselves after sloughing their skins several times a year, one would grasp the markedly suggestive reasons why serpents are associated with immortality and with divine beings.

Again, the uncanny ability of serpents to appear and disappear with baffling suddenness, and their ingenious capacity of camouflaging themselves disconcertingly fills man with such dread that it leads him to think of them as creatures both cunning and sly and wise and all-knowing. Yet again, their sinuous movements, so akin to that of a rapidly-flowing river, and their ability of propelling themselves swiftly and silently before breaking movement abruptly to stare with unblinking look, so unnerves man that they are equated with some proverbial sage, who dispassionately contemplates all and sundry with inscrutable eye and unfathomable mind.[4]

It might help to bear in mind that snakes were associated with Athena, the Greek goddess of wisdom, and that representations of serpents on the croziers of Coptic and Byzantine bishops used to symbolize the prudence that had to characterize their pastoral ministry. Furthermore, the instinctive choice of graveyards, cremation grounds, and abandoned houses, for their abodes makes one think of snakes as closely related to the world of the spirit, while the holes in the ground, in which they are almost invariably to be found, relates them to the earth and inclines one to consider them as symbols of earth divinities. Since many centuries past, several peoples have come to view snakes and their abodes in holes as sexually-expressive symbols of life, power, and fertility. The ability of snakes to strike mortals with sudden, agonizing, and unsuspecting death, often with disastrous consequences, also led people to think of them as lords of life and death and arbiters of human destiny.

On their plus side, since serpents most abound during the monsoon and harvest seasons, (let us note that Nagpanchami is celebrated at the height of the monsoon season) and since they help in no small measure to keep in check the hordes of rodents, frogs, insects, and other pests, that destroy fruits and crops by the hundreds of thousands of tons, snakes render an incalculable service to farmers in particular and to people in general. For this reason they are held in great reverence, appreciation, and esteem.[5]

Also to be borne in mind is the fact that even today snakes play a notable part in the areas of health and healing. It is possible today to find snakes (elaphe longissima) play a role in the 'Schlangenbad' ('snake bath') at many German spas. That there was a close link between Asklepios (in Greek) or Aesculapius (in Latin) and snakes is well-known.

Indeed, the snake was the god himself in his theriomorphic (or animal form) manifestation, for Asklepios was essentially a chthonic deity. The consort of Asklepios, Hygieia (=health, from which is derived the English word 'hygiene'), also played a part in the well-being of mortals. In human form Asklepios appears as a tall, bearded man with a white cloak and a serpent staff (the emblem even today of healers, physicians, and other medical practitioners).[6]

2. Ritual Elements of the Feast

The celebration of this feast begins with a fast which serves as an act of penance to purify the devotees from their sins, to dissociate them from the profane world, and to insert them into he world of the Sacred. Bathing melas are often organized on the banks of rivers. Live snakes, especially cobras, are procured, or in lieu of these, cloth, metal, stone or clay effigies of these are fashioned, or painted presentations of the same are prepared to represent Sesha, Ananta, or some other mythological snake that is then worshipped by the devotees. These are bathed in water, presented offerings of flour or cooked food (or the same are placed before the abode of snakes), and water and milk are poured on them or offered to them to drink.

Prayers are offered so that the devotees may not only be unharmed by snakes but rather be blessed by god with prosperous lives and bountiful harvests. Snake-charmers are very much in evidence in towns and villages on this day, as they go about their trade with a variety of snakes so that people may fulfil their religious duties of piety, penance, and petition. On this day, too, people scrupulously abstain from ploughing their fields lest they inadvertently harm or even kill a snake and thereby suffer the real or supposed evil consequences of their actions.[7]

3. Significance of the Feast

Through the celebration of this feast devotees glorify God

in and through the snake-world and hope to be blessed with good health, increased life, and prosperity. By honouring snakes — and ultimately God — people acknowledge that these mysterious, silent, and lowly creatures, play an important, though not readily evident, role in the maintenance of a healthy, balanced, and flourishing world. The ritual elements go to implore God's blessing, so that the devotees may be unharmed by snakes and may be the grateful recipients of manifold benefits.

4. Points for Reflection

The feast of Nagpanchami should remind all people of goodwill that :

a. Each and every creature, howsoever small, lowly or insignificant it may appear to be, plays a precise, constructive and, in its own way, irreplaceable role in God's beautiful creation, helping, as instruments of his presence, power, and providence, to bring it to its appointed perfection, and that no one has a right to thwart this God-determined plan.

b. Therefore, any wanton destruction or harm to any one of God's creatures is verily a crime against the goodness and bounty of God.

c. According to experts, there is no animal in India more closely connected with popular religion and folklore than the snake, and none regarding which more general ignorance prevails. Our beloved country, India, has been immensely blessed by God not only with every type of climate in the world but also with a very large part of its fauna and flora (to say nothing of much more precious treasures). "The reptilian fauna of India", acknowledges Sir G. Watt, "is remarkable for the great variety of generic types and number of species. The latter amounts to no fewer than 450, which is nearly one-third of the total number of species known in the world. They refer to 100 genera, of which the majority are not found beyond the limits of India."

And the beauty of it is that: (a) most of the snakes in India are not only harmless but very beneficial to humanity; (b) only the so-called big four are considered to be really dangerous: the cobra, (including the king cobra or hamadryad whose main diet consists of other snakes), the Russell's viper, the krait, and the saw-scaled viper. We ought, therefore, to learn to recognize them, to respect them and to keep a healthy distance from them since snakes in general are by nature shy and timid creatures that readily avoid man's presence and never or hardly ever attack him unless harmed or cornered; (c) although around 30,000 people are estimated to die of snake-bite every year, this number, considering the huge population of the world, is only a tiny fraction of the living beings on earth.

d. Furthermore, it is important to remember that even in cases of presumed poisonous snake-bite, most victims die of shock rather than of actual snake-bite poisoning. Genuinely venomous snakes seldom bite even when molested, and if they do bite they may not poison the victim. One of the most important medical dictums to be borne in mind is: "Poisonous snake-bite is not synonymous with snake-bite poisoning". The snake's objective is more to get away from a potential enemy; not to kill him. Most bites even from venomous snakes, therefore, may be completely harmless or at worst sub-lethal.

e. Snakes do an enormous amount of good to mankind. The world-renowned late Dr Salim Ali declared that 20-50% of our country's food crops are destroyed by rodents every year. This is a huge loss by any measure. By destroying rodents, snakes save India at least 25% of its annual food grains, and this is admittedly an immense boon. Moreover, it is worthwhile remembering that a single rat snake will kill and eat hundreds of rats and mice in one year.

f. When God created the beautiful world and gave it to man, he handed it over to him to use and not to abuse, to till but not to spill, to utilize but not to vandalize, to consecrate but not to desecrate. In God's world men and women are not owners; they are merely stewards and stewardesses. One alone is the earth's owner — God; and to him will every creature have to render a faithful account of conscientious stewardship. Snakes play an important part in maintaining ecological balance and well-being. This is proving to be an increasingly vital and desperate concern today, and in this task of preserving nature's wealth snakes are far from being destroyers. On the contrary! The real destroyer, unfortunately, is the voraciously greedy, aggressively selfish and wantonly destructive modern man and woman. To pillage and to destroy has never been the way of nature. Its benign law has always been: "to give respect and to receive respect; to live and to let live". Every one of us should imitate nature and learn to live in harmony with her. Or else, we shall only be signing our own death sentence, and, what is worse, that of the rest of humanity and creation as well.

Endnotes:

1. Cf. Kane, Pandurang Vaman, History of Dharmasastra, Poona (Bhandarkar Oriental Research Institute), 1974, vol. V,1, pp.124-125; Crooke, William, Serpent-Worship (Indian), in Hastings, James (ed), Encyclopaedia of Religion and Ethics (ERE), Edinburgh (T.& T. Clark), 1981, vol. xi, p.418b.

2. Cf. Kane, P.V., op.cit., p.126; MaCulloch, J.A., Serpent-Worship (Introductory), in ERE, XI, pp.399-411; Crooke, William, art. cit., in ERE, XI, pp.411-419; Welsford, Enid, Serpent-Worship (Teutonic and Balto-Salvic), in ERE, XI, pp.419-423; Walker, Benjamin, Serpent--Worship, in Hindu World, London (George Allen & Unwin), 1968, II, pp. 387-390; Zimmer, Heinrich, Myths and Symbols in Indian Art and Civilization, Delhi (Motilal Banarsidass Publ.), 1990, pp.77-90; Sahi, Jyoti, Symbol of the Serpent, in The Child and the Serpent — Reflections on Popular Indian Symbols, Bangalore (Asian Trading Corporation), 1994, pp. 159-169.

3. Cf. Kane, P.V., op.cit., pp.126-127; Crooke, W., op.cit., in ERE XI, p.414b;

Dange, Sindhu Sadashiv, <u>Hindu Domestic Rituals,</u> Delhi (Ajanta Publ.), 1985, pp.88-94; Rao, S. K. Ramachandra, <u>Serpent and the Mountain,</u> in <u>The Folk Origins of Indian Temples,</u> Bangalore (IBH Prakashana), 1980, pp.37-65; Sahi, Jyoti, op.cit., pp.161, 167.

4. Cf. MacCulloch, J.A., art. cit., in ERE XI, pp.399-411; Crooke, W., art. cit., in ERE, XI, pp.411-419; Lurker, Manfred, <u>Snakes,</u> in Mircea Eliade (Ed-in-Chief), <u>The Encyclopedia of Religion,</u> N.Y. (Macmillan Publ. Co.), 1987, XIII, pp.370-374; Crooke, W., <u>Snakes,</u> in <u>Things Indian,</u> New Delhi (Oriental Books Reprint Corp.), 1972, pp.439-444; Crooke, W., <u>The Popular Religion and Folklore of Northern India,</u> New Delhi (Munshiram Manoharlal Publ.), 1978, under <u>Tree and Serpent--Worship,</u> II, pp.121-145; Heiler, Friedrich, <u>Erscheinungsformen und Wesen der Religion,</u> Stuttgart (Verlag W. Kohlhammer), 1979, cf. Index under <u>"Schlange"</u>; Kristensen, W. Brede, <u>The Meaning of Religion,</u> The Hague (Martinus Nijhoff), 1971, cf. Index under <u>"Snakes"</u>; Stidworthy, John, <u>Snakes of the World,</u> N.Y. (Bantam Bks.), 1972, pp.148-150; Sahi, Jyoti, op.cit., pp.159-161, 166.

5. Whitaker, Romulus, <u>Common Indian Snakes,</u> Bombay (Macmillan Indian Ltd.), 1978, pp.xiii, 8, 11, 13, 31, 86-88; Whitaker, Zai, <u>Snakeman,</u> Calcutta (Penguin Bks), 1990, pp.29ff; Heiler, Freidrich, op.cit., cf. Index, under <u>"Schlange"</u>; Kristensen, W. Brede, <u>The Meaning of Religion,</u> op.cit., cf. Index under <u>"Snake"</u>; Miller, Harry, <u>Slimy But Not Satanic,</u> in <u>Science Express,</u> Indian Express, 8 December 1967, p.1, cols 1-8; Sahi, Jyoti, op.cit., pp.165-166.

6. Cf. MacCulloch, J.A., art. cit., in ERE XI, pp.403a, 403b, 404a, 406b; Crooke, W., art. cit., in ERE XI, pp.417a, 417b; Meier, C.A., <u>Asklepios,</u> in <u>The Encyclopedia of Religion,</u> op.cit., I, pp.463-466; Lurker, Manfred, art.cit., in <u>The Encyclopedia of Religion,</u> XIII, P.373a; Stidworthy, John, op.cit., p.150; Sahi, Jyoti, op.cit., p.150; Sahi, Jyoti, op.cit., pp.163,166.

7. Cf. Sharma, Brijendra Nath, <u>Festivals of India,</u> New Delhi (Abhinav Publ.), 1978, pp.24-25, 89; Kane, P.V., op.cit., p.125; Dange, Sindhu Sadashiv, op.cit., pp.88-94; Crooke, W., <u>The Popular Religion and Folklore of Northern India,</u> op.cit., II, pp.317-140; Sahi, Jyoti, op.cit., pp.165-167.

SHRAVANA — 8TH DAY OF THE DARK FORTNIGHT

JANMASHTAMI
or **Gokul Ashtami** or **Krishna Jayanti**

Humans in every age have believed that under special circumstances and for special reasons, God appears in the world in a material form. Whenever there is much unrighteousness and confusion and disorder set in and baffle the well-ordered progress of humankind; whenever the balance of human society is upset by selfish, ruthless, and cruel beings; whenever the foundations of social organisations are undermined, then God appears in order to re-establish righteousness and restore peace: the Kingdom of God, the Khuda Raj, the Ramrajya or the Golden Age.

Shekinah, Avatar, Incarnation, are words used respectively among Jews, Hindus, and Christians, in referring to such "theophanies", though they differ substantially in their full meaning. All these three religions, however, agree that the "descent of God" is for the "ascent of man". The words and the deeds of the divine Incarnation produce a benign influence on human beings and help them in their upward divine unfolding and self-realisation. The Incarnation comes to reveal the divine nature of man and makes him rise above the petty materialistic life of passion and egoism.

Hindus believe that Lord Krishna is the 8th avatar of Lord Vishnu. (Cf. Part I, ch. 4, pp. 36,37 for a list of the avatars). Once a year we can witness in many places the joyous scene of young men forming a human tower, by climbing one upon the other, to reach and to break the earthen pot with curds (dahi-handi), that is suspended at a great height on a rope. As the pot is broken and its contents eaten as prasad, loud acclamations of "Govind ... Govind" are heard. It is the birthday of Lord Krishna (also called Gopal or Govind). This festival falls on the 8th day of the dark half of the month of Shravana. It is one of the greatest festivals among Vaishnavite Hindus, celebrated in some of parts of India almost like Christmas!

1. Who Was Krishna?

In all probability, Krishna was a name of some historical personage, but the "Lord Krishna" that is now venerated as divine seems to be a composite figure of various personages in the religious literature of Hinduism. The name first appears in the Rig Veda but is not connected with divinity. A Krishna is a war hero in the Mahabharata. In the Bhagavad Gita, this hero becomes a transcendent being, an object of devotion and adoring surrender, the supreme dispenser of grace and salvation. It is, however, in the Bhagavad Purana, written many centuries later (9-10th A.D.), that we have a more complete story of Krishna. There is an attempt here to synthesize different traditions, some that held him to be of royal blood and others that considered him to be of humbler pastoral background. At any rate, he now begins to be fully identified with Lord Vishnu (Hari) himself: *"Krishnastu Bhagavän svayam"* (As for Krishna, he is the Lord himself!) and will continue to be increasingly an object of "bhakti" among a large section of modern Hindus.

A king of Mathura, on the banks of the river Yamuna, had a son, Kansa, and daughter, Devki. The king got his daughter married to a high-ranking officer, Vasudev. On the very day of their marriage, Kansa had a vision that the eighth son of his sister Devki would kill him. He, therefore, took every precaution to see that all Devki's children were destroyed at birth. In spite of the fact that Devki and Vasudev were imprisoned by Kansa, on the night their eighth child was born, the gates of the prison miraculously opened and Vasudev was able to take his son safely out. He crossed the river and went to Gokul to the house of a friendly shepherd couple, Nanda and Yashoda, and exchanged his son for their daughter whom he took back to the royal prison.

There is then a succession of wonderful happenings in the life of the little Gopal. He kills the demoness Putanä who, disguised, was suckling him. Together with his elder brother, Balaräma, and his other cowherd friends, he has extraordinary adventures, first in his own village, Vraja, then in Vrndävana, where his foster-parents have removed him for reasons of security. Many frightful demons and rakhshasas, and Kansa himself are killed by the child Krishna, and a great snake, Kälya, is vanquished by him, after a long struggle in the waters of the Yamuna. Pranks also, some of them of doubtful symbolism, are played by him, who together with some other children steal the clothes of the gopis, while these are bathing! (To teach us, some say, that all shame and human respect must be put aside in our approach to the divine!) The women of Vrndävana grow more and more enamoured of the child. The Räs-lílä, the love dance, during which Krishna assuming a thousand bodies plays with all the gopis and showers his love upon each and every one, is the highest point of the tenth part of the Bhagavad Purana, where the story of Krishna is told.

After all these exploits, where we are never quite certain whether Krishna is a divine spirit enacting a symbolic play or man of flesh and blood, Krishna and his brother Balaräm leave Vrndävana and go to school! New demons and giants are encountered, new feats, new displays! Then there are his various marriages (to Rukmini, Satyabhämä, etc.), his struggles, his journey to Dvärakä, and his death.

2. The Celebration of the Festival

This festival is celebrated differently in different parts of the country. The breaking of "*Dahihandi*", as described above, and the playing of "*räs lílä*" are the most common social functions. As it is believed that Lord Krishna was born at midnight, a twenty-four hour fast is observed on this day, which is broken at midnight. Temples are decorated for the occasion. Specially in the North, Christmas-like cribs are made to depict the birth of Krishna. Kirtans are sung, bells are rung, the conch is blown, and sanskrit hymns are recited, in praise of Lord Krishna. At Mathura, the birthplace of Lord Krishna, special spiritual gatherings are organised at this time. Pilgrims from all over India attend these festive gatherings.

3. The Meaning of the Krishna Legend

The "original" Krishna was probably a historical personage, an Indian Ulysses who liberated Mathura from the clutches of a tyrant. It is only years later, through a process of gradual apotheosis, that he became the Supreme Being of the Bhagavad Gita and the Bhagavad Purana. This transformation of Krishna from a human to divine being appears to have been a part of a human longing for a more personal than a philosophical focus for religious devotion. As one Christian author wrote: "It is a projection of a deep and insatiable need of the human soul for a living God whom, when revelation is absent, man must needs seek in a human image raised above all human standards."

4. A Christian Reflection

One can notice many apparent similarities between Krishna and Christ: both are expressions of God's love and concern for suffering humanity; both were born at midnight, one in a prison and the other in a cave; both were sought to be killed by the local rulers and were saved through exile; both taught a path of "bhakti"; both performed miracles on behalf of the suffering... but the similarities end there. Krishna killed Kansa, Christ did not kill Herod. "I came not to destroy but to save," he said. In fact, he was killed for our sins!

This festival offers us an invitation to reflect on the purpose of our lives and of God's plans for each one of us. It also challenges us to reflect on our unique mission and the ways in which we can be instruments of God's saving action in the world of our times.

This festival also reminds us of the truth that God protects his devotee. He protects in a special way the one whom he sends to establish his kingdom and fulfil his plans. Finally, the festival puts us in touch with God's faithfulness and love for humankind in the mystery of the incarnation.

SHRAVANA — FULL MOON

NARALI PURNIMA (Coconut Day)

With the conclusion of the rainy season, festival life in India increases in intensity through the relatively cool and dry months that follow. The months of Shravana (July-August) and Bhadrapada (August-September) are filled with religious fairs held at shrines and temples, where images of deities are displayed for darshana (auspicious viewing) and worship. The full moon day (*purnima*) of the Shravana is special because it is an occasion when two popular festivals are celebrated — Narali Purnima and Rakhi Purnima. Even though they bear no particular connection with each other, it is an occasion for people to celebrate both the horizontal and vertical aspects of their relationship respectively with God and with their fellowmen.

After one or two months of heavy rains and strong winds, the sea becomes calm. On this same day, the full moon day of Shravana, boats are launched into the sea again. But, before doing so, it is customary on the Western coast, not only for Hindus but also for members of some other merchant and fishing communities, to offer flowers and a coconut (*naral*) to Varun, the sea god.

From time immemorial human persons have sought union with God. Unable to see Him directly, they are inclined to find Him in nature. In this way they develop an instinctive sense of God's presence in their lives. God's presence, His immensity and His power are experienced in a special way by people who spend a great part of their life in the sea (See Psalm 107, vv. 23-32). We turn to God more

106

easily when we feel insecure. Varun is the personification of God as manifested through the sea. Inner faith needs to be expressed through some concrete and meaningful external action. Throwing the coconut into the sea is the action intended to express the inner faith of the devotee.

1. Significance of the Coconut Worship

The coconut is a fruit full of symbolism in Hindu culture. The coconut's three eyes represent the three-eyed Lord Shiva. It is also a symbol of God's generous care for the material needs of His people. Therefore it plays an important role in all Hindu festivals and offerings made as part of worship, and on occasions like the laying of a foundation stone, the inauguration of buildings and various projects, the launching of ships, etc.

The coconut is known as "*Shriphal*" or "divine fruit". Within its hard shell, it contains food and drink, the two essential elements God has placed in creation for our nourishment. The hard shell expresses God's desire that we should enjoy the fruits of the earth through personal effort.

The coconut is the most common fruit used as an offering to God. The effort needed to break the shell represents the element of sacrifice. The kernel and the water are offered to God and then shared by those present as "prasad" or food blessed by God.

2. Some Reflections and Suggestions

This could be an occasion to build up an eco-spirituality and a day to count God's many blessings to us through the gifts of nature. It is also an occasion to renew our trust in the God who shares our concerns and takes care of us. A prayerful reading of Psalms 29, 33, and 107, should be conducive to obtain the fruits of this festival: reverence for the majesty of God revealed in his creation and prayer for protection in time of danger.

SHRAVANA — FULL MOON

RAKSHA BANDHAN

A friend of mine was in hospital recently and desperately needed blood before the operation. Many were alerted about her condition but everyone had one excuse or the other to make. It was in that hour of dire need that I received the following phone message — "Sister, if you need any help or if you require blood for your friend, you can count on my support." You see, that was a call from Sunil, my *rakhi* brother".

1. The Ritual and its Meaning

This ancient festival has come a long way changing its colour and character with changing times and circumstances. How and when this ritual of tying the *rakhi* (amulet) to express an emotional bond of brotherly love and protection for a sister is not known, but history is replete with incidents when rakhi in its most colourful and decorated garb has served as the harbinger of peace, harmony, fraternity, and friendship.

It was customary from time immemorial, especially in North India, for a maiden to send a rakhi to any person addressed as a "brother", but generally in contingencies of grave danger or urgent necessity. For example, during several foreign invasions, starting from Greeks to Mughals, Hindu women, as a matter of expediency, utilised rakhi to communicate sisterly love and relations even to the invaders sometimes, in anticipation of no harm or damage to self or to the kingdom. It is said that Alexander the Great

108

during his invasion of India had received a rakhi and request from King Puru's wife to save her husband's life in the battlefield.

According to Rajput usage, by dispatching or presenting a rakhi, a Rajput maiden conferred on anyone whom she so adorned with it, the title and respect of an adopted brother. If such a gesture of affection was recognised, it entitled her to all the protection of what has been called a "cavalier servente" and no scandal was attached to it. Humayun received such a rakhi from Queen Karnavati of Chittoor when her kingdom was invaded, and leaving his conquests in Bengal, he rushed to her rescue and drove away her foes. Akbar and Jehangir also followed this practice which was introduced in the Mughal court by Hindu ladies.

Girls and married women tie a rakhi made of a few, twisted, golden or simple yellow threads, on the wrist of the right hand of their brothers, close male friends and neighbours, and pray for their welfare and protection from any evil influence.

This age-old festival is a means of strengthening the bond of love between sisters and those whom they claim as their rakhi brothers. On this day, members of the Hindu family bathe very early and go to the market to purchase beautiful rakhis from colourful stalls. The males clothed in their best and females in their bright costumes first offer prayers to their family deity. In some places, before tying a rakhi, the arati is done by waving a plate with a lighted lamp, betel-nut and leaves and a few rice grains in it, three times before the brother. After which some rice grains are sprinkled on the head of the brother and vermilion powder is applied to his forehead. In some places he is also presented with a flower and sweets. The man considers it a privilege to be chosen as "brother" by a girl who ties a rakhi on his wrist. If the "brother" is not at hand, the rakhi is sent to him by post or through some person and in return the sister receives various gifts and cash.

Through this ceremony the person on whom the rakhi is tied assumes certain sacred duties (almost like the god--parents at Baptism among Christians). The "rakhi brother" undertakes to protect his "sister" in time of danger and to help her in time of need. By tying rakhi on one's blood--brother, the fraternal relationship is enhanced to a sacred bond.

2. The Religious Connotations of the Custom

A practical and an inspiring social custom was, in the course of time, made sacrosanct by religious myths.

It is interesting to note that in ancient times on this very day, the full-moon day of Shravana, the Brahmins tied mauli (red-saffron thread) round the wrist of their *Yajmanas* (patrons and clients) and recited hymns for their safety, and in return got something in cash or kind. On the sunrise of that day, after offering worship to gods and sages, they got prepared a protective packet (amulet) containing whole-rice grains and mustard decorated with gold thread. The royal priest tied the amulet on the king to the accompaniment of the mantra : "I tie on you that whereby Bali, the very powerful king of demons, was bound. O protective amulet don't slip off, don't slip off." All the people were then given an amulet by the priest who was honoured according to their ability. This practice of Brahmins tying the sacred thread is in vogue even today in many Hindu religious places and families.

Many and different legends are told of the origin of this custom. According to one, goddess Indrani tied rakhi to her husband Lord Indra when he was dethroned from his heavenly kingdom by an invading demon. It is said that, with the power of his wife's rakhi, Indra could defeat the demon and could regain his lost paradise. Another legend has is that Lord Vishnu's wife tied such a bracelet around the wrist of her husband as a charm, when he took on the Vamana (dwarf) avatara to slay the demon Bali. After her

110

rescue, Sita tied a rakhi around the wrist of her brother-in-
-law Lakshamana as a symbol that he should protect her
against future dangers.

3. Some Reflections

Nowadays, the observance of rakhi has become more
confined to one's family or social circle. The ceremony has
almost lost its broader transcultural applications and deeper
spiritual meaning. Yet, there is much we can learn from this
festive custom. In spite of the progress made in our times,
we still have with us the legacy of systematic discrimination
against women. It is embedded within the economic, social,
political, religious, and even linguistic structures of our
society. Today, the conscience of society needs to be aroused
to give justice to women.

A festival like Raksha Bandhan invites us to take up the
mission of bringing about God's Reign in our midst by
accepting everyone as a brother and a sister. It is a challenge
to us to do our utmost to break down barriers created by sex,
class and caste differences, and to respond to God's plans
of building a world where "there is neither Jew nor Greek,
there is neither slave nor free, there is neither male or female,
where all are one in Christ Jesus" (Gal 3:28).

The festival of Raksha Bandhan is therefore an
appropriate occasion to promote the values of sisterly and
brotherly concern — to build and strengthen the bonds of
true friendship and to appreciate the complimentary gifts of
men and women. This can also be an occasion to be
appreciative of priests and to show our gratitude for their
selfless services they render to people everywhere.

This day could also be a day of celebration for men and
women — a time to acknowledge with gratitude the positive
impact we have on one another's lives. It could be a day
when couples renew their marriage vows. It could also be a
day when women express their expectations of their rakhi

brothers, a day when men pledge to support women in their endeavour to break down unjust social structures that bind and discriminate them and to be supporters of God's plan for a loving relationship of respect, mutuality, and equality between men and women.

On the occasion of this festival, Catholics may be enlightened by reflecting on the following Scripture texts which witness to the attitude of Jesus towards women:

➢ His active concern and willingness to help women in need — Lk 7:11-16.

➢ His openness to listen and to dialogue with them in a spirit of partnership — Mt 16:21-28; Jn 4:1-26.

➢ His appreciation of their unique gift of generosity, faith, and love — Lk 21:1-4; Lk 8:40-48; Lk 7:36-50.

➢ His acceptance of their collaboration in his ministry — Lk 8:1-3.

➢ His commitment of the cause of their liberation and the destruction of unjust social structures — Jn 8:1-11; Lk 13:10-13.

112

BHADRAPADA — 4TH DAY OF THE MONTH

GANESH CHATURTHI

1. The Festival

The most popular Hindu festival in Goa and Maharashtra is undoubtedly the Ganesh Chaturthi. It falls on the 4th day of the bright half of the month of Bhadrapada and is considered to be Ganapati's "birthday".

The Ganesh festival coincides with the harvest season. By the 5th or 6th century A.D., this was celebrated, in some places, in thanksgiving for the early crops; and in propitiation for the later ones. That is why in the Ganesh puja agricultural products are used: *durvas* (grass), flowers, *panchamrit* (five cow products), laddus, and neureos. The rat is depicted under his belly as his *vahan* (vehicle). This has reference to Kal, the destructive god, whom Ganesh had conquered. Thus the "rat" has been subjugated and the harvest protected.

New attributes were also given to this god. Besides being the god of prosperity and auspiciousness, he now came to be looked upon as the god of wisdom and knowledge. That is why a Hindu child begins its school career by performing Ganesh puja and the first words taught to the child to pronounce are: "*Shri Ganeshya Nämah*" (Praise to Lord Ganesh), and on this festival students keep their books before the image, and artisans their tools.

It was at the dawn of this century, that the erudite

113

scholar and great patriot, Lokmanya Tilak, stimulated the national spirit of the masses of India, by organizing an annual festival in honour of Ganesh, beside celebrating the Shivaji Jayanti (birthday). He popularized these festivals through the columns of his paper "Kesari". Thus Ganesh came to be celebrated with great pomp and gaiety in South India, especially from Maharashtra to Madras, with elaborate and often artistic, neighbourhood, Ganesh *pandals* and cultural and religious programmes during the festival.

The festival is preceded by a day of fasting. And the family does not taste any food before the deity is installed and consecrated. The image is made from mud (*chikal*) brought from the river bed or sea and is colourfully painted. Once the image is consecrated by the mantras of the *pujari* (priest), God is supposed to have come to dwell in that statue and to have visited the house, and so beautiful prayers are addressed to Him. The puja may last sometimes 36 hours, sometimes three days, sometimes seven or more days, according to the decision of the *dha zan* (elders) of the village or in fulfilment of vows. At the end of the festival, the presence of the deity is "removed" by a special ceremony, and the image is immersed in a well, river, or sea, as the case may be, returning it to the dust (*chikal*) from which it was made.

For the uninitiated, the image of Ganapati may appear somewhat strange and even absurd: half-man and half--elephant, with four hands and a pot-belly. But obviously it is not meant to be a statue of a historical figure! Many ancient religions, like those of Assyria, Egypt, Greece, etc., had in their mythology such therianthropic (part man, part animal) beings — winged lions with human heads, winged demons with the head of an eagle, the Sphinx of Egypt, Greek gods like Pan and Satyr, the living creatures in the vision of prophet Ezekiel (Ez 1,8-10) — that symbolized divine or demoniac attributes like power, immortality, generosity, benevolence, or malevolence, revengefulness, etc. They too had social origins, with religious myths attached to them in a later more sophisticated age.

2. Social Origins of Ganapati

Hinduism has two distinct currents: popular or folk Hinduism and literary or classical Hinduism. Both these currents form part of one religion. Folk Hinduism denotes the sum of customs and beliefs as actually practised in the life of an ordinary Hindu. Literary or classical Hinduism indicates the more scholarly and higher values and cultural traditions.

Folk Hinduism has its roots in the Indian village where the Aryan civilization initially rested and flourished. For the original nomadic Aryan the thin jungle on the hill plateaux, where he roamed in search of food, was a familiar world. He knew its beasts and their habits and could pit his brain against their ferocity. At that time many tribes worshipped a kind of "King of the Animals", whom they considered in a sense the owner of the forest and its folk. In the later years, however, when the Aryans had become settled peasants, their new way of life brought with it changes in their psychological outlook. Natural surroundings were now divided into friendly and unfriendly. The friendly were now the village where they now lived, and its surrounding fields, all very well known and hospitable; whereas the unfriendly were the jungles and mountains, now unknown and dangerous!

The beasts and other forest dwellers that were once familiar and friendly to the nomadic Aryan, gradually came to appear more than natural. They were now looked upon as spirits, ogres, and monsters, against whom the peasant Aryan had to seek protection. One way to do this was to place the "King of the Animals" at the entrance of the village so that, propitiated by regular sacrifices, he would keep away from the village all those evil "spirits". He thus became the "Protector of the Village", *Kshetra-pal* or, in later Hinduism, *Gram Devatā*.

115

In the Deccan, one of the most popular Kshetra-pals was Gajendra (Lord Elephant), known also as Ganesh or Ganapati, a name which means "the master (*pati or isha*) of the hosts (*gana*) of evil spirits" (symbolised by the rat at his feet). (Another such popular Kshetra-pal is Hanuman, the Monkey God.)

This way of understanding was not exclusive to the folk religion of the Aryans. Many other ancient tribes too around the world represented protecting divine beings by a "totem" which was initially an image of an animal or plant. Gradually, as man developed and became uncomfortable with an animal god, the totem representation also changed, first to a half-human half-animal form and finally to a fully human form, with the original animal finding some place in the myth or in the image itself. Thus the eagle became Garuda, the vehicle of Vishnu, and the bull became Nandi, the vehicle of Shiva.

It has also been suggested that Ganapati and Hanuman owe their animal heads to the masks used by the dancers who impersonated them in their ritual dances.

3. The Ganapati Myth

Vedic Hinduism had eventually become a religion of sacrifices, entangling man's life from the cradle to the grave. A revolt followed. Buddhism, Jainism, and the Upanishads, began to question the value of exterior rites performed by the Brahmins, and laid emphasis on inner life of self-control, non-violence, meditation, and penance. The sages in the forests founded their own philosophical schools and began to discuss problems of soul, God, life after death, nature of the world, etc. Their ideas were propagated; kings like Ashoka patronised Buddhism, and so most of folk India went over to Buddhism.

In order to stop this exodus from Hinduism, Brahmins began to compile the Puranas. (See Part I, chapter 3 of this

116

volume.) Stories about gods and goddesses were introduced to make Hinduism attractive to the masses. Ganesh too was presented as a god, one among the many others. Different Puranas, originating from different Hindu communities, give different versions about the origin and worship of Ganesh. For example, in the following account given in Shiva Purana, the birth of Ganesh was a "virgin birth", hence he is sometimes called *Vinayak*, which means "born without a husband":

Parvati wanted to find a way to prevent Shiva from entering her apartments while she had her bath. So she collected the dirt from her body and with it formed a child! Proclaiming him as her son, she appointed him to be her gatekeeper. When Shiva was making his rounds and wanted to enter Parvati's apartment, he was stopped by Ganesh at the door. A fight followed, and after much bloodshed Ganesh was beheaded. The goddess became infuriated and herself entered the arena. Her wrath threatened the whole universe. At this Shiva and his followers asked her forgiveness, but Parvati demanded that her son be restored to life. Shiva sent his attendants to get the head of any living being they could find. The attendants went and then returned with the head of a single-tusked elephant. This Shiva joined to the lifeless trunk of Ganesh and Ganesh came back to life!

4. How the Enlightened Understand Ganapati

Such beliefs were accepted by folk Hinduism; the enlightened Hindus, however, have a different explanation. For them the Puranas are not of great value because these were added later on to make Hinduism popular. For the enlightened Hindu and the philosopher, God is a Supreme, all-powerful, omnipresent, omniscient, formless, spiritual Being who cannot be truly represented in any human form. However, since man needs something to concentrate on, to reach the knowledge of God and to meditate on Him, the

117

supreme being's divine powers are depicted in the different images of gods and goddesses and in various forms consonant with his particular culture.

Ganesh, therefore, is merely a human representation of some of God's powers. The trunk of an elephant is the most powerful part of his body, with which he can uproot big trees and carry the heaviest loads. Now God is all-powerful, and representing him as having an ordinary human nose would not depict him as he really is. So he is not only given the trunk of an elephant but also four, six, or even eight or more hands, to show that there is no limit to God's power.

With his trunk resting on his one tusk and with his eyebrows, Ganesh symbolises the eternal mystic ॐ "AUM". God's omnipresence and omniscience are depicted in Ganesh's small sharp eyes that penetrate everything, in his long ears that can hear the least whisper from the hearts of men, and in his broad forehead that is the seat of wisdom. Thus the idea of an omnipotent, omnipresent, and omniscient God is meant to be expressed in the image of Ganesh.

5. Points for Reflection

Although Ganesh Chaturthi is a Hindu religious festival, according to Brahmavaivarta Purana, hospitality is the hallmark of that festival. The festival is, therefore, a powerful reminder of one of the most cherished values of our Indian tradition, a value that needs to be maintained and fostered. Hence, Catholics are encouraged to visit their Hindu friends and neighbours on this occasion. In fact, Hindus consider such a visit, even by Christians, as very auspicious, a blessing from God, a sign of friendship.

Even the contemplation of the idol could remind us, on the one hand, of the omnipotence, the omniscience and the omnipresence of God — the Alpha and Omega (Christian equivalent of AUM) and, on the other, that "man is a beast in search of humanity" — and divinity! He can realise this only with the blessing of the Lord of Hosts.

ASHWIN BRIGHT — THE FIRST NINE DAYS

NAVRATRA

The month of Ashwin begins with the "novena" of Navratra (lit. nine nights), during which the "feminine" aspect of God is celebrated and venerated. This feminine aspect is represented both by Saraswati, the gentle, lovable, and refined wife of Brahmä, who is depicted with the *vina* in her hands and a swan or peacock as her *vahan* (vehicle), and by Durga, the warrior-goddess, who is variously represented either as sitting on a lion (symbol of strength), with various weapons in her hands and killing the buffalo--shaped demon Mahishasur, or as fierce-looking Kalika killing the mighty demon Shumbha. During the Navratra, Saraswati is venerated mainly in the West and the South, whilst Durga is venerated in the North and the East, especially in West Bengal.

1. Saraswati Pooja

During the Navratra, special prayers are offered in honour of Saraswati, the goddess of wisdom, literature, and the fine arts. On the first night the ghatsthapana takes place. In the midst of the recitation of Vedic verses, a vessel of water called "*kalash*" is put before her image; if not, before a dish of rice topped with a coconut and surrounded with books and toys. During the nine days the image of the goddess and the "*kalash*" must not be touched. The devotees must fast or take only one meal a day. An oil-lamp must be kept burning throughout. This lamp is called *"nandadeep"*. Every day a garland of fresh flowers is presented to the goddess.

On the last three days of Navratra the goddess is more elaborately worshipped. At noon the head of the family performs puja, and in the evenings Saraswati's praises are sung from the holy book *"Saptashati"*. Then *"arti"* is performed with great solemnity and sweets and pan passed around. Many people also go daily to visit the temple of the goddess.

2. Durga Pooja

Whilst the Saraswati worship in Western and Southern India is rather sober and quiet, the Durga festival is celebrated in the North with much pomp, surpassing even the pomp of the Ganesh festival in Maharashtra and Goa. There are different daily ceremonies to venerate the goddess in her different manifestations, until she "leaves" the statue, which is then immersed in water on Dassara Day.

Durga is the personification of the "Power of God" (Shakti). She typifies a woman who, far from being subservient to male domination, takes on the role of punishing the wicked and destroying evil, thus collaborating with God and man for the destruction of evil and the establishment of divine reign. She is also known by other names like Mother Goddess, Kali, Laxmi, Chandika, Bhavani, Ambika, etc., each with its own meaning and myths. (See Part I, ch. 4.)

A Reflection

Catholics familiar with the Bible will not be very much surprised at these personifications of God's attributes as "females". The Bible itself personifies the Wisdom of God (Sapientia) as a "female", and King Solomon speaks of her as if she was a living person. (See Wisdom ch 7-8.) In the early Church, especially among the Greeks, also, the Holy

Spirit (Pneuma) was referred to as feminine and sometimes, though rarely, even depicted as female. God who is spirit is neither male nor female, and thus one can understand why even among Catholics some people relate (and at times refer) to God as "mother" as well as "father".

Catholics will also not be surprised that a woman with extraordinary powers undertakes to destroy evil. Sin came into the world through the action of both man and woman, and divine providence has ordained that salvation be wrought also through the action of man and woman, in the persons of Jesus and of his mother Mary. Christian faith, however, refuses to attribute to Mary an equality with God. Hers was a role that was supportive of her Son's redemptive action which alone brought about the salvation of the human race. Only Jesus "is the image of the invisible God... for in him dwells the whole fullness of the deity bodily." (Col.1,15; 2,9)

ASHWIN BRIGHT — THE 10TH DAY OF THE MONTH

DASSARA

Dassara (lit. "the tenth day") follows immediately the Navratra and commemorates the victory of Rama over Ravana who had kidnapped his wife Sita and taken her to Lanka. Rama, along with his brother Lakshmana and devoted follower Hanuman, and an army of monkeys (?) fought a great battle to rescue his lovely wife Sita. The war against Ravana lasted for ten days and the story of Rama and Sita is recounted with affection and love in the great epic Ramayana. Rama was a great believer in the powers of goddess Durga, and he is supposed to have prayed to her for nine days before he himself entered the battle-field on the tenth day and killed Ravana. People proclaimed it as the greatest victory of good over evil.

Huge effigies of Ravana, his brother Kumbhakaran and his son Meghnad are made, and filled with large quantities of crackers and fireworks. At just about sunset, an actor depicting Rama shoots an arrow from his bow, which hits the Ravana effigy in his navel where a pot of nectar, the reason for Ravana's invincibility, was stored. Then all three effigies are set alight, and there is much merry-making.

There are some other legends attached to this festival, that have given rise to various practices and ceremonies that marked the festival especially in the past. According to one legend, when Pandav went to dwell in the forest, on the way he hid his weapons in the hole of a "*shami*" tree. A year later, when he was returning from the forest, he reached the tree on the Dassara day and recovered his weapons and as he did so, he worshipped both the shami tree and the weapons. Hence the custom of worshipping weapons on this feast-day.

Another legend has it that King Raghu of Ayodhya, an ancestor of Rama, wanted to help young Kautsa with gold coins that the young disciple wanted to give as "*gurudakshina*" to his guru. As the King did not have the required amount, he decided to invade and loot Amravati, the wealthy city of Indra. Knowing the strength of the King's army and in order to avoid bloodshed, Indra, the protector of Amravati, miraculously showered gold on all the "shami" trees of Ayodhya. This happened on the day of Dassara. In remembrance of this event, the custom is kept of "looting" the leaves of the shami (apati) trees, and presenting them to each other as sone (gold).

Some students of religious sociology have tried to interpret the myth in terms of North-South, Arya-Dravid conflict. In fact, in ancient times, kings in India would cross the boundaries of their kingdom on this day and make war against neighbouring kings. It was the beginning of the war season and it was customary on the occasion of this festival to worship weapons of war.

A Reflection

Weapons today are too deadly to be "worshipped", and people no longer look forward to wars. So the significance of Dassara has rightly been shifted from fight against neighbouring rulers to fight against injustice, from war to peace. Hence, instead of worshipping weapons, tools, instruments, vehicles, pens and pencils are worshipped, because they are the means of fighting injustice, ignorance, and evil.

"Armies" with adorned horses and caparisoned elephants march in a pageant across the city limits (e.g., in Mysore), not in order to wage war but to proclaim peace and harmony. Dassara is a day to cross man-made barriers and to extend to all the hand of fellowship and friendship. Today we do not worship weapons but ask God to bless all instruments which are helpful for the betterment of society. To worship weapons with which brother kills brother would be an aberration, the very opposite of religion. We are reminded of the words of Prophet Isaiah: "It will come to pass in the latter days... they shall beat their swords into plowshares, and their spears into pruning-hooks; nation shall not lift up sword against nation, neither shall they learn war anymore." (2, 2-4)

ASWHIN — DARK 13TH TO KARTIKA — BRIGHT 2ND

DIVALI

Divali or Dipavali, which means a row or cluster of lights, is the festival of lights, fireworks, rejoicing and fellowship, that is most widely observed in India. The origin of this festival is shrouded in the dense mists of hoary antiquity. That is why one should not be surprised to find differences regarding beliefs, ritual observances, social practices, duration of the festival, or even regarding the deity in whose honour this festival is kept.[1] Although there are not wanting people who celebrate Divali for one, two, three or four days, most devotees believe that this festival is to be celebrated for five days: from the 13th of the dark half of Ashvin to the 2nd of the bright half of Kartika.

1. The Festival Rituals

There are five principal items or elements that constitute the Divali festival: worship of wealth, celebration of Vishnu's victory over Narakasura, worship of Lakshmi and dice-play, celebration of the victory of Vishnu over Bali, and the exchange of brotherly and sisterly affection. Illuminations and fireworks characterise all the days of Divali. However, in addition, each of the five days has some cultic features particular to it.

(a) Yama-trayodasi (Yama's 13th day)

On the eve of this festival and on the first day of it too,

courtyards are cleansed, houses are freshly painted and vessels are washed and burnished. The day begins with a ritual bath and a pledge taken by the devotee to partake of saltless food and to sleep on the floor. These acts are symbolic of one's desire to mortify oneself and to make a new beginning in one's relationships with God and neighbour through inner cleansing. This day is spent in special devotion to Krishna. In the evening a lamp is lit and offered to Yama with a prayer that the devotee be preserved from sudden and untimely death. Although it is specially dedicated to Yama, people on this day also worship coins and ornaments and purchase new utensils. Hence this day is also called *Dhana-trayodasi* or *Dhana-teras*.[2]

(b) Naraka-chaturdasi (Naraka's 14th day)

On this day is celebrated in a special manner Vishnu's or Krishna's victory over Naraka who had been guilty of committing much evil. The 13th of the dark half of Ashvina is observed to procure for oneself protection against sudden and untimely death, whereas the 14th has for its principal objective deliverance from sickness and sin. Indicating this are the many ritual gestures and words used on this day: the oil-bath in the morning, the waving of the apotropaic medicinal plant *apamarga* during the bath, the libation of water to *Yama*, the lighting of a ceremonial lamp to keep *Naraka* away, the lighting of many lamps in several places in and around one's house, the crushing underfoot of a bitter cucumber simbolising Naraka, and the many prayers offered for deliverance from personal sins or those of one's deceased ancestors. A solemn memorial of one's departed relatives is made in and through the *parvana-shraddha*, and a meal is given to Brahmins.[3]

(c) Lakshmi-puja

This day, as the title itself indicates, is one especially dedicated to the worship of Lakshmi, the goddess of wealth.

It is a day given to merry-making with dancing and music, and is known as *Sukha-ratri*. Devotees prepare for this day by worshipping their account-books, closing old accounts and opening new ones. Houses and their surroundings are brilliantly illuminated with rows upon rows of lamps, and people dressed in all their finery go around joyously greeting relatives, friends and neighbours, while exchanging gifts. The womenfolk make arati to their family members to implore God's blessings on them, and beat winnowing baskets and drums to symbolically dispel evil and misfortune from their midst. On this day cows are specially honoured in the govardhana-puja, as an expression of gratitude to God for the prosperity that has come to their farming communities through them. They are tastefully decorated with coloured designs, festoons and garlands. And are not milked on this day nor made to bear any burden. At night, people gather to read edifying passages from their sacred books, to sing songs to Vishnu, and to pass their time gambling: one way of acquiring wealth![4]

(d) Bali-pratipada

The 1st of the bright half of *Kartika*, is regarded as one of the three most auspicious days of the year. The most important event of this day is the worship given to Bali, a good and popular king of a past golden age in India, who became the important personage in a myth that is the original nucleus of the festival of Divali (See below No.3).

After an oil-bath, a picture of Bali and his wife Vindhyavali is drawn in five colours on the floor of the house, puja is offered in which, besides the usual gifts, *kumuda* (lotus) flowers and also meat and alcohol are presented, accompanied by appropriate prayers. In the afternoon, a proclamation is made: "Today is the Rule of Bali, enjoy yourselves!" Devotees make it a point to offer alms on this day, as such an act of mercy is believed to be specially meritorious. The night is spent in prayerful vigil and in edifying people through sacred dramas.

(e) Yama-dvitiya (Yama's 2nd day), better known as Bhaiya-dooj or Bhai-beej.[5]

This day, the last of the Divali festival, commemorates the meal Yama had at the house of his sister Yami or Yamuna. On this day no man should eat in his own house. Rather, he should go to his sister's house (or, in case he has no sister, to the house of a close female relative) where she serves him a meal with great affection, and in return receives gifts and ornaments from him. A ritual bath is prescribed, as well as libations of water offered for the departed, for their deliverance from the bondage of their sins. With these expressions of love and concern for both the living and the dead, the festival of Divali comes to a close.

2. Significance of Divali

In order to understand the underlying meaning of Divali, a consideration of three things seems to be necessary, namely, the myth regarding Bali, the five-day celebration which begins and ends with the commemoration of Yama, and Divali as a festival of lights.

The myth of Bali is central to the celebration of Divali. According to this myth, Bali, who had become very powerful, had incurred the displeasure of the gods. One day, as he was offering an ashvamedha sacrifice, Vishnu appeared to him in the avatar of a dwarf Brahmin student, Vamana, and begged him for as much land as he could cover in three paces. Bali, notwithstanding a warning from his teacher that the request was an insidious one, generously acceded to it. Thereupon, Vamana grew larger and larger and in two steps covered heaven and earth. When Vamana asked Bali where he could place his foot for his third step, Bali told him to plant it on his head. Vamana at once did so and thrust Bali into the netherworld! However, Vishnu was so pleased with

Bali's adherence to his pledged word that he raised him to the status of Indra.

But who is Bali? Some Puranas refer to him as the lord of the demons. Others speak of him as a great, good, and powerful king in South India, under whose rule people once enjoyed unbelievable prosperity and bliss, and later on looked forward year after year to its return. Bali may have also been the mythical representation of some great beneficial change in nature, for the annual return of which people longed for. In the myth Bali is said to be the son of Virochana, and Virochana is one of the many names of the Sun. Indra is also closely connected with the Sun.

As Divali occurs at the end of the monsoon, when all of nature bursts into vibrant life bringing prosperity to all, and at the time when the sun crosses the equator to go down to the southern hemisphere, this festival could very well be a form of intense prayer both of thanksgiving and of petition to the Sun-god. As men, cattle, forests, and fields, need his life-giving light, prayers are offered for his return to their hemisphere, which is now gradually growing "dark" through the recession of the sun. Then, the experience of their prayers being heard naturally cause the people to explode in a festival of lights, in gratitude, joy and fraternal affection, that embraces even the deceased relatives, the friends, and the well-wishers.

Secondly, the consideration of the reasons why this festival begins and ends with a commemoration of Yama could be even more relevant. Yama is the lord of the dead[6]; but he is also the Lord of Righteousness (*dharma-raj*). He is the first of mortals to die, the first to venture forth into after-life, to walk the path of the fathers and to show the same to many others [14]. The commemoration of him, at the beginning and the end of Divali, reminds devotees that life is short, precarious, and serious, and that, if one is to share in the truly happy days of the reign of Bali, one has also to live in righteousness, without being attached to anything created, which would only be vain idolatry. It also reminds people that he who would wish to share in true life and light should be prepared to die to things created in order to live to reality uncreated.

Thirdly, Divali is rightly the **festival of lights**. It firmly emphasises where true wisdom and values lie. Light symbolises wisdom, truth, certitude, joy, and life. He, therefore, who always strives to live a life of godliness is the one who is eminently qualified to truly and rightly celebrate this great festival (*maha-utsava*) of Divali. Furthermore, one who strives to experience God in everyone and everything rejoices in the brotherliness and sisterliness that bind not only human beings here on earth but also those who have passed over to a better life; not only cows, animals, and other mute creatures, but also inanimate creation.

Endnotes:

1. Cf. Kane, Pandurang Vaman, History of Dharmasastra, Poona (Bhandarkar Oriental Research Institute), 1974, vol. V, Part I, p.194ff.

2. Cf. Subhash Anand, Major Hindu Festivals — A Christian Appreciation, Bombay (St Paul Publications), 1991,op.cit., p. 106.

3. Cf. Kane, P.V., op.cit., pp. 196-199; Subhash Anand, op.cit., pp. 107--108.

4. The gambling that takes place occurs only during the days of this festival and is kept within reasonable bounds, according to Om Lata Bahadur, The Book of Hindu Festivals and Ceremonies, Bangalore (UBS Publishers' Distributors Ltd.), 1999, p.211. However, Kane avers that entire fortunes are made or lost during these gambling bouts — cf. Kane, P.V., op.cit., p. 203.

5. For a charming story that glorifies the affection that should bind brothers and sisters together, cf. Om Lata Bahadur, op. cit., pp. 66--73.

6. Cf. RV X.14.1; 16.9; 135.1.

7. Cf. RV X.14.1-2.

11

KARTIKA — 12TH DAY OF THE MONTH

TULSI VIVAH

The festival commemorates the marriage of Krishna to Rukhmini, both of whom are considered to be the avatars respectively of Vishnu and Vrinda, the wife of a famous warrior demon, Jalandhar.

The legend attached to the marriage is interesting, though not very edifying. Jalandhar had become invincible because of the virtue of his faithful wife, Vrinda. He was a threat to the gods who therefore used deceit to make her lose her virtue!!! They first deceived her with the news that her husband had been killed in battle. To convince her of the fact, they placed in front of her the severed head and body of two monkeys. Vrinda was plunged in grief. Then a sadhu came by and, reciting some mantras, he re-joined the head and the body, and there stood in front of her Vishnu, looking exactly like her husband Vrinda. In her joyous excitement, Vrinda embraced the look-alike and thus lost her virtue, for having touched the body of a man not her husband! Soon Jalandhar was indeed defeated and killed.

When Vrinda came to know the truth, she was wild and cursed Vishnu: "Your wife will be taken away from you and you will have to ask help from monkeys to recover her." This curse was literally realised when Vishnu took the avatar as Rama whose wife was taken away by Ravana and had to be rescued with the help of Hanuman and his monkey brigade.

Vrinda then prepared the funeral pyre for her husband and herself became sati. Now it was the turn of Vishnu to grieve and he remained seated at the side of the pyre as a "madman". To remove his "madness", the gods planted three trees in the cremation ground: a *tulsi*, an *avala*, and a *malti* (jasmine). Of these, the tulsi became very dear to Vishnu, because like Vrinda, she is endowed with all qualities.

Although Vrinda, in a moment of rage, had cursed Vishnu, when the latter took avatar as Krishna, she took avatar as Rukhmini, and on this 12th day of the bright Kartika they became husband and wife!

On this day the place where the tulsi is planted known as Vrindavan, is cleaned and smeared with cowdung. Sugarcane is buried in it, and *avale* and wet tamarinds are put on it. Round the vrindavan a pandal is raised with sugarcanes. Then at the recitation of mantras, the "marriage" between tulsi and the idol of Vishnu is performed and beaten rice with jaggery (*lohyo*), puffed rice (*chirmulio*), and pieces of sugar-cane are distributed to those present.

A Reflection

Whatever be the myths surrounding the celebration, the tulsi with its innumerable medicinal properties is indeed a "consort", the healing hand of God. God has provided us with an abundance of such healing plants and grass, which often animals recognise, but the humans have forgotten. There is a return nowadays to "nature"-cure methods. The Tulsi Vivah is an occasion to thank God for his generosity and to commit ourselves to discover his various gifts in nature.

12

JANUARY 12-14

MAKAR SANKRANT

Introduction

According to the Hindu religion, the Creator has knitted the universe so intricately and ingeniously that everything created, no matter how diverse, lives in unity and harmony. Hence, every little change in the universe or in nature affects every cell and every fibre of our life. From time immemorial our ancestors had discovered this eternal truth, and they lived it out by celebrating every changing event in nature. Their songs and dance, and their entire culture were expressions of this great mutuality and oneness. That is why their feasts were mainly astronomical, commemorating the revolutions of the planets, the alternations of the seasons, and the recurrence of cyclical intervals of longer or shorter durations.

The Festival of Makar Sankrant

Makar Sankrant (called 'Pongal' in South India) is a clear example of such a commemoration. 'Sankrant' denotes the passing of the Sun from one sign of the zodiac to another. For Hindus every 'sankrant' is a holy day that is to be celebrated mostly by prayer and fasting, but the Makar Sankrant, when the Sun passes from 'Dhanush' (Sagittarius) to 'Makar' (lit crocodile, corresponding to Capricorn) is the most solemn. It is the only Hindu festival that follows the solar movement, and is celebrated from sunrise to sundown. It falls usually between 12th-14th of January. In many parts of India it coincides with harvest and hence it is celebrated differently.

The religious aspect of this festival consists in the worship of the Sun god, which is often depicted in courtyards under the form of red diagrams. Specially in the North, bathing in holy rivers like Ganga and Yamuna particularly at Prayag near Allahabad, or in any sacred streams or ponds, is recommended. It is also customary to offer sweetmeat made of sesame and jaggery (till-gul) to the ancestors, household gods and to the village deities. In this season sesame is considered to have especial nutritive and medicinal qualities.

Visiting friends and relations and sharing sweetmeat with them is part of the festival. In Goa and Maharashtra, a handful of "till-gul" is exchanged on such visits, with the greeting in Marathi: "Till-gul ghya ani godd godd bhola" (lit. Accept till-gul and speak sweetly).

Pongal is the corresponding feast in the South, especially in Tamil Nadu, and it is celebrated with great pomp. Children rush home for holidays. New pots are bought for the household and in the finest one rice is boiled with milk and sugar. Members of the family anxiously watch operations as quick boiling means good luck for the coming year. When it is completed, everyone shouts: *Pongal!*, i.e., "it's boiling!" Rice is offered up and eaten by the family group with all sorts of sweet foods. On the next day, the Mattupongal, cows, bullocks, and buffaloes, are washed, decorated, paraded, and fed with sweet cooked rice.

A Feast of Victory of Life Over Death

As the sun moves from the northern hemisphere towards the southern hemisphere, the nights gradually grow longer and colder, and the days become shorter and shorter. As a result, the northern hemisphere faces winter and the whole atmosphere in the North becomes cold, gloomy, and lifeless — a death experience!

But from Makar Sankrant onwards, the sun starts moving towards the North. The days start to grow longer and nights shorter, and the cold gradually lessens with the increasing warmth of the sun. Spring gently sets in. The whole of Nature throbs with life; the plants, the animals, and the human beings are once again rejuvenated — a time to bloom, a time to sing, and a time to share love. That's what Makar Sankrant is all about: a triumph of life over death.

Makar Sankrant, therefore, has a threefold dimension: spiritual, social, and environmental. The spiritual dimension refers to the special bathing done on this occasion to signify the casting out of darkness by the purifying waters. Then the worship of the Sun, as the Lord of Light, signifies the welcoming of light into one's life. From the social point of view, Makar Sankrant is a time to receive and share love. The giving of sweetmeat symbolises sweetness in human relationship. All bitterness in life is sweetened by the celebration of the feast of love. Finally, the festival celebrates the spirit of harmony and interdependence that exists in nature. Indeed, everything on earth — flora and fauna — throbs with pristine glory, as it was intended by the Creator — a friendly ecology.

A Reflection

In the Hindu understanding of "dharma" and according to the Rig Veda (X, 90), the world is related to the Cosmic Person (Purusha) as his body. It is, therefore, the duty of human beings to keep this body healthy. Over this century, however, this body has fallen sick; it is plagued by the deadly germ of "ego-centritis" which has been rapidly destroying the immunity system of the world. As a result the world is suffering from various "cancers": blood cancer called "oceanic leukaemia", skin cancer called "ozone perforation", lung cancer called "air pollution" and a general cancer called "deforestation". It cannot rest on account of hallucinations caused by the deafening noise around, and it continually cries tears of acid rain. All the time it runs a very a high temperature, the global warming. The urgent question is: "Will the world ever survive to celebrate Makar Sankrant in future?" The answer lies with each of us. We could provide the antidote!

13

MAGH — DARK 13TH

The 13th night of the dark half of every month of the Hindu calendar is considered as 'Shivratra' — the night of Shiva. But the 13th of the Magha month (around January-February) is observed by Hindus as Mahashivratra, the great night of Shiva. This night is celebrated all over India as a festival of great importance, dedicated to Lord Shiva under the symbol of Linga.

1.   The Myths about the Festival

There are many myths in the various Puranas connected with this festival. According to one story, the world was coming to an end. It was the end of an era. All around there was thick darkness. In the midst of limitless water Vishnu was reclining on the coiled Ananta, the primordial serpent. Brahma appeared on the scene and questioned Vishnu's identity. Each claimed to be the Supreme Lord of creation. As they were contesting to prove their claim, they saw a flame rising in the northern direction. Slowly the flame became bigger and bigger, till its either end could no longer be seen. Brahma became a swan and went in search of its upper end, while Vishnu became a boar and dug deep into the earth. Not finding either its upper or lower end, both returned to the starting point. They then saw the Linga in the middle of the flame and heard a voice uttering "AUM". Vishnu and Brahma then realized that they were in the presence of Shiva, and that he was the real Supreme Lord. That was the moment of their enlightenment!

Another story has it that once a hunter set out for a hunt.

138

He came near a pond and, for the purpose of hunting, he climbed a "*bel*" tree (sacred to Shiva). Sitting on a branch he waited for the game, but since the leaves obstructed his vision, he began to pluck a few which accidentally fell on a Shiva Linga ("*pindi*") that was under that tree. Just then, a herd of deer came to drink water and the hunter took aim at a `hind' (female deer). The poor creature noticed the movement of the hunter and cried out, "Please wait a moment; before you shoot, let me go home and meet my young ones for the last time. Then you may take my life at your pleasure."

The hunter gave the hind permission to go home, and remained sitting on the tree, waiting for her to return. As he waited the whole night, he was forced to observe a fast! Inadvertently, therefore, he had performed the three devotional acts that now make up the observance of the Mahashivratra: He had offered the "*bel*" leaves on the Shiva Linga; he uttered the name of Shiva with his mouth; and he had kept a fast! As a result, his heart was changed and he was filled with sentiments of mercy, and he spared the hind when she returned in the morning. Shiva was so pleased that immediately he carried both the hunter and the herd to the heavenly realm.

According to other stories, it was during this night that Shiva married Parvati. Others still connect this celebration with Shiva's action of saving the whole universe, by drinking the dreadful poison that emerged when the *devas* and the *asuras* were churning the ocean.

2. Ritual Observances

The Puranas that describe the celebration of Mahashivratra commonly indicate the following observances: *upavasa* (fast), *jagarana* (keeping vigil during the night), *snapana* (bathing the linga), *archana* (offering bilva leaves and other gifts), and *japa* (reciting the name or the litany of Shiva). When the celebration is given a community form there may also be *katha* (narrating the story of Shiva) and a suitable *pravachana* (exhortation).

3. A Christian Reflection

The above-mentioned stories symbolize various aspects of divine action as regards humankind. Symbols of light/fire are common to many religions. Jesus himself says: "I am the light of the world. He who follows me, will not walk in the dark." We are called upon to walk in that light and thus attain salvation.

True, our devotion ought to be a conscious act, but does not the Lord himself say in that parable: "I was hungry... thirsty, and you gave me to eat...to drink." And the righteous answer: "Lord, when did we see you hungry...thirsty..." (Mt 25, 31ff).

Keeping a vigil is what every Christian is advised by the Lord to do, because no one knows when the "Bridegroom will come"! (Mt. 25, 1-13).

Finally, when our Hindu brothers and sisters celebrate the moment when Shiva is said to have saved the world from the poison, we Christians can join them by celebrating the salvific mystery of Jesus Christ, the Lamb of God who takes away the sin of the world. Let us rejoice and be glad for Jesus, the Son of God, has saved us from eternal damnation!

14

PHALGUNA — DARK 5TH-14TH

HOLI — SHIGMO

The Fire-and-Colour Festival

"There is a time and a season for everything under heaven" — thus says the Holy Bible in the Book of Ecclesiastes (3:1). That is why religious calendars of all religions provide an eternal architecture through which time, as the experience of irreversible duration, may pass. Every year is new and different from the previous one, yet, through the observances of sacred festivals and fairs, each year repeats the enduring and paradigmatic forms of religious experience and community life.

As the weather begins to warm up again during the months of Phalguna (Feb.-March) and Chaitra (March-April), Krishna is venerated with the Dionysian festival of Holi, when devotees dance, play pranks, and douse one another with coloured water. Although the new year does not actually begin for another fortnight, Holi serves as the event of chaotic renewal that includes the end of the old year and beginning of the new year marked with appropriate exuberance.

Holi is one of the major and perhaps the most popular Hindu festivals, and is celebrated by all. The gaiety that marks the feast is unequalled. It commences about ten days before the full moon of the month of Phalguna, but is usually observed only for the last three or four days before the full moon. It is known by other names in different parts of India — Holi in the North, Kamadahana in the South, and Shigmo in the Deccan.

141

Its Origin

This is a very ancient festival. According to Kane, the great historian of Hindu Law, "it prevailed at least some centuries before Christ". Its very great antiquity seems to be further corroborated by the fact that there is quite a bit of confusion as regards both its origin and the mode of celebrating.

The earliest written record, Bhu Pu, refers to the festival of Holi as Sita-usna which points to the transition from winter to summer. It is therefore, in its origin, a Spring Festival and thereby the festival of love and life, because it stresses the creative force of generation. The burning of Holi on the last day of Phalguna is a symbol of the ending of one year and the beginning of another. The ancient rituals and blessings connected with this festival all refer to its origin as a Spring Festival.

The same ancient text refers to Holi as a celebration to ensure the protection of children. Children are the visible evidence of human fertility and as such their safety is the safety of humanity. Hence Holi, from ancient times, has been a celebration of life in all its forms.

Medieval Appropriations

It is not an uncommon phenomenon in the history of religions that some rite/institution continues to be part of the life of people, even when its original significance is forgotten. Then the community tries to invent some explanation for what it continues to practise. This has been the lot of Holi too. Different stories and legends have subsequently been put forward to explain its meaning. Even though they may not give us an insight into the original intention, they definitely help us to understand the religious beliefs and aspirations of the people who formulated these associations.

The story of Dhaundha, a demoness who caused harm to children, is one of the ancient myths associated with the

Holi festival. This demoness indicates some infantile disease. According to this story, Holi is referred to the medicinal fire which was meant to bring about healing to the patient struck by this disease.

For some, Holi celebration is a commemoration of the burning of Kama by Shiva. The feast therefore is known as "Kamadahana" (the burning of lust) or Madandahana (burning of Madan, the god of lust). It is associated with a prophecy that only the son of Shankar (Shiva) would be able destroy the demon Tarkasur (Narkasur). So Madan decided to tempt Shiva by drawing his attention to Parvati. Shankar, who was in deep meditation, was annoyed at this disturbance, opened his third eye and cast a fiery look on Madan who was reduced to ashes.

Another story associated with this festival is the story of Prahlada, the son of a demon king Hiranyakasipu. Prahlada was a great devotee of Vishnu, much to the father's distress. Since all efforts to wean him away from his devotion were futile, his father told Holika his sister to take him in her lap and enter the fire. Holika was, however, burnt, but Prahlada, the devotee of God, emerged unhurt from the fiery ordeal.

Another story that is commonly narrated on the occasion of Holi is about the killing of Putana by Krishna when he was still an infant. This tradition identifies her with Holika. Kamsa who was after the child's life got her to go and offer the infant her poisoned breast. Krishna sucked the very life out of her. The villagers burnt her body on a pile of wood. Holi is a very important Vaishnava festival. This is best seen in Bengal where as part of the celebration the images of Radha and Krishna are placed on a swing. Originally two different festivals, it is from the sixteenth century that the Swing Festival and Holi on the one hand, and Krishna and Holi on the other, have been associated with each other. If today Holi is so much a Krishna festival, it is because it expresses the clear association of the Divine Player par excellence with India's most rollicking festival.

The Holi Festival Today

The 'Rang Pashi', falling three days before the full moon of Phalguna, heralds Holi into the household, when all members of the family get together in the evening. There is no puja associated with this part of the festival, except the putting of a little colour on the faces of the gods. The household priest or the eldest male member begins the function by formally sprinkling colour on the faces of all the members.

In some places, where this festival is combined with the dol yatra or the swing festival, the image of Krishna as a babe is placed in a swing cradle and decorated with flowers and painted with coloured powders. The innocent frolics of little Krishna with the merry milkmaids of Brindavan are commemorated; so religious people chant the name of Krishna and sing Holi songs related to those frolics. A dinner is then arranged where special eatables are served. The married daughter of the house is presented with the gift of a special saree called the *dandia* which is worn on that day.

Then comes the day of Puno when Holi is burnt in the evening. Usually it is a community celebration. Bonfires are lit with huge heaps of firewood on crossroads. People venerate the Holi fire by dancing around it, beating drums, and blowing conches. Games representing the frolics of Krishna also take place round the fire. People take a little fire from here to their houses, because they believe that it renders their houses pure and free from diseases.

The next and third day, which is called Parva, is the climax of the Holi festival. The head of the family worships the fire in the centre of which a mango tree or a coconut tree, a plantain or castor-oil plant is buried. From the morning onwards people gather and "play" Holi. They visit one another's houses, carrying colour and water, drenching one another as they visit different places. It is a day when relatives are visited; or some just enjoy celebrating this festival with their neighbours. There is much singing and merriment and everyone, both young and old, join in the fun. Lunchtime heralds the closing of the festival.

Significance of the Festival

As a spring festival, Holi contains the elements of wonder that we experience when we behold the earth clothed with the splendour of vernal bloom. It proclaims the glory of God and not only inspires joy and new life, but stirs us on to find its Creator who is "hiding" Himself in all these forms. This festival can be an invitation to reflect on colour as one of the beautiful things of God's Creation. Light which is colourless breaks up into a variety of hues, when the sunlight goes through the raindrops producing the rainbow. Our artistic nature seeks harmony in colour and in sounds. The feast of colour can be an occasion to encourage and develop our aesthetic sense. This festival is an invitation to appreciate beauty in its varied forms and to the development of good taste.

The call of Holi is to keep always ablaze the flame of God's love manifested in our love for others. Holi therefore brings people of different age groups, communities, castes, and walks of life together. It is the uniting or embracing of the great and the small, of the rich and the poor. The festival teaches us to forget the outgoing year's ill-feelings and begin the new year with love, sympathy, co-operation, and equality.

The Holi fire is the new fire, symbolic of a new year and more specially of new life. New fire, not only in the hearth but also in the heart! Fire in this festival is experienced as the source of purification and health. It is an invitation to burn all the impurities of the mind like egoism, vanity, lust;

and it is an invitation to soar to greater heights of spiritual freedom. It challenges us to ignite the values of cosmic love, sympathy, co-operation, mercy, generosity, selflessness, truthfulness, and purity, through the fire of Yogic practice. This festival therefore can be an occasion for Christians to join hands with their Hindu sisters and brothers in their common cause of building up a new and just world order where everyone is a brother and a sister.

PART III
WORSHIP AND RITUALS

PART III
WORSHIP AND RITUALS

WORSHIP IN HINDUISM

Worship is a unique expression of one's relationship to divinity. Giving praise and thanks, seeking forgiveness and grace — these are the immediate goals of worship. It presupposes, however, an I-Thou relationship which is found in the Bhakti Marg of Hinduism but not in the Jñana Marg of the Vedantists, which admits only an I-That relationship.

Bhakti postulates a personal God (*Ishwara*) with different attributes (*saguna*), and relationship with him is visualised at three levels *prarthana* (intercession), *puja* or *aradhna* (worship) and *upāsana* (contemplation). The Vedantists, on the other hand, admit only *upāsana* of the non-dual and attribute-less Brahman, even if at times they too offer prayer and worship.

In speaking of the worship of a deity, it should be remembered that Hindus have usually three categories of deities to be considered: their village deity (*grāma devatā*), the family deity (*kula devatā*), and the personal deity (*ishtta devatā*). The first is worshipped in the village temple and the second in the house sanctuary; whereas the worship of the last is entirely an individual affair, without any fixed ritual. Besides these, there is the periodic worship of other deities, especially on their respective feastdays. A most popular and elaborate puja, because considered to be most effective in obtaining divine favour, is the Satyanarayan Puja in honour of Vishnu.

When performing puja, much attention is paid to the proper enunciation of the formulas and performance of the ritual actions. On the other hand, there is an immense variety in the way Hindus worship either at home or in the temple. It depends on one's caste, sect, region, place of residence; whether a village or a city, etc. There are, however, certain common features that can be mentioned.

I. HOME WORSHIP

In an old article reprinted in RELIGIOUS HINDUISM (St Paul's, Mumbai, 1997), Robert Antoine, S.J., points out that a Brāhmin is by caste the Hindu whose existence is completely under the sway of ritual. The other castes model their religious practices on the pattern of Brāhmin life. If, therefore, we follow the course of a Brāhmin's daily life, we shall have a general idea of the ritual duties of all Hindus. The following is Antoine's own description of the daily religious life of a Brahmin:

Rising before sunrise, a Brāhmin is careful to avoid the sight of inauspicious persons or objects. A widow, a sweeper, a barren woman are inauspicious. A ring, a cow, a little child, are auspicious. His right foot must touch the ground first. Once out of bed, he rinses his mouth three times and winds his holy thread round his neck and over his right ear. After the morning toilet, he wears his holy thread round his neck and is allowed to break silence. He cleans his teeth, rinses his mouth, and bows to the sun. The morning bath follows, preferably in a river, concluded by a prayer to the sages, the gods, and the ancestors. Then begins the *Prätah-sandhyä* or morning prayer, which must be completed before the sun rises.

Seated on a low stool and facing the east, with his sacred thread hanging from his left shoulder, he sips water, pronounces sacred formulas (mantras) over the ashes which he has brought with him and marks his forehead, his arms, ribs and knees with them. He ties his hair. Closing one nostril after the other, he exhales and inhales, repeating the sacred *Gäyatrï mahamantra*:

AUM, Bhoor Bhuvah Swah
Tat Savitur varennyam
bhargo devasya dhïmahi
dhiyo yo nah
O Supreme Lord,
the Source of Existence, Intelligence and Bliss!
We meditate on the lovely light
of the god, Savitri;
May it stimulate our thoughts!

Then closing both nostrils and bending his head, he repeats mentally the same mantra four times. The whole process is repeated three times. He then formulates his intention (*sankalpa*) to be purified of his sins. Water is sprinkled to dispel the demons. More water is poured as a symbol of the bath to free the earth from demons so the Sun can rise. A prayer to the Sun follows. The *Gäyatri mantra* is repeated 108 times on a rosary counting as many beads. Often the morning worship is concluded with different positions of the fingers which symbolise different petitions.

The morning *homa* (oblation) is an offering of ghee, curds and rice to the fire, and must precede the first meal. *Homa* is followed by *svädhyäya*, or spiritual reading: the right hand is placed successively in front of the mouth, the eyes, the ears, the nose, the lips, the top of the head, the chin, the forearms, the navel, and the back, in order to obtain the protection of the gods. The Gäyatri is repeated and the reading of a sacred book begun.

The ceremony of triple *tarpanna* (propitiation) follows. After sipping water, the worshipper sits facing the east, his sacred thread hanging over his left shoulder, and pours water from his straightened fingers. This is *Deva-tarpanna* (propitiation of the gods). Then he faces the west, his sacred thread hanging round his neck, and he pours water between his two little fingers, the hands being held in the form of a cup. This is *Rshi-tarpanna* (propitiation of the sages). Then he sits facing the south, his holy thread hanging from his right shoulder, and pours water between the base of the thumb and the first finger of his right hand. This is *Pitr-tarpanna* (propitiation of the ancestors).

The next item on the daily programme is the *Deva-püjana* (worship of the deity). Usually a small room is reserved in the home as a kind of private oratory where the image of the favourite god (*ishttadevatä*), the image of other gods and the various utensils used in worship (bell, copper vessel, spoon, sandal-wood paste, incense, conch-shell, etc.), are also kept. The water used in the *pujä* must be blessed. The blessing of water is done as follows: the worshipper holds his right hand above the copper vessel containing the water and, bending down the fore-finger, moves the hand up and down, mentioning the names of the great pilgrimages and holy rivers. Then he holds his hand in the form of a cow's udder over the water, symbolising thus the coming down of nectar. The water thus blessed is sprinkled over the utensils of the worshipper. The special prayers and gestures of the worship depend on the deity who is worshipped. The worship is usually completed by a prayer asking for the forgiveness of sins.

Such are, in short, the morning devotions of a devout Brähmin: *snäna* (bath), *sandhyä* (morning prayer), *homa* (sacrifice to the fire), *svädhyäya* (spiritual reading) and *devapujana* (worship of the deity). It is evident that many Brähmins do not have the time necessary to perform all these duties entirely. For their sake, an abbreviated ritual is foreseen. Many Hindus who have given up the long morning ritual remain faithful to the daily recitation of the Gäyatri.

Besides *pujas*, pious brahmins perform daily *sandhyas*, morning and evening prayers, said by the side of a river or lake, in honour of the sun god. It must also be noted that all the members of a family are not bound to perform the rites. Usually, the head of the family alone does it in the name of all.

152

II. TEMPLE WORSHIP

The temple worship may consist either of a prayer service like *bhajan*-singing, *kirtans* (preaching in song), or in offering puja to a deity by venerating his/her idol in specific ways. It may be noted that an image of a deity is a mere object until it is "consecrated" (*pränna pratishttä*). This consecration may be done once for all (e.g., images in the temple), or each time there is a puja (e.g., the image of Ganesh for the Ganesh Chaturthi).

There are various formulas for the consecration of the image, some long and others short. The common feature in them all is the invocation (*ävähan*) to the particular deity to come and indwell in the image, each limb of the image being touched by the consecrating priest and made to become a limb of the deity. As soon as the consecration is over, the devotees look upon the image with awe and adoration (almost comparable to the Consecration at the Catholic Mass). They believe that there is a real *sämnidhya* (presence) or *ävirbhäva* (self-manifestation) of the deity in the image. It is no longer a mere statue or an idol, but an "image" (*pratimä* or *pratikrti*) of the god.

When the consecration is temporary, there is a de-consecration (*visarjana*) ceremony: the deity is thanked for having dwelt among the worshippers and asked to depart till the following festival. After this, the statue, because it has been a dwelling place of the deity, is taken respectfully to some sacred river and thrown into the water.

The Puja

The puja of the various sects is determined by their respective sacred texts called "*angamas*". The following features of the puja of *Panchayatana* (Shiva, Vishnu, Surya, Ganapati, and Devi) are common to almost all pujas:

A. Preparation Rite. First of all, objects for offering are collected. They consist of flowers, sandal paste, certain leaves (e.g., tulsi, bilva), water, fruit, and sweets. Puja vessels are prepared and the ground where the puja will be performed is washed and wiped. These tasks belong mostly to women. At the correct time, worshippers squat facing north or east.

The pujari begins by performing the rite of purification of mouth (*āchamana*) by sipping water thrice and reciting certain *mantras* (formulas) and the 24 names of Vishnu. He then expresses his resolve (*sankalpa*) to perform the rite and declares its purpose, that is, makes the intention for the rite. Then follows the consecration of the water to be used in the puja, and finally, there is the salutation to the line of teachers.

B. Purifications. The objects of worship are purified by sprinkling water and reciting mantras and a prayer of exorcism.

C. Consecration of the Worshipper. Through chants and certain gestures (*mudras*) the worshipper himself is then purified. At times he may imagine that his sinful body and mind (*pāpa purusha*) are consumed in the mystic fire, that a new heavenly body, free from sin, is created out of that mystic fire (*bhuta shuddhi*). He then invokes the deity in the heart of this new divine body (*jivanyāsa*).

D. Mental Worship (*Mānasa puja*) of the deity is performed individually and privately, in one's heart.

E. External Worship consists of various parts:

a. *Nyāsa* — consecration of hands and body by certain mudras and mantras;

b. *Āvāhan* — invocation of the deity that dwells in the heart, now called to come out and inhabit the object of worship (an image, a stone emblem, a flower, etc.);

c. *Upachāra* — worship proper, done by offering 10 or 16 "gifts" (*soddashopachāra*) to the deity, while reciting appropriate formulas:

1. *āsana* (seat),
2. *svāgat* (welcome),

3. *pädya* (washing of feet),
4. *arghya* (rice, durba grass, flowers, etc.),
5. *ächamaniya* (rinsing),
6. *snäniya* (milk and honey for bath),
7. *vastra* (clothes in the form of tulsi leaves),
8. *upvastra* (blouse and ornaments, also in the form of tulsi leaves),
9. *gandha* or *chandana* (perfumes and sandal paste),
10. *pushpa* (flowers to wear),
11. *dhüpa* (incense),
12. *deepa* (light),
13. *nivedya* (food),
14. *pradikshana* (religious circumabulation),
15. *mantrapushpa* (flowers with mantras), and
16. *namaskara* (final adoration).

F. Conclusion. Before the deity is sent back to his or her celestial abode (udväsana), the following or similar prayer is said, which is somewhat similar to the prayer said by the catholic priest of the Syrian-rite at the end of the Khurban (Mass):

"Veneration to the Infinite and Eternal Male (Purusha), who has thousands of names, thousands of forms, thousands of feet, thousands of eyes, thousands of heads, thousands of thighs, thousands of arms, and who lives for ten million ages.

"O great god, pardon my want of knowledge of the right way of worshipping thee. Sin, misery and poverty are removed; happiness and purity are obtained by thy presence. O great god, I commit thousands of faults every day and night; forgive me as I am thy servant. There is no other protection but from thee; thou only art my refuge; guard me therefore, and defend me by thy mercy; pardon my mistakes and defects in syllables, words and actions; O mighty lord, be propitiated. I offer flowers with prayers. Let the five gods, of whom great Vishnu is the first, be pleased with the worship I have made. Let all this be offered to the Supreme Being. I offer thee with my mouth, O Vishnu, the sacred salutation Vashat. Be pleased, O Sipivishta, with my oblations;

155

let my songs of praise exalt thee; protect us ever with thy blessings."

The puja ends with the distribution of *prasad*. (see next chapter), which not only promotes the psychological sense of participation, but is meant to "purify" body and mind, as it proceeds from the deity.

III. SACRIFICES

The great Vedic sacrifices are no longer celebrated. They have been replaced by the puja of home and temple deities. There are, however, five great sacrifices which have preserved much of the Vedic tradition and are occasionally performed by wealthy Hindus anxious to assure their liberation or that of some relative or friend.

The *Mahārudra* sacrifice is believed to wash away the sins of the person for whom it is offered, whether he be alive or dead. Eleven Brāhmins officiate at sacrifices *(hotr)*: one as *āchārya* (guide), one as *brahmā* (protector), one as *sadasyapati* (scriptural guide), one as *ganapati* (supervising the proper recitation and pronunciation of the mantras), one as *upadrastr* (general supervisor). Four more Brāhmins act as doorkeepers, to keep demons away. The fire lit at the beginning must burn continually for the five or eleven days during which the sacrifice lasts. The god Rudra and attendant deities are installed. Worship goes on the whole time and every evening there is *ārati* (waving of lamps.)

Gāyatrī-purascharana. A householder is expected during his life to repeat the Gāyatrī 2,400,000 times. Towards the end of his life, if he has doubts regarding the fulfilment of that duty, he may perform the Gāyatrī-purascharana. A number of Brāhmins are invited who will recite the gāyatrī during several days until the number is completed. The ritual resembles that of the Mahārudra. While the mantra is recited, ghee is continually poured into the fire.

There are finally three great sacrifices meant to propitiate

156

Chanddi, the consort of Shiva. Brähmins are employed to recite the *Chanddi-pätha* (a passage of the *Märkandeya Puräna* containing 700 stanzas) in honour of the goddess. The simplest form of the sacrifice is to repeat the 700 stanzas 100 times. The second and better form is to repeat them 1,000 times. The third and best form is to repeat them 100,000 times.

The word 'sacrifice' *(yajna)* is also used in a broader sense for the five great sacrifices *(mahäyajna)* which a householder must offer every day. According to the Manu-smrti, they are : *Adhyäyanam brahmayajnah:* "reading the Holy Scripture is the sacrifice to Brahma"; *Pitryajnastu tarpanam:* "the sacrifice to the ancestors is the propitiation" (see above); *Homo devayajnah:* "the *Homa* sacrifice is offered to the gods"; *Balirbhutayajnah:* "the feeding of animals is offered to the elements"; *Nryajno thitipujanam:* "hospitality is the sacrifice offered to men".

IV. PUJA AND THE EUCHARIST

Christians will be interested to note the difference between Puja and their own Eucharist (the Mass):

1. Puja is a simple rite of human adoration and service to God, involving a certain amount of personal self-sacrifice. The Eucharist, on the other hand, is believed to be an act of God sacrificing himself for man, a mystical immolation of Christ to the Father. It is essentially an act of "thanksgiving" (literal meaning of *"eucharistia"*), which the puja is not.

2. The Eucharist is a commemorative rite, bound up with salvation history —the passion, death, and resurrection of Jesus—, whilst puja is an expression of the timeless aspiration of the human soul, an essentially mystical rite.

3. The Eucharist is a rite of communion with God, through which God's grace is infused in the worshipper; whereas puja is a purificatory rite, besides being a rite of adoration. Communion may take place only if the person is

enlightened by contemplation, and not through the puja itself.

4. Finally, the Eucharist is both central to Christian life and the corporate worship of the entire community, through the priest.

Puja, however, is peripheral to Hindu life. It is contemplation, which sometimes is considered the lowest form of religious life, that is more central and effects union. Idea of corporate worship is lacking in the puja.

THE PRASADA

Is It Correct for a Catholic to Accept It?

Noel Sheth, S.J.

I.   What Is Prasada?

Prasada is the remnants of food (usually fruits or sweets) offered to a deity in a Hindu ritual called *puja*, in which the deity is worshipped as an important guest. The food is believed to be partly consumed by the deity and thus blessed by it. After the puja the devotee partakes of this offering. The eating of this food creates a bond of communion between the deity and the devotee, who obtains the deity's favour or grace.

The word *prasada* has the following connotations: sedateness, calmness, good temper, propitiousness, graciousness, kindness, favour, gift, grace. Etymologically, it is derived from the indeclinable particle *pra*, and the causative of the verbal root *sad*. In the present context, the particle *pra* denotes 'intensity', 'excess', 'completion', 'perfection', 'satisfaction', 'excellence', 'adoration', 'respect'. *Sad* means 'to sit', and the causative therefore means "to cause to sit down, recline, rest, settle". The original idea seems to have been the propitiation of the deity by making a propitiatory offering: the deity who is angry and excited is as it were respectfully and completely *(pra)* caused to sit back and relax, to become sedate and tranquil, pacified and placated *(sada)*. In this way the deity, being pleased, becomes kind, favourable, gracious towards the devotee.

159

Prasada is, therefore, the food offered to a deity, which then becomes 'blessed' or 'graced food' for the devotee. It should be noted that, in the ritual performance of the puja, the water and other materials used in various libations to, and ablutions of, the image of the deity constitute a sacred mixture *(tirtha)*, and it is drunk by the devotees. Similarly, the flowers and/or leaves offered *(nirmalya)* to the deity are holy and are respectfully placed on their head by the devotees. In all these three cases — the food, the aqueous mixture, and the flowers and leaves — the devotee partakes of the leftovers of the offerings to the deity.

In Hinduism there are major deities and minor deities. The former are truly divine: they do not have imperfect, material bodies, are not subject to ignorance and rebirth and, in view of those Hindus who belong to the bhakti traditions, can grant salvation. The minor deities are finite souls who, due to their past deeds, are reborn in godly, but imperfect bodies: they are ignorant, subject to birth and death, and can grant only this-worldly rewards, but not salvation. They are only temporarily and accidentally "superior" to human beings, but essentially there is no difference, for when they die they can be reborn in godly, human, animal, or plant bodies.

A Hindu may perform a puja to a Supreme Being or to a minor deity (who is regarded as a manifestation of that Hindu's Supreme Being). Nowadays Hindus are monotheists or absolutists, believing that there is only one Supreme Reality, and all other minor gods and goddesses (and indeed all other finite beings too) are either real or unreal manifestations or reflections of that Supreme Being. Some Hindus may regard the neuter Brahman as the Absolute, others may consider Vishnu as the Supreme Being, others Krishna, others Shiva, others Durga, and so forth. (Due to this diversity and also because of many other reasons, Hinduism is not really one religion; it is rather a "federation of faiths".) So when a Vaishnavite (one who

160

believes in Vishnu as the Supreme Being), for instance, worships Shiva and offers food to him, the Vaishnavite regards Shiva as a minor god and ultimately a manifestation of Vishnu.

In this context, it should be remarked that the word *puja* (worship) is used rather loosely, for it can be accorded to the Supreme Being, to minor gods and goddesses, or even to inanimate objects like weapons, implements of one's trade, etc. Christians, on the other hand, use different terms: *latria* is employed only when we adore God; *hyperdulia* is reserved for the Blessed Virgin Mary because she is the Mother of God; and *dulia* is exclusively for the veneration of angels and saints.

In many places in India it has become quite a common practice for Hindus to bring some *prasada* to their offices, factories, and workplaces, and distribute it among their colleagues. Generally they do not bring the *prasada* from their 'daily puja' but they frequently share the *prasada* from "occasional pujas", such as the *Satya Narayana Puja*. Similarly when people visit Hindu homes, especially on feast days, they are often offered prasada by their Hindu hosts. In this context Catholics sometimes find themselves in a dilemma: on the one hand they would like to be polite and maintain good social relationships with their Hindu colleagues and friends, and on the other hand they want to be orthodox Catholics, and wonder whether it is all right to accept the Hindu prasada.

II. Why is Communion not Given to Non-Christians?

Catholics hesitate all the more to take the Hindu prasada when they remember that Hindus are not allowed by Catholics to receive Holy Communion which, in many Indian regional languages, is called *Krist-prasad* or *Param-prasad*. How is it that, unlike the Hindu *prasada*, the Christian prasada is not shared with others?

The present Catholic understanding is that by receiving the Eucharist, people are not only expressing their faith in Jesus Christ as God, but are also united with the Christian community, sharing in the life, and accepting the basic doctrines, values, etc., of this community. Hence it would not be proper to offer Communion to non-Christians, for, in doing so, we would be forcing them to acknowledge Christ as God and also to accept our beliefs and doctrines. So one could tell our Hindu brothers and sisters that it is precisely out of respect for them that Communion is not given to them.

In the case of Hindus, on the other hand, when people accept prasada from a Hindu belonging to a particular sect, they may commune with the deity to whom it is offered, but they are not thereby considered to be members of that particular Hindu denomination and, naturally therefore, are not obliged to accept and live by the beliefs of that group. It may be remarked, incidentally, that, for a variety of reasons, Hindus are generally not so restrictive as Christians, although one does find even nowadays some Hindu temples which prohibit non-Hindus or even Hindus of low castes from entering those temples.

III. Would Hindus Misjudge Christians Who Accept the Prasada?

One may ask whether Hindus will get the impression that a Christian by accepting the prasada is acknowledging or worshipping the Hindu deity to whom the food has been offered. As has been pointed out above, prasada is not always offered to the Supreme Deity. It is therefore not likely that a Hindu will think that, by eating the prasada offered to a particular minor deity, the Christian is necessarily recognizing that Hindu deity as the Supreme Being. And even when the prasada was offered to a deity that an individual Hindu considers to be the Supreme Being, it does not necessarily imply that, by receiving the prasada, one is

162

acknowledging that deity as the Supreme Being. For just as a Vaishnavite who offers this prasada to Shaivites knows that they are not thereby recognizing Vishnu as the Supreme Being, so also the Hindu is all the more aware that Christians are not changing their religion and acknowledging the Hindu's deity as the Supreme Being, merely by taking the prasada.

Even though Hindus may not explicitly express it or even consciously think of it, yet if they were asked about it, they would probably say that they regard the acceptance of prasada by a Christian as an act of social etiquette, rather than a religious act. Incidentally, one notices that even Hindus who are actually atheists politely accept the prasada offered by a believing Hindu, without making any fuss.

There is of course a slim chance of Hindus misinterpreting Christians who may receive the prasada while being present for a puja for, unless it is clear to them that the Christians are there only as observers, they may be mistaken to be participants. (It should be noted that the Church forbids participation in the rites, "communicatio in sacris", of non-Christians.) Normally, however, Christians are not present at these pujas, whether in the temple or at home: we are mainly concerned here with the distribution of prasada in the workplaces or homes, after the puja is over.

IV. Is Prasada an Offering in the Context of Idolatry?

In many places the Bible warns us not to eat food offered to idols, i.e., material images which are regarded as deities, and not merely as representations or symbols of deities. Is the Hindu prasada offered to idols and, if so, would it be wrong for a Christian to eat it? In this context one should note the following points:

1. In modern times, a number of Hindus think that the image of clay or wood or stone, etc., is not a deity: it is only

163

an inadequate, human way of representing or symbolizing the deity. When sons or daughters kiss the photograph of their mother or father, they are surely not showing their filial love and affection to the picture, but to their father or mother whom the picture represents. When Christians light a candle in front of a statue of Jesus or Mary or a saint, they are definitely not adoring or venerating the material image. Many of these Hindus are even against the performance of pujas.

2. On the other hand, there are many Hindus who believe that, after an image is "consecrated" through a ritual called the *prana-pratistha* (establishment or infusion of life into the image) ceremony, the deity enters into, and dwells in that image until the latter is "de-consecrated". Hence these "consecrated" images are not like the statues of Jesus, Mary and the saints, which are blessed (and thus sacred) but not "consecrated" in the Hindu sense.

For some of these Hindus the material statue, after being "consecrated" becomes the abode of the deity, just as the tabernacle in the case of the Eucharistic Jesus. In this case, it is clear that the image is not the deity itself, and that food, etc., is offered not to the image but to the deity dwelling in it. For many other Hindus the image is transformed into a body of the deity. This transformation, however, is not a transubstantiation, as in the case of the Eucharistic Bread and Wine: the material of the statue still remains imperfect matter (*prakriti*) but is now alive, since the living deity is present in it just like a soul which is said to have transmigrated into a body.

Note that the relationship between the deity and the consecrated material image is not so intimate as in the Christians' understanding of the intrinsic union of the soul and body, which together form one being. In the Hindu view, human beings, for example, are essentially only spirits, without material bodies. The human soul and its body do not form one being, the body does not really belong to the human person. When the ignorant human soul attains salvation, it realizes that it never had a body, that it had only a mistaken, apparent, extrinsic relationship with a body! In this case, the food is offered not merely to the deity, but to the deity who has the image as its living body, just as in daily life Hindus may offer food to a guest, who is then not merely a pure spirit, but a soul ignorantly in contact with a living body. Even so, it is not idolatry in the strictest sense, for the material statues or pictures are not, in themselves and by their very nature, considered to be deities; they become the living bodies of the deities only through the transformation that takes place by the deities entering into them after the consecration ceremony.

There are of course Hindus who do not in any way distinguish the consecrated image from the deity. In this situation, too, it should be remembered that if, in the case of a puja offered to a minor deity, some Hindus identify the consecrated image with that of a minor deity, they are not practising idolatry, for they are not regarding the statue as the Supreme Divinity, but only as a finite being temporarily superior to human beings.

3. In some Hindu sects there are special idols and objects which, even without the consecration ceremony, are regarded as the deity itself. But even here the understanding is not that they are worshipping some inert matter, but the deity who exists in that form: it is something like the Second Person of the Trinity taking on human form, or somewhat like the Eucharistic Bread and Wine being Jesus Himself. For Christians, who have a different world-view from that of these Hindus, these images are not divine, but just ordinary material idols, and hence Christians would consider these Hindus to be idolatrous. (By the same token, of course, Hindus who do not share the Christian faith may wonder how Christians believe that the consecrated host is Jesus Christ, when it looks and tastes like bread.) Further, according to some Christian scholars, even the earlier group

of Hindus which considers the consecrated image to be the living body of the deity is practising idolatry. These scholars would of course be all the more emphatic in their judgement in the case of Hindus who identify the consecrated statue with the deity, especially the Supreme Deity.

Let us now suppose that we have a case where a Christian believes that a Hindu is offering prasada after practising real idolatry. What then? Would it be sinful to receive and eat that prasada? Biblical scholars tell us that the religious leaders of ancient Israel were afraid that the polytheistic beliefs and practices of Israel's neighbours would contaminate and weaken its strict monotheism, and so they repeatedly engaged in vehement polemics against idolatry. However, after the Exile (6th century B.C.), once Jewish monotheism was theoretically well-established, the Old Testament did not attack idolatry so forcefully as before. There was a clearer realization now that the idols were in themselves powerless and useless, but there was also the fear that through partaking of the food offered to false gods or evil spirits, one was in danger of becoming spiritually blind and being led astray from the true faith.

This same basic belief prevailed in the period of St Paul, and his condemnation of idolatry must be viewed against this background. During St Paul's time there were two groups of Christians who were sharply divided on the question of eating food sacrificed to idols. One group felt that, since the idols were non-entities, there was no harm in eating the food placed before them. The other group was mortally afraid of touching such food, fearing the malignant influence of the demonic spirits that they believed inhabited such food. In 1Cor 8, 13, St Paul agrees with the first group, stating that idols do not really exist, since there is only one God. (It is worth remembering here that each Hindu sect also believes in the only one Supreme Being, just as Christians do.) Hence, he says, we are free to eat or not eat food offered to idols. However, he cautions us to be careful not to scandalize, mislead, or confuse others who may be ignorant and have weak consciences.

One would, therefore, have to judge whether any Christian who is in the vicinity is likely to be scandalized or led astray. One would think that this is a rather remote possibility nowadays since even illiterate Christians generally know that a material idol is not God. However, as mentioned earlier, in the case of being actually present at the performance of a puja, there is a greater chance of the consciences of other Christians there being scandalized or damaged by the taking of prasada by one or other Christian. While forbidding participation in the temple feasts of non-Christians (1Cor 10, 20-22) St Paul also warns of the danger of ruining the conscience of the weak by eating the food in the sacrificial feasts (1Cor 8, 10-12). But, as has been pointed out, it is rather rare that a Christian is present at a puja, and it would be still more rare for more than one Christian to attend the same puja. Our discussion focuses more on the accepting of prasada in the workplace or home, without having been present for the actual performance of the puja.

IV. Conclusion

It would seem, therefore, that in general there is very little chance of people, whether Christians or Hindus or even others, misunderstanding a Catholic taking the prasada. However, if some Catholics do have qualms of conscience, I am sure the Hindus will understand these Catholics, if they politely decline, saying, e.g., that due to religious restrictions they would prefer not to take the prasada, at the same time being careful to indicate that they do not thereby want to belittle the Hindu religion and practices. It would be similar to a Jew or a Muslim refusing to eat pork, or a vegetarian Hindu not accepting meat. In fact, there are a very few orthodox Hindus, who do not eat in a restaurant or even a Hindu house of a different sect from the one to which they belong. Hence, Hindus would not take it amiss if one respectfully mentions one's difficulty in taking the prasada.

Perhaps a better approach might be to tell the Hindu in a nice way that "even though as a Christian I do not worship other deities, I shall still accept this prasada as a sign of my sharing in your joy and celebration." Hindus would not be offended because, when they offer *prasada* to Christians, they certainly do not expect them to accept their beliefs and doctrines. However, since the chances of misunderstanding and scandal are practically nil, it might be best to accept the prasada in a spirit of fellowship and friendship. Partaking of and sharing in the same food, whether one believes that food to be blessed or not, builds up communion, brotherhood, and sisterhood. After all, as we say in Sanskrit, *vasudhaiva kutumbakam:* the whole earth is but one family.

3

THE RITUAL OF ĀRATI

Apollinaris Pinto, S.J.

In every Hindu ritual worship, there is invariably the *ārati*. Though various scholars believe it was a pre-Aryan word, many others derive it from different Sanskrit roots. According to some it is linked with the word, *"araryanti"* (to praise), which is perhaps connected with *"ri"* that means to go, to move, to rise upwards. *"Aratrika"* is referred to the light which is waved at night before an idol, or kept before it the whole night.

Another word for arati is *"niranjana"* which means waving a light before an idol as an act of worship or adoration. *"Deepadan"* is also a word used and it means presentation of light. Therefore, arati is the repeated waving of light in a circular form either before a sacred idol or a human being.

Arati is offered to God, to saints, to human beings and, on certain occasions, even to animals. When the arati is offered to God and to the saints, it expresses respectively praise and worship of God, and respect to the saints who are embodiments of divine ideals and therefore worthy of respect and veneration.

The arati is done also to human beings, namely, to an honourable guest, to show love and respect. In other instances it is done to newly-married couples, to brides at their departure from the paternal homes, on the occasion of the *"raksha bandhan"*, at the "thread ceremony" (*upanayana*), to avoid evil eyes, etc. In ancient books there are references that arati was offered to elephants and horses of the king.

In the temple as also at home, the arati may be performed at various times: early in the morning, with wicks (*kākāda arati*); before lunch, with eatables (*mahanaivedya*); in the evening; before dinner; and at night, before going to bed (*shejārati*).

There are special reasons why the arati is performed, especially at the end of a puja: it "completes" the puja! In a puja the arati is the last item of the ritual, and the purpose is to supplement or complete whatever is lacking, either by omission or disrespect. "When puja is performed without a proper mantra, or a proper ritual, it reaches its completeness through arati" (*Devi Devataon ki 101 Aratiyan*).

Even at other times, the arati is supposed to lead the devotees to the supreme state of God. "He who sees the arati of the lord of lords, Vishnu, will be a brahmin for seven births and at the end will reach the supreme state of God." (Ibid.) It liberates the kulam (clan). "He who looks at the incense and arati, and receives or respects it with two hands, redeems or liberates crores of kulas and reaches the supreme state of God."

Different elements are required to perform the arati, which in the homes are generally prepared by women in a prayerful mood and with their minds set on God:

a) *Mula-mantra*: the basic mantra of the deity or saint that is being worshipped;

b) *Pushpanjali*: flowers;

c) *Mahavadya*: beating of drums or blowing of trumpets or striking of cymbals to announce the arati;

d) *Jaya-stavana*: praising the Lord with the word "Jay!";

e) *Karpur or ghrita*: camphor or ghee light;

f) *Shubha-patram*: a clean plate for the articles of arati;

g) *Vishvamaneka vartikam*: arati-stand with uneven (*vishama*) number of lights (usually the arati stand has five or seven lamps).

170

Whether done at home or in the temple, the arati requires a ceremonial or ritual purification by bath. Then, wearing a wet or fresh cloth, the pujari removes the old flowers and washes (*abhishekam*) the idol reciting the appropriate mantras, and then decorates it. After that, he rings the bells with an invocation:

agamartham tu devanam	:	That gods may come,
gamanartham tu rakshasam	:	that rakshasas may go out —
kuruve ghantaravam tatra	:	I ring this bell.
devata-ahvana-lakshanam	:	The aim is to call upon God!

When performing the arati, the worshipper follows certain steps. There is the *Deepamala*, waving of lights to form a garland; *Sa-udaka-abja*, offering of water from a conch; *Dhauta-vasasa*, waving with washed cloth; *Kuta-asvathadi-patraiha*, waving with the mango and peepal leaves; *Panipatena sastangena*, prostration at the feet of the deity.

The waving of the "*shubha-patram*", with its ritual contents, has to be done in small circles at certain points or positions of the one who is being thus venerated, e.g., near the feet, navel, face, and finally over the entire body. It can also be done in the agamic tradition, that is in the form of AUM.

It should be noted that a triple arati is also done to the people attending the puja: for the good of the entire world, the good of the village, and the good of each individual soul. After this the devotees "receive" the arati flame by rotating their hands over it and then placing them on one's head as if to anoint themselves with the light of God.

Christian Understanding of Arati

For some years now, ever since the Church began to encourage "inculturation" in worship, within certain limits, arati is being performed in various churches of North India and in houses of priestly and religious formation. In the churches it often replaces the western-style incensation done on various occasions (see the Indian edition of the **Roman Missal**).

a) *Pushpārati*, with flowers and a lamp in the middle, is done at the entrance of the church or the sanctuary, to welcome the celebrant and the congregation and also to create an atmosphere of God-awareness, or to make the people God-oriented. After the priest is welcomed with the arati, he sanctifies the sanctuary, the altar (*vidhi arati*) and the people (*jana arati*) by going in their midst, and making the arati to them. (See the "Order of Mass", in the Roman Missal, Indian Ed., No. 2)

b) A double arati — *Pushparati* (with eight flowers) and *Dhuparati* (with incense) — is done over the gifts at the Offertory (*naivadh arati*). "The celebrant makes the *pushparati* by waving three times the tray of eight flowers and then placing the eight flowers around the gifts in eight directions invoking Jesus Christ each time by one of his attributes." (Ibid. No. 22).

c) A triple arati (*maha arati*) — *Pushparati, Dhuparati and Deeparati* — is done by three members of the assembly at the Great Doxology: "through Him, with Him, and in Him...", accompanied by the ringing of the bell. (Ibid. No. 52) In some places, arati is also performed during various para-liturgical services, like the Benediction of the Bl. Sacrament, veneration of relics and images, etc., and also at some other parts of the Mass: to the Holy Bible before the proclamation of the Gospel (*granth arati*); during the "anaphora" (the Eucharistic Prayer); at the "epiclesis" (calling down of the Holy Spirit); and again at the Elevation when Jesus is adored as Lord and God. *Deeparati* is also offered to people (*jana arati*) at the final blessing — to protect them, their village, and the whole world from all evils and to sanctify them for their mission in the world.

Jesus the Arati

There are Christians who find in the arati a meaningful representation of Jesus, "the image of the invisible God" (Col. 1, 15).

1. Just as at the waving of light around the image which is normally kept in the dark place of the sanctuary, the face of the deity radiates light, so does Jesus "reflect the glory of God and bears the very stamp of his nature" (Heb. 1, 3). Jesus is the *antarjyoti*, the inner light, that enlightens every person coming into this world (Jn 1, 9).

2. The arati completes worship. So is Jesus the completion of both the human act of divine worship and of the divine act of revelation to the humans.

3. The arati leads humans towards the supreme state of God. Jesus is the light and he leads us to the Father. "No one comes to the Father but by me" (Jn 14, 6).

4. The arati liberates not only the devotee but the entire world. Jesus takes away the cause of pain and suffering, the sin of the entire world. "He is the expiation for our sins and not for ours only but also for the sins of the whole world" (I Jn 2, 2). The arati also suggests the "kenosis" of Jesus: the arati-flame by burning itself out before the sacred image in order to show the face of the divine. By his kenosis Jesus glorified God and became the redeemer and mediator of the world.

Conversely, the Eucharist itself is our *Maha-arati*. Before leaving this world Jesus gave the command that his memory should be celebrated until his second coming: since he is an arati offered, first, to God in total worship to do the Father's will and to be obedient unto death, and, also, an arati offered to humanity for the total removal of evil, his memory is our own maha-arati.

4

THE SANSKĀRAS

The entire life of an authentic Hindu, from conception to birth, is accompanied by *sanskäras*, rituals by which a person is sanctified and thus qualified for performing the sacred actions of the Brahminic community. The accepted number of sanskaras differs from school to school. Generally 16 are accepted at least on principle.

1. *Garbhädhäna* (impregnation) performed on the 4th day of the marriage, prior to the couple having intercourse. Though not very common nowadays, the ceremony is quite meaningful. In a gesture reminiscent of Tobiah of the Bible (see Tobit 8, 5-9) the officiating priest prays: "Let Vishnu prepare her womb; let the Creator shape its form; let Prajapati be the Impregnator; let the Creator give the embryo." The final plea of the husband is "Oh faithful wife, give birth to a son who will live long."

2. *Pumsavana* (prayer for male offspring) is performed in the 3rd month of pregnancy. Certain texts require that the mother keep a fast. She is then fed by her husband with two beans and a grain of barley, mixed with a handful of curds, and made to pray three times for a son. Along with this rite went the Anavalobhana for the prevention of miscarriage. Some drops of the juice of a stalk of fresh darbha grass are put in the mother's right nostril, with the recitation of certain mantras.

3. *Simantonnayana* (parting of hair), during which scented oil is put on the mother's head and her hair is parted at the centre with three stalks of Kusha grass bound into one, in preparation for the great birth event. The stalk is drawn

174

three times from the forehead by the priest, each time repeating the sacred words *bhoor, bhuvah,* and *swah,* and the mystic *AUM.*

4. *Jata Karman* (birth ceremony) performed soon after the baby is born and before cutting the umbilical cord. The father touches, with a golden spoon containing mixture of honey and ghee, first, the lips of the infant, with the prayer "Oh long-lived one, mayst thou live a hundred years in this world, protected by the gods"; then ears: "May Savitri, may Saraswati, may the Ashwins, grant thee wisdom"; and finally the shoulders are rubbed with the mixture: "Become firm as a rock, sharp as an axe, pure as gold; thou art the Veda called a son, live thou a hundred years. May Indra bestow on thee his best treasurers."

5. *Nama Karana* (name-giving), performed usually on the 10th or 12th day of a child's birth. It is also a ceremony of "purification" of the household, ritually polluted by the childbirth. This is done by bathing the mother, and washing the walls of the house with cow dung, and adorning them with flowers, etc. Various names are suggested by the family astrologer based of the child's horoscope and the father chooses one among them. The ceremony ends with the distribution of sweetmeats.

6. *Nishkramana* (carrying out) is a simple ceremony, not always observed by all. The child is carried out by the parents in the fourth month and presented to the Sun, with the words: "That eye-like luminary, the cause of blessings to the gods, rises in the East. May we behold it for a hundred years. May we hear, may we speak, may we be free from poverty for a hundred years and more." After this, the child is taken to the village temple and presented to the deity there.

7. *Anna Prasana* (food giving). In the presence of a few family friends, some solid food is given to the child for the

first time, in the sixth month, whilst the priest recites sacred texts. After the child, the friends too are feasted.

8-9. *Kshaura* (shaving of head) and **Kesanta** (tonsure) are often performed together. Among Brahmins the ceremony is performed in the third year, but at times delayed by even 4-5 years. In orthodox families, the child is placed in the mother's lap to the west of the sacred fire, whilst the father sits opposite holding 21 stalks of Kusha grass. With these he sprinkles the child's head three times with a mixture of warm water, butter, and curds. Then he inserts three stalks seven times into the child's hair on the right side, saying: "O divine grass, protect him!" Then he cuts off a portion of the hair and gives it to the mother, whilst reciting various texts, leaving a tuft (*shikha*) of one, three, or five locks.

10. *Upanayana* (initiation). Also called the "Thread Ceremony", it is one of the most important of all Hindu ceremonies. Prior to this ceremony, the boy is not considered a member of any of the three higher castes, and is not allowed to participate in Brahminic rites or to recite the Vedas. An orthodox Brahmin father may not admit him to eat with himself. The ceremony takes place usually between the age of seven and ten. An auspicious date and time are fixed. Prior to the ceremony, the boy is shaved, anointed with perfumed oil, and bathed. At the appointed time and place, the boy bows to his parents and the guests who shower blessings upon him. Then he is made to sit on a stool, opposite his father, and the officiating priest sitting at the side recites the sacred texts. The boy then bows and touches the feet of his father and receives his blessing. The guests, too, bless the boy by showering rice or some other grain on him for luck. A fire is lit with sacred twigs and is fed continuously with ghee.

Once these preparations are completed the priest takes out the white sacred thread made of three, white, cotton threads, each consisting of three finer threads, intertwined into one. The three threads represent the trinity and the white colour purity. For Kshatriyas hemp is used instead of cotton, and wool for the Vaishyas. The thread must be consecrated by Brahmins before the ceremony. The priest hangs the chord on the left shoulder of the boy and passes it across the body and the ends are tied under the right arm into a sacred knot called *Brahma-grandhi*. The Brahmins join the officiating priest in the recitation of sacred texts. The boy then is taught the mysterious *Gayatri Mahamantra*. All guests leave the room, and the Gayatri is whispered three times into the boy's ear by the priest or the father, both being wrapped up in a shawl, and the boy repeats it each time.

Then the three *vyāhrtis* (sacred utterances): *Bhoor, Bhuvah, Swah,* are taught and repeated after AUM. Finally the Gayatri is recited in a proper liturgical way, the way the orthodox Hindu would recite throughout his life:

> *AUM, Bhoor Bhuvah Swah*
> *Tat Savitur Varennyam*
> *Bhargo Devasya Dhimahi*
> *Dhiyo yo Nah Prachodayat.*
> Thou, O Supreme Lord,
> the Source of Existence, Intelligence and Bliss,
> the Creator of the Universe!
> On that lovely splendour of Savitri (the Sun),
> on that splendour of the god, we meditate;
> our minds may he himself stimulate.

In ancient times, the boy retired to a *gurukul* (guru's abode) soon after the Thread Ceremony to begin his education. *Upanayana* means leading one to one's guru. Such a student had to beg for his food. That is the meaning of the staff given in his hand at the end of the ceremony.

The sacred thread is the distinguishing mark of the "twice-born", a symbol of regeneration. It is believed to have mystic powers, and in all forms of worship and daily life, it is given an important place. Its position is altered from left shoulder to right shoulder and around the neck, according to variations in the ceremonial. The thread is never taken away from one's body, but may be replaced if worn out, without any public ceremony.

11. **Samavartana** (return home). Since nowadays the boy does not retire to a gurukul, this ceremony is performed immediately after the Upanayana ceremony. The boy is dressed like a householder and the beggar's staff removed from his hand. Instead, he is given an umbrella, sign of prosperity and dominion (!). After reciting some sacred texts, the officiating priest declares: "Till now you have been a *Brahmachari*, now you are a *Snatak*, a householder." Then the feasting begins!

12. **Vivah** (marriage). The date and the time of a marriage are decided according to the partners' horoscope. The details of the ceremony differ from place to place, but the essentials are the same. The ceremony usually has two parts: the giving away (*sampradāna*) and the marriage proper (*pännigrahanna*)

a) *Sampradāna*. The bride sits in her room, all decked up and surrounded by her female relatives and friends, and receives gifts and presents from the invitees. When the groom arrives, there is rejoicing and he is taken to another room prepared for him. At the given time he is conducted to the place of the ceremony and made to sit on a low stool opposite the bride's father (*sampradātā*). The ceremony is conducted under the direction of two Brahmins representing each of the families. Family trees of the couple are recalled and the bride's father officially expresses his choice of the young man as his son-in-law. He then gives the boy various symbolic objects.

The bride is then brought on a flat seat carried on the shoulders of some relatives and shown to the groom (*shubhadarshana*) with the top part of her sari being thrown over the head of the groom (applause!). A married woman with living sons ties the right hands of the couple with *kusha* grass, whilst the girl's father, holding her left hand, sprinkles her with scented water, saying: "*Enäm kanyäm väsoyugächaditäm sälankäräm prajäpatidevatäkäm tubhyam aham sampradade.*" (I give away to you this my daughter, decked with clothes and ornaments and devoted to Prajäpati.) The groom accepts her with the word *Svasti*.

b)*Pännigrahanna*. The marriage takes place before a blazing fire, symbolizing Agni, the most truthful and straight-dealing among the Hindu gods. The couple sit side by side, with the bride's face usually veiled. After the veneration of Ganapati, the remover of obstacles, the officiating priest takes a piece of consecrated linen and ties one end to the bridegroom's clothes and the other to the bride's. Sacred texts are chanted, during which at a certain point, the priest joins the hands of the couple under the consecrated cloth (*pännigrahanna*). Later he takes a consecrated chord and winds it around their necks. At various times he asks the couple to throw rice, coconut kernel, etc., into the fire; at other times he does it himself. There is sprinkling of water, throwing of gulal (red powder), and other similar activities, at the direction of the priest. Finally, there is the irrevocable *Saptapadi* (Seven Steps) around the fire, that seals the marriage contract. As they go around, the couple recite: "Take thou one step for the acquirement of force; take thou two steps for strength; take thou three steps for the increase of wealth; take thou four steps for well-being; take thou five steps for offspring; take thou six steps for the season; take thou seven steps as a friend; be faithfully devoted to me; may we obtain many sons; may they attain to a good old age."

Catholics will recall similar prayers in their own marriage ceremony: for example, the special prayer for the bride after the Our Father, and the Solemn Blessing at the end of the Mass.

The marriage ceremony is the last Sanskara in the life of a Hindu. According to Hindu conception, a man's perfect life span is 120 years. Hence the 60th birthday (*Shashitipurti*) is an occasion for special celebration, but there is no special ceremony attached to it.

Funeral Rites

Though they are not considered sanskaras, funeral rites are carefully observed as their proper performance affects the fate of the dead person. The date and time of one's death is determined according to Hindu belief one's *karma* of previous life. After death a person either attains *moksha* and returns to become Brahma or, after a brief sojourn with the gods, comes back to this world in some other body to pay for its sins. Hence, everything possible is done at the last hour to ensure that the person is fully purified for the moksha.

A dying person is taken from his bed and laid on the floor to ensure that he escapes the evil spirits that roam between earth and heaven. Immediately after death, the body is washed and wrapped in a new cloth, gold or silver is put in its mouth, and loud lamentations announce the death to the neighbourhood. The body is then laid on a stretcher and carried to the burning ghat on the shoulders of four or six men, preceded by the chief mourner, usually the eldest son or a close relative, who goes barefoot and carries a fire-pot in his hand.

At the burning ghat, the body is sprinkled with "Ganga" water and kept on the funeral pyre. The chief mourner takes fire from the pot he had carried and lights the pyre on the head side in case of males, and on the side of the feet in case of women. The fire is kept alive by pouring ghee on it. Those present see to it that the skull of the dead person bursts while the body burns (else it is cracked by a cudgel), because Hindus believe that the soul gets locked up in the skull after death, and gets trapped there if the skull does not burst open. The chief mourner then walks round the pyre four times, with his left side close to the body. After this the mourners go for a purificatory "bath" and return home.

The mourning continues for ten to thirty days, at the end of which there is a solemn memorial (*Shräd'dha*) service. On the first day after the cremation no food is cooked in the house; relatives and friends may send it, though many adults would prefer to fast. On the following days, some simple food may be cooked and eaten. It is believed that during these days, the departed begins to acquire a "subtle frame", one limb each day, and unless the funeral ceremonies are performed properly, he may become a deformed evil spirit wandering in space.

Three days after the cremation, there is the simple "ash gathering" ceremony. A low-ranking priest sprinkles holy water on the spot and collects the ashes in a vase and presents them to the son or nearest relative. The ideal is to immerse them within the period of one year in the River Ganges at sacred places like Haridwar, Benares, Prayag (Allahabad), and Gaya, where professional priests are available in hundreds to perform the ceremony for a stipend. The River Godavari at Nashik is also a favourite spot for the immersion of the ashes for the people of Maharashtra. In this case, the vase containing the ashes is kept buried near the cremation spot and dug out on the day of Shräd'dha and handed over to the family. If, for whatever reason, ashes are not be carried to the above sacred places, they are immediately immersed in any water-hole.

The *Shräd'dha* (memorial) is an important and expensive ceremony, for on it depends the destiny of the deceased. Gifts and feasts are given that are believed to reach his soul. The ceremony is to be performed by the son (hence the eagerness to have one!) on the 10th and the 31st day of the cremation. The rituals begin early in the morning and continue until mid-day when a sumptuous meal is served first to the Brahmins, who represent the ancestors, and only after they are "satisfied" to the rest. It is common on this occasion for the son to make balls of cooked rice (*pinddapradāna*), and to offer them to the soul of the departed saying: "This food is for you, my father... Oh fathers, regale yourselves here, come as bulls each to his share." The pindas are then decorated and worshipped with the prayer: "Oh fathers, go away by the sombre ancient paths, after bestowing on us wealth, and endow us here with auspicious prosperity and valiant sons." Invocations are made for all the deceased members of the family and for the prosperity of all living members. The Brahmins are accompanied to the door and the ceremony ends with this mantra: "If the ancestors are in the world of gods, they are gratified by the food offered in the fire; if they are in the world of ancestors, they are gratified by the dinner given to the Brahmins; if they are in hell they are gratified by the pindas offered on the ground."

5

HOLY PLACES AND HOLY MEN

I. PILGRIMAGES

Hindus and Catholics agree on the importance of pilgrimages (*yātrā*) to holy places (*tīrtha*). Religious motives to undertake them vary: penance, fulfilment of a vow, merit, intercession, etc. It is an occasion to experience and promote religious fervour, to participate in solemn ceremonials, to listen to the reading of the scriptures or good sermons, etc.

Important Places

Among the Hindu pilgrimage places there are, first of all, the sacred rivers, where one goes for a "holy dip". Although every water-hole is sacred to the Hindus, water being the source of life, the most sacred are the Mother Ganga who carries straight to heaven any one whose ashes she has received; the Godavari, along whose banks Rama hunted; the Kaveri, a favourite resort of the apsaras; the Narmadā and the Krishna. The confluence of the Ganga and Yamuna at Prayag (Allahabad) is an important centre where thousands of pilgrims congregate every 12 years to participate in the "Kumbhamela". Water from these holy rivers is carried away reverently, as many Catholics take water from Lourdes, and kept at home for a long time and used on special occasions.

Among the holy cities, the most sacred is Varānasi (Benares) with over 2,000 temples. Mathura on the river Yamuna, known as the birthplace of Krishna, has especially sacred spots like the Vrindavan groves and the Kadamba forests, both associated with Krishna and his Gopis.

Ayodhyä, the birthplace of Räma, Haridwar, where the Ganga leaves the hills and enters the plains, and Gaya further down on the Ganges in Bihar, are some other popular pilgrimage spots.

A pilgrimage joining the four sacred spots: the Badrinath in the Himalayas in the North, the Rameshwaram in the extreme South, the Dwarka in Kathiawar in the West, and the Jagannath temple in Puri, famous for its Rath Yatra, in the East, would bestow moksha on the pilgrim.

Higher up on the Himalayas there are, besides Badrinath, the Rishikesh town and the Amarnath cave some 70 km from Srinagar in Kashmir.

Popular among some sects are the Vaishnodevi cave temple north of Jammu, the Meenakshi (wife of Shiva) temple in Madurai, the temples of Chidambaram and Tanjore popular among South Indian Shaivas, and those of Kanjivaram and Srirangam favourites of the Vaishnavas. Panddharpur is a popular Vaishnava temple in Maharashtra dedicated to Vitthoba, whereas the Kandoba temple of Jejuri is a popular Shaiva temple. Nashik on the Godavari is as sacred to Maharashtrians, as Gaya on the Ganges is to the North Indians.

Any Christian who has witnessed Hindus going on a pilgrimage will not fail to be impressed by the religious fervour with which the pilgrim prepares himself, often by prayer and fasting for a number of years. If pilgrimage to Vaishnodevi (7,000 feet above sea level) could be taken as an example, the pilgrims will start by reverently kissing the ground at the starting point at Chatra and whispering *"Jai Mata Di"*. Then, as they walk up the well laid-out and spotlessly clean 12-km track, the only sound one hears is the acclamation *"Jai Mata Di"*. Almost all go up on foot; and, whilst there are a few who are carried on palanquins or go on the horseback, one comes across, though rarely, someone or another who "measures the road" literally, by lying flat on the ground with his hands stretched forward and then stand where the tips of his fingers had reached and repeat the process, until he reaches the holy cave.

Once they have reached their destination, the pilgrims are given the number of the group they could join for the *darshan*. They can during this time visit one or two shrines that are around, or eat a simple meal at one of the restaurants whose rates seem to be subsidized. The atmosphere is very quiet and prayerful. When the turn of the group comes, the members stand in a queue to enter the cave through a short tunnel. For most of the pilgrims, the entrance into the cave is a deep spiritual experience. Depending on the crowd waiting outside, one might get 30-60 seconds to be inside the cave, after 6-8 hours of walking to come there! The darshan consists in venerating the holy ground by touching it with the two hands which then are touched to one's forehead, whispering a quick prayer of thanksgiving or intercession to the "deity" and receiving the bleessing of the pujari there with some prasada and/or a medal. The "deity", Vaishnodevi Mata, in this case resides in a simple millennial rock formation that resembles the tops of three heads that are duly garlanded. The visit for many is a life-time experience, whilst others do it regularly, even every year.

II. PRIESTS, GURUS, AND SADHUS

A. Priests

During the Vedic times, the position of priests was pre-eminent. Besides being repositories of knowledge and wisdom, they exercised considerable mastery over the mighty and the lowly alike, on account of their familiarity with mystery. Though the priestly ideal was challenged from the time of the Upanishads, it survived due to the later codification of *varnnas* (castes) and *āshramas* (life-stages), the ritualist approach to religion promoted by karma-mīmāmsā and theistic revival around Shiva and Vishnu.

Eventually Brahminhood dissociated itself from ritualistic duties, and it was said that only those who could not find better occupations took up the priesthood with its ritual duties. As a consequence the priests in Hinduism (*purohit*, *yājak*, *pūjāri*) enjoy little prestige, possess little education, and are not expected to be especially zealous or disinterested.

The most respected among the priests, is the *kula-purohit* (family priest) who ministers to the orthodox and well-to--do families for a fee, in performing ritual acts on various occasions. Poor people, who cannot afford their own purohit, and many individual villages, have one in common. Often he is also their astrologer, physician, exorcist, and spiritual adviser.

Temple pūjāris are regarded even less, although nowadays there may be among them some learned people who take up the temple service either part-time or in addition to some professional work.

B. Gurus

Unlike the *pūjāri*, the *guru* is a highly respected person among Hindus. It is the guru who, at the time of the Thread Ceremony, admits a boy to Brahminhood and whispers into his ears the sacred mahamantra Gayatri. From then on the young initiate must enter the guru's household (*gurukul*) for a minimum of twelve years and attend to the guru's needs, whilst the guru imparts to the *chela* all the knowledge and wisdom he needs to face life. This actually happened very rarely even in the past, and the entire process was reduced to some symbolic ritual action in the Thread Ceremony, but the ideal demonstrates the position that a guru holds in Hindu society. The guru's responsibility towards the *chela* is lifelong, and is always received very respectfully when he comes to visit his *chela*.

There is a more important value implied here. No one can progress in the spiritual life and attain salvation (*moksha*)

186

without a *guru*. This is where many Christian ascetical writers would agree, and require not only the guidance of the Maha Guru, Jesus Christ and his Holy Spirit, but also an experienced, human, Spiritual Director. But there is a difference here. The Hindu guru must be a *jivanmukta*, someone who has already obtained liberation in this life, is infallible, and holds the keys of *mukti*. The Christian guide, on the other hand, is himself on the way towards salvation and can only assist the work of divine grace by his advice and experience. (See Hebrews 5, 1-3)

C. *Sādhus, Sanyāsis, Yogis*

In ancient times, every male when his hair turned white had to go through the stage of *vanaprastha* (hermit) and *sanyāsi* (homeless wanderer). It was not done generally, but even now individuals retire themselves to Varanasi and other hallowed places to lead a solitary life. There are even some who lead such a life residing in a little hut in the neighbourhood of their own family compound.

While there are wandering Sādhus, many ascetics live in matths and whilst leading ascetical lives themselves, instruct others in the spiritual life. We may distinguish a few categories among them:

1. ***Shaiva Sadhus*** may be recognised by their sect mark: generally three horizontal lines or a broader band drawn with ashes on the forehead and other parts of the body. Rosaries of rudrāksha beads, a trident, a leopard skin, are among the usual insignia.

Dashanāmī Sanyāsis were founded by the great philosopher-ascetic Shankaracharya, with centres in Puri (East), Dwarka (West), Joshi (Himalayas) and Shringeri (South). They are real fortresses of Hindu and Advaita orthodoxy. Their head is the Swami of Shringeri. The term *dashanāmī* refers to their being divided into ten branches. They are also called *ekadannddi* as they carry a one-knotted staff. *Dashanämï Nagäs* are a militant branch of sadhus attached to the *Dashanämï Sanyäsis*, who concentrate mostly on bodily asceticism and gymnastics. Their centres are called *äkhädäs*.

Yogïs are followers of Gorakhnäth (10 cent. A.D.) who was a populariser of Hattha-yoga, a special type of yoga which aims at mystical liberation by physiological means. It is heavily mixed with Tantrism and Saktism. They indulge in magic and are often addicted to intoxicants as a stimulant for their yogic trances. Whilst *Gorakhnäthis* (also called Khänphätta yogis because their ears are pierced for huge ear-rings) are more respectable, the *Äghori Yogis* are most disreputable. They drink out of a skull, preferably human, make it a point to eat dung and flesh of corpses, and would offer human sacrifices if not refrained by the country's laws.

Jangamas are the ascetics among the Lingäyats of Karnataka.

2. **Vaishnava Sadhus** came up later than the Shaiva Sadhus and, unlike these, do not have a common theology. There are, therefore, followers of Ramanuja, Madhava, Nimbarka, Ramananda, Vallabha, Chaitanya, Kabir, etc.

These *Vairägis* (detached persons) differ little from the laity, as do the Shaiva ascetics. Their sect mark consists of two white lines in the shape of a V; a third line, either white or red, is often added in the centre. Their dress is usually white and the beads are of tulsï.

These too have their own *Vaishnava Nagäs* for protection against their Shaiva counterparts.

Among the more modern orders of Vaishnava Sanyasis may be counted the Ramakrishna Mission founded by Vivekananda (1899) and the Prajapita Brahma Kumaris founded (1937) by Dada Lekh Raj, later called Prajapita Brahma. Accounts of these have been given in Part I, ch. 6.

3. **Recruitment and Initiation**. Ideally future sadhus are

recruited from among grownup boys. But given the scarcity of "vocations", even children are often recruited. The initiation into the order is preceded by a sufficiently long training.

The rites of initiation vary from sect to sect: a new name, a sacred mantra, and the monastic dress, are central to all rites, just like in Christian religious orders. Sometimes a funeral ceremony is performed to signify death to one's caste. Here or later, the initiate takes the vows to practise *ahimsā*, not to engage in trade, not to take employment, etc. The vow of celibacy is not compulsory in all orders.

Sadhus may live in the matth of the *mahant* (abbot) or be wandering. Hospitality is the hallmark of a matth, and so a wandering sadhu may stop at a matth of his own order or any other, and is sure of a meal and a place to rest. Fresh news, therefore, is always circulating as sadhus from all over come and go.

The daily routine of a matth would include worship in the temple, various tasks about the house, some practice of yoga, religious reading and discourse, and at times service to the neighbourhood like health and education services. Visiting sadhus too may take part in these activities. Many sadhus take only one meal a day and after death, a sadhu is buried, not cremated.

HOLY DAYS AND AGES

An orthodox Hindu is steeped in religion (often read as superstition) and for him every day is a holy day, since it is under the influence of some deity. There is also a widespread belief in muhurts among Hindus. According to this belief, certain times, certain days, certain astronomical occasions and occurrences, are either auspicious or inauspicious. In our country, even the launching of a satellite may be determined by a *muhurt*! Certain observances are indispensable to those who wish to be in peace with the gods on that day, and avoid the malefic influence of some of them.

1. The Weekdays

Each day of the week is, in a sense, holy because it is dedicated to a particular deity. Besides the deities indicated by the name of the respective weekday, devotees of Ganesh, Hanuman, and other puranic deities, have a particular day dedicated to each of them and special prayers and fasts are practised by those seeking a particular boon, like a husband, or a child, or success in an enterprise.

Ravivar (Sunday) is dedicated to the Sun (Ravi) god. He is known as a luminous red person driving in a chariot drawn by seven horses. His charioteer is the lame Aruna (Dawn). Ravi is normally a malefic being and it is unlucky to be born on his day. However, it is a propitious day to begin undertakings like the construction of a house, to start a business, etc. (Auspicious colour: Green.)

Somavar (Monday) is sacred to the Moon (Soumah, also Chandra). He is a handsome, male deity riding an antelope.

190

It is auspicious to be born on a full-moon day. Monday is also sacred to Shiva, as the moon is part of his adornments, and killing bugs on this day is considered an act of merit, as it is an offering to Shiva. As Shiva is an ascetic, it is a good day to fast. The day is, however, unauspicious for shaving — the man might lose his son! (The moon has no favourite colour and to prevent jealousy among the gods, multicoloured dress is recommended.)

Mangalvar (Tuesday) is sacred to Mangala (planet Mars), the god of war, also identified as Kumara or Kartikeya, the second son of Shiva. In some myths he is considered rather hostile to women; thus it would be unlucky for a girl to come of age on a Tuesday. Planet Mars is feared to have malefic influence and persons born under it will be really unlucky. Hence he should be propitiated by special worship. (Ironically "*mangala*" means the auspicious one!) Of course, it is a lucky day for wars, but unlucky for business, journey, construction of a house, etc. (Auspicious colour: Red.)

Budhvar (Wednesday) is sacred to Budh (planet Mercury), illegitimate son of Chandra (moon) and Tara (star) whom he — Chandra — had abducted from her husband Brahaspati (Jupiter). It is interesting how he got that name. Neither force nor persuasion from the other gods would induce Chandra to give up his adulterous life and return Tara to her lawful husband. At last at the insistence of Brahma, Chandra reluctantly agreed to return Tara to Brahaspati who, however, noticing that she was pregnant refused to accept her. Nor would Chandra take her back. In this predicament, Brahma forced early birth and the son born was so beautiful that both Chandra and Brahaspati claimed fatherhood. Tara was asked to declare who the real father of the child was. She hesitated out of delicacy. The child suddenly found speech and commanded her to speak the truth, which she did and indicated Chandra as the real father of the precocious boy. Chandra was so proud of the wisdom of his son that he called him Budh. Budh is neutral, as far as astral influence is concerned, which will be determined by the position of other planets in relation to Budh. (Auspicious colour: Yellow.)

Brahaspativar also called **Guruvar** (Thursday) is dedicated to Brahaspati (Jupiter), the Guru of the gods. A Brahmin by caste, his influence is benefic, and a person born under his influence will be lucky and a girl coming to womanhood on a Thursday will be the mother of many sons. (Auspicious colour: White.)

Sukravar (Friday) is dedicated to Sukra (Venus) who, however, is not a beautiful woman like in the West, but a kindly old Brahmin, very wise and very learned. As a planet he is the most auspicious and a person born under his influence will have the faculty of knowing the past, the present, and the future. He is believed to know the magic formula which can bring the dead back to life. He is blind in one eye, an affliction caused by Vishnu because of Sukra's extraordinary loyalty to his king. (Auspicious colour: White.)

Sanivar (Saturday) is sacred to Sani (Saturn). The most malicious of planets, Sani is depicted as a lean, ugly, lame old man, riding a vulture. He is evil incarnate and everything that comes under his influence is doomed. Naturally, it is an auspicious day for robbers and murderers to do evil! One legend has it that he casually looked at the new-born baby of Parvati and this resulted in the head of the baby flying off from its trunk. It had to be replaced by the head of an elephant — the origin of Ganesha! Sani may be propitiated by worship and if pleased he may even bestow some boons. (Auspicious colour: Black.)

2. The Months and Years

The Hindu calendar divides the year into 12 lunar months, each beginning with the full moon (*purnnima*), according to some reckonings, and with the new moon (*amavasya*, that is, "living with" the sun!) according to others. These months are:

Chaitra (Mar.-Apr.)
Vaishäka (Apr.-May)
Jyaistha (May-Jun)
Asädha (Jun-Jul.)
Shrävana (Jul.-Aug.)
Bhädrapada (Aug.-Sep.)
Ashvina (Sep.-Oct.)
Kärttika (Oct.-Nov.)
Märgashirsa (Nov.-Dec.)
Pausha (Dec.-Jan.)
Mägha (Jan.-Feb.)

Phälguna (Feb.-Mar.) Each month is divided into 15 *tithis* (lunar days). Since these days are slightly shorter than 24 hours and the lunar year is shorter than the solar by 11 days, every three years an extra month (*Adhikmasa*) is added. It is marked by special rituals and pilgrimages.

The months are divided into two *pakshas* (fortnights) called the *Shukla Paksha* (bright half) and the *Krishna Paksha* (dark half). The 14 days of each *paksha* are in ascending order: *Prathama, Dwitiya, Trithiya, Chaturthi, Panchami, Shashti, Saptami, Ashtami, Navami, Dashami, Ekadasi, Dwadasi, Thrayodasi,* and *Chaturdasi.*

The solar reckoning of the Hindu calendar corresponds to the Greek system:

Mesha	Aries
Vrishabha	Taurus
Mithuna	Gemini
Karka	Cancer
Simha	Leo
Kanya	Virgo
Tulla	Libra
Vrischika	Scorpio
Dhanu	Sagittarius
Makara	Capricorn
Kumbha	Aquarius
Meena	Pisces

The solar day is divided into 60 *ghatikas*, each ghatika being equivalent to 24 minutes. A ghatika is sub-divided into 60 *palas*, a pala into 60 *vipalas*, and a vipala into 60 *prativipalas*. The prativipala is the smallest division of time and is equivalent to about 0.006 seconds.

3. The Kalpas and Yugas

Whilst *Prativipalas* are the smallest units of time according to Indian astronomy, the *Kalpa* or the day of Brahma, is the largest. According to this astronomy, a Kalpa is equivalent to 4,320,000,000 of our years. It is divided into 1,000 *Mahayugas*, each of which is divided into four *Yugas* or Eras: the *Kritayuga*, the *Thretayuga*, the *Dwarparayuga*, and the *Kaliyuga*.

The Kritayuga is the Golden Age when all men are equal and good, and evil is entirely absent from the world. Its length is 1,728,000 years. In *Thretayuga*, whose length is 1,296,000 years, evil appears for the first time. Though men of this age are not so happy as earlier, they are far better than those in *Dwarparayuga* in which good and evil, both equally strong, struggle for supremacy. At the end of this age, which lasts 864,000 years, evil overcomes good and the world enters *Kaliyuga*, the age of strife, sweat, and toil. The **Kaliyuga** is to last 432,000. As this age progresses, evil gathers momentum till good is entirely destroyed, and the redemption of the world can be brought about only by its destruction and reconstruction by a Supreme Being. It is for this purpose that Vishnu will take avatär as Kalki, the destroyer, and will bring about the end of the world by a deluge or by fire. Presently we are living in the sixth millennium of Kaliyuga, and there are yet more than 425,000 years for the end of the world.

In place of the Kaliyuga reckoning, different Hindu sects follow either the **Vikram Yuga** or **Saka Yuga**. In Kerala they also have the **Kollum Yuga**.

The Kali Yuga is the classical era of the Hindus and is

194

used all over the country mainly for religious and literary purposes.

According to this mythical reckoning, the life-span of Brahma is 100 Kalpas. Then will come the death of Brahma and the universe will be engulfed in the Great Chaos (*Mahapralaya*) which destroys all gods, demons, and humans. After one hundred years of the Chaos, another Brahma is born, and the cycle is thus continued without end.

The Vikram Yuga is used mainly in North India (except in Bengal where they have their own Bengali Era), and more particularly in Gujarat. It is supposed to have started with the coronation date of the semi-mythical King Vikramaditiya in 57 B.C. According to this calendar, the year 2000 A.D. corresponds to year 2056-57 of the Vikram Era.

The Saka Yuga is even more extensively followed in India, though of a later origin. It is supposed to originate from the coronation in 78 A.D. of King Salivahan who, as a little boy born miraculously without a father and from a little girl, killed the king who was doomed to die by a divine ordinance, and seized the throne of Ujjain. By this reckoning, year 2000 will be year 1923 of the Saka Era.

4. The Vratas

Vratas are special days for prayer and fasting and giving presents to Brahmins. It is meritorious, both in this life and in the next, to keep the vratas as prescribed by various ritual texts like the Puranas. Their neglect might bring about bad luck and even disaster. Going by different texts, for a pious Hindu almost every day of the year would be a *vrata*.

The most commonly observed vrata is the Ekadasi or the eleventh day of each fortnight of the month. There are two in each month: the bright half (Shukla Paksha) and the dark half (Krishna Paksha) (See p. 195). Most women of the three higher castes and some men who are not prevented by work fast on this day. The Ekadasis falling during the four months of the monsoon have great importance. They are kept in honour of Vishnu who, during this period of time, had to rescue the Vedas from the demon Hiranyaksha at the bottom of the ocean, by taking the form of a boar.

The full-moon day of the month of Vaisakha is observed as a *vrata* in honour of Ganesha. Those who do so will have their obstacles removed, ambitions fulfilled, and wishes gratified by Ganesha.

The third day of the month of *Bhadrapada* is dear to unmarried girls and the vrata is called *Haritalika* (abducted). When Parvati, trying to avoid marriage to Vishnu, as her father had planned, ran away to Shiva, her father thought that she had been abducted by him. Those who keep the vrata may eat only plantains, and must spend the day in prayer and in performing the prescribed pujas. By worshipping Parvati on this day, unmarried girls will marry men that they love. Girls who do not observe this vrata may remain unmarried for successive lives! Married women too who do not keep the vrata may become widows in seven lives.

Every *Sankrant* (the day on which the sun passes from one sign of the zodiac to another) is a *vrata* of some sort. But there are some that are most important: the Makar Sankrant (when the sun enters Makar-Capricorn) and every Mangal Sankrant, that is, the Sankrant that falls on Tuesday of every even month of the calendar.

All full-moon days (*purnimā*) are holy, but the one of the month of Jeshta is observed as vrata in honour of Savitri, and the vrata is called Vat Savitri or Vat Purnimā. (*Vat* being the banyan tree that is worshipped on this day.) Savitri was a model of conjugal fidelity, and married women keeping the vrata on this day ensure long life for their husbands.

YOGA AND THE CHRISTIANS

Yoga is much more than what many people, especially Christians, imagine it to be, after seeing children "doing yoga" in the school or after hearing about "yoga classes" conducted by some expert. The bodily postures popular in modern yoga, the "Indian gymnastics" as someone called them, have a tantric basis and only a tenuous connection with the classical Yoga, which is one of the systems of Indian philosophy.

"Yoga", with a certain linguistic affinity to the English word "yoking" literally means "union" and it refers to the final stage of "meditation" in which the meditator becomes one with the object of his meditation.

Yoga is one of the six orthodox schools (*sad'darshanas*) of Indian philosophy: *Nyāya* and *Vaishesika*, *Sānkhya* and *Yoga*, *Mimāmsā* and *Vedānta*. It is also counted among the five Indian systems of mysticism that arose in the course of history: the sacrifice system of the Vedas and especially the Brahmanas; the Upanishadic system, the Yoga, the Buddhist system and the Bhakti system. To these may also be added the Tantric system.

The basic text of Yoga is the *Yoga-sutra* attributed to Patañjali (2nd cent. B.C.), which was expanded by later authors with their own authoritative commentaries. Yoga is closely related to the dualistic philosophy of Sāmkhya, according to which the *Purusha* (Self) is distinct from *Prakriti* (Matter). Yoga, however, assumes the existence of *Ishwara*; that is why it is also called *Seshwara-Sāmkhya* or theistic Sāmkya.

Yoga is the organised effort of self-deliverance and union with the Self. It holds that spiritual liberation occurs when the Self (*purusha*) in me is freed from the bondages of Matter (*prakriti*), that originated from ignorance and illusion. Yoga attempts to reverse the process going back through the very same stages through which the bondages were brought about. The final outcome of this process will be a return to the original state of purity and consciousness or oneness (*yoga*) with Self, the object of the yogin's contemplation.

The Eight Stages

The Yoga process is said to go through eight stages (hence *ashttänga yoga*), of which the first four are external aids to Yoga, and the remaining four are internal aids.

The first two stages are **moral preparations**: yama (restraint), that is, abstinence from injury (*ahimsä*), truthfulness (*satya*) abstaining from stealing (*asteyä*), continence (*brahmachärya*) and abstaining from avarice (*aparigraha*), all of which are meant for social good and safety; and niyama (observance), which includes cleanliness of body (*shaucha*), contentment (*santosha*), austerity and penance (*tapas*), study (*svädyäya*) and devotion to God (*Ishvaraprännidhäna*), intended for individual and personal discipline and improvement.

The next two stages are **physical preparations**: äsana (posture), a series of exercises in posture, intended to enbale the seeker to hold one posture for an extended period of time, without distraction; and prännäyäma (breath control), a series of exercises intended to stabillize the rhythm of breathing in order to encourage complete respiratory relaxation. Breath is considered as manifestation of individual vitality: whereas accelerated breath means a state of excitement, retarded breath means the slowing down of individual vitality and the approach to pure consciousness. This understanding leads some yogins to wall themselves up at the end of their life and the closed tomb where their breathing comes to an end is called their *"samädhi"*, the final stage of Yoga.

The fifth stage, *pratyähära* (abstraction from the senses), is a **mental preparation** and it involves control of the senses, or the ability to withdraw the attention of the senses from outward objects of mind. The sixth stage is *dhärannä* (concentration), the ability to fix the mind on any object, material or otherwise, for a long period of time (e.g., fixing the mind on the tip of one's nose or navel, the lotus of the heart, the light of the brain, or even on Ishwara or his image); the seventh, *dhyäna* (meditation), is the uninterrupted contemplation of the object of meditation, beyond any memory of ego.

The final stage, the goal of Yoga, is *samädhi* (trance), when all mental activity is stopped and the object of contemplation and the contemplative become one. Here too there are degrees: in the *savikalpa* (object-bound) or *sabïja* (seed-containing) *samädhi* the subjective consciousness still persists, whereas in the *nirbïja* (seedless) *samädhi* even this consciousness of the subject, or of the object, or of the process of knowing, disappears.

Obviously, for the attainment of the samädhi, some schools of Yoga emphasise the physico-physiological approach (**Hatha Yoga**) through *äsanas* (postures) and *prännäyäma* (breath control); whilst others prefer the psycho-spiritual approach (**Raja Yoga**) through *pratyähära* (abstraction from the senses), *dhärannä* (concentration) and *dhyäna* (meditation).

In recent years Yoga Therapy has become quite popular both in the East and in the West. It follows naturally the Hatha Yoga approach and prescribes a certain Yogic diet, Yogasanas, and understanding of life, environment, society, etc.

A Critique

Yoga is one of the various ways (others being sacrifice,

tapas and sannyasa) of responding to the Absolute. There is no doubt that *yama* and *niyama*, as explained above, are very beneficial for personal and social well-being. Many have also realised benefits from some of the pshycho-physiological stages of Yoga. Clasical spiritual guides like St Ignatius of Loyola and modern spritual directors, speak of the usefulness of postures (*asanas*) and of breathing exercises (*prännäyäma*), as helps for prayer and contemplation. Meditation too is widely recommended for relaxation and peace of mind. However as a philosophy and a process for union with God, Yoga is very questionable. According to Yoga philosophy, man's highest aim is the isolation of the spiritual element in himself. The *purusha* shines in his own light, free from the disturbance of the world, free mainly of the restless psychic processes in man himself; but there is no positive content in this freedom. As Fr J. Neuner says in RELIGIOUS HINDUISM, we cannot conceive of the real destiny of man, and particularly of his spiritual nature, as a splendid isolation. It must consist in commitment and devotedness. The yogin withdraws from the world into his own sphere; he is no longer concerned with what happens around him.

Another criticism that may be levelled against Yoga is that, although it admits the existence of Ishwara, Ishwara is not the creator and the last end of man, in whose service and love man finds his fulfilment: he is only one of the many possible objects of contemplation, a "model" of the "pure consciousness" which the yogin should achieve. Man remains the centre of his own interests and efforts.

Finally, it must be questioned whether the state of absolute and objectless consciousness which Yoga claims to achieve, can indeed be reached, even though it is distinct from the vision of and union with God. A true mystic experience consists essentially in God's self-communication to man, and this He does of his own free choice. No human effort alone can bring it about.

Yoga and the Christians

Efforts have long been made to integrate various elements of Yoga, in particular the psycho-physical techniques, into Christian asceticism. See, for example, *Christian Yoga* by J.M. Dechanet. These techniques can help to bring about the disposition of a calmed body, of quiet nerves, of a balanced mind, of an atmosphere of silence, not only for our prayer and contemplation but for our whole life.

However, the first question that comes to the mind of a Christian is whether the Yogic experience is a religious experience. Traditional theology has much difficulty in accepting Yoga as a means to attain union with God, for it seems to claim that liberation is brought about by "knowledge" (gnosis) attained by personal effort, and not by a freely-given grace (charis) of God. The most that those theologians are ready to grant is that Yoga may help to dispose the person to receive that grace.

Other theologians, following the statements of Vatican II and of the recent Popes, take a broader view. According to them, "knowledge", both in Hinduism and in the Bible, is a religious concept in the realm of experience, which seems to be an expression of the operation of grace. Though "nature" and "grace" are theoretically different, in the existential situation "nature", they say, may be already affected by grace. In fact, in the Indian context, everything comes from God, everything is maintained in and by the Lord, and finally everything will merge back in God.

One reason for hesitation on the part of Christian theologians, writes Fr T.K. John S.J., to regard Yoga--experience in the context of the religiosity of Hinduism is due to the impression that Yoga techniques and samadhi--experience seem to be only casually linked. Nowhere is it said that one produces the other. He insists that the samadhi cannot be engineered by any techniques or practices. "The man who faithfully adheres to Yoga, as well as the man who turns to God in other ways, both share experiences that are to be understood in a religious context." For this we should recall the basic understanding of the present existential state of man to which Karl Rahner referred when he wrote, "Preaching is the awakening and making explicit of what is already there in the depths of man, not by nature but by grace. Grace which enfolds man, the sinner and believer too, as his very sphere of existence which he can never escape from."

It is by following this line of thought that Fr Neuner writes in the above-mentioned book, "Spiritual self-discipline among Christians will not develop into self-concentration but into greater readiness to hear God's word, to meditate on it, to be silent in His presence, to surrender to God a body and a mind which are only trully controlled and prepared to be spent in His service."

PART IV
OTHER RELIGIONS

MOHAMMED AND ISLAM

"In the past," says the Holy Bible, "God spoke to our ancestors many times and in many ways through the prophets, but in these last days he has spoken to us through his Son." (Heb 1, 1-2). The Jews and the Arabs both believe that their ancestry goes back to Abraham: the Jews through his son Isaac born of his lawful wife Sarai, and the Arabs through Ishmael born of his Egyptian slave-girl. According to the Bible, they were both blessed by God who promised to make each of them into a great nation.

The Jews were committed to the worship of the One True God in the Temple of Jerusalem, so too the Arabs but in their own Temple at Mecca, the Ka'bā, which they believed Abraham himself had built.

The Jews had their prophets, many of whom the Muslims also recognise as such, but the latter further believe that Mohammed, son of Abdullah, son of Abdul Muttalib, of the tribe of Qureysh, was specially chosen by God to be his prophet. In fact, for them he was the final prophet and messenger of God, "the seal of the prophets", but nothing higher. When, after about 30 years of intensive missionary work, he finally died on June 8, 632 and some of his followers were overwhelmed with grief, his friend Abu Bakr proclaimed the real belief of the Muslims when he said: "Whoever worshipped Mohammed, know that Mohammed is dead; but whoever worships God, know that God is living and shall never die."

205

1. The Prophet

Of rather humble origin, Mohammed was born at Mecca in A.D. 570 or 571. His birthday (**Id-e-Milad** or **Milad-un-Nabi**) is celebrated by Muslims on the 12th day of the third month of the Hejira Calendar, Rabi'ul-Awwal. Mohammed's father died before his birth and his mother died when he was barely six years old. So he grew up in the care, first, of his grandfather and later of his uncle Abu Talib.

As a young boy Mohammed travelled through Arabia with his uncle in the merchants' caravans and, when they rested at night, probably heard people of different faiths express their ideas. At the age of 25 he was employed as her business agent by a rich widow, Khadijah, 15 years his senior. So faithfully did he do her work and so exemplary was his behaviour that the widow soon married him and they lived happily and holily together for 26 years.

Mohammed was deeply upset by the idolatry, the low moral standards and social injustices around him. The Meccans had once believed that their temple, the *Ka'ba*, had been built by Abraham himself for the worship of the One True God, but now, like in the Jerusalem Temple at one time, idolatry had crept in and, though still called the House of Allah, the chief objects of worship in it were some 360 idols which were called daughters of Allah and intercessors. Distressed by this situation, Mohammed would retire with his family to a desert cave on Mt Hira during the hot month of Ramadan. There he sought to discover by his own inner consciousness the way of truth. God, however, made him realise that all true wisdom comes from Above. As the Holy Bible says, "Trust in the Lord with all your heart, on your own intelligence rely not." (Prov 3, 5).

Islamic records describe the experience. It is said that one night, when Mohammed was 40 years old, toward the end of his quiet month, the first revelation came to him. He was asleep or in a trance when he heard a voice commanding

206

him three times to read. He tried to excuse himself as he was illiterate, but when finally he surrendered, he was ordered to read: "In the name of the Lord Who creates, creates man from the clot," and to read: "It is Thy Lord the Most Bountiful Who teaches by the pen, teaches man that which he knew not." (Sûr.xcvi, 1-5) When Mohammed awoke, the words remained "as if inscribed upon his heart." He went out of the cave on the hillside and heard the same awe-inspiring voice say: "Oh Mohammed! Thou art Allah's messenger, and I am Gabriel." And when he raised his eyes, he saw above the horizon the angel in human form.

But was the call genuine or was he merely dreaming? Mohammed belonged to a group of seekers of truth who distrusted any intercourse with spirits. Further, he was too humble to consider himself chosen as God's messenger to mankind. He undertook a serious spiritual discernment with the help of his wife Khadijah and her cousin Waraqa ibn Naufal, a very old man who had become a Christian. The latter declared his belief that the heavenly messenger who came to Moses of old had now come to Mohammed, and that he was indeed chosen as the Prophet of his people. The hesitation, however, persisted until with the subsequent revelations and the conviction that they brought, Mohammed finally accepted as divine the call to be Prophet.

When Prophet Mohammed died in A.D. 632, a majority of Muslims elected his disciple Abu Bakr to be his successor (*caliph*). They claimed that they followed the "example" (*sunna*) of the Prophet in their faith and life. They were called the Sunnis. A minority, however, held that the leadership should have gone to Ali, Mohammed's cousin and husband of Fatima, the prophet's daughter. These formed the *Shiah Ali* (Ali's Party) and became the Shiites.

2. His Teaching

There is a wide similarity between the teachings of Mohammed and those of the old prophets of Israel.

Confronted like them with idolatry, Prophet Mohammed taught "submission" (*Islam* in Arabic) to One God, and those who did submit to Him were called *Muslim*. The words that came to him regularly when in a state of trance were transmitted to his disciples who held them sacred, memorised them and finally committed them to writing. They have come down to us in their Sacred Book which is known as *Al-Qur'ân* (the "Reading"), because the angel he saw on Mt Hira insisted on his "reading", though he was illiterate.

The Quran is a comprehensive guide for Muslims on all aspects of their lives: spiritual, moral, social, economic, and so on. It contains many stories that appear in the Bible, including the birth of John the Baptist and the virgin birth of Jesus who is described as "the Word of God". (Sûr. xix, 20-21) However some details of the Quranic stories differ from the Biblical version. For example, the Quran denies that Jesus died by crucifixion: "but Allah took him up unto Himself. Allah was ever Mighty, Wise."(Sûr.iv,158)

Like the Bible, the Quran denounces money-lending for profit; it forbids lying, stealing, adultery, and murder. Punishment for some of these can be severe, like in the Old Testament. It mitigates, however, the old law of retaliation ("an eye for an eye, a tooth for a tooth") by urging forgiveness; it lays down measures to restrict slavery; whilst it does not ban marriage to more than one wife — a common practice in his society — it limits the maximum number to four, provided they can be given a fair and equal treatment, otherwise only one. In marriage, the husband is the head of the family, but the wife has rights that protect her from abuse. Men are often urged to treat their wives with kindness. The ideal marriage is one in which there is love and mercy. The Quran teaches respect for parents, protection for orphans and widows, and charity to the poor. It teaches the virtues of faith in God, kindness, honesty, industry, courage, and generosity.

In Islam there are **five essential articles of faith:** belief in One God, His Angels, His Holy Books, His Messengers, and the Hereafter. According to Islam, there is only one God and his revealed name is Allah. He is the same God who is worshipped by Christians and Jews. The belief in Angels too is very similar to that of the Christians. Among the Holy Books are the Psalms of David, the Torah of the Jews, and the Gospels; but for Muslims the Quran is God's final message to mankind. Messengers are the prophets that God sends to every nation. Nearly 30 are mentioned in the Quran, including Moses and Jesus who, however, is said to be only a prophet and not an incarnation of God. Muslims believe that Mohammed was the final prophet and messenger of God, "the seal of the prophets". The "Hereafter" corresponds to the Heaven and Hell of the Christians, though the description of Heaven varies.

Together with the faith in one God, Allah, the Muslims perform **five main religious duties** known as *arkanuddim* (the five "pillars of religion"). They are:

(1) Profession of faith (*Shahada* or *Tashahhud*), that the muezzins proclaim regularly in Arabic from the masjids: "There is no God but Allah, and Mohammed is His messenger";

(2) Prayer, especially the five ritual prayers (*Salat* or *Namaz*) to be performed respectively at dawn, at noon, in the afternoon, and at nightfall, whilst facing Mecca;

(3) Observance of fast during the month of Ramadan (*Roza*);

(4) Almsgiving to help the poor and the needy as also to support social, educational, and health institutions (*Zakat*); and

(5) Pilgrimage to Mecca (*Hajj*).

4. His Character

The sayings and actions of Mohammed were painstakingly preserved by early Muslim scholars and so we can learn much from these writings about his character. Even non-Muslim scholars do not doubt his sincerity in his mission: in the early years of his ministry, he bore much ridicule and even persecution rather than forsake his task. He also refused to fall to the enticements of the Meccan chiefs who offered him rank, power, and wealth, to stop preaching against idolatry at the Ka'bah, that was bringing them economic and political benefits. He had dignity and commanded respect without being distant. He combined heavy leadership duties with an intense spiritual life, spending generally two-thirds of the night in prayer. In spite of being the head of a large and growing community, Mohammed always lived life of extreme simplicity, living on a diet of water, dates, and barley, sleeping on a sack filled with twigs, and possessing only one change of clothes. In the midst of his official duties, he found time to help with household tasks and was known to patch his own clothes and mend his own shoes.

After the death of his first wife, Khadijah, Mohammed married several wives, many of them widows of warriors that had fallen in the battles. By marrying them, he was able to support them and provide them with a new life.

As a prophet Mohammed considered his duty to take up military leadership, not to impose his religion on others but, if Muslims themselves were not allowed to follow their religion in peace, then to defend it by arms if necessary.

Muslims believe that God revealed Himself and His will for mankind through Prophet Mohammed. Though not infallible, he was chosen by God because of his exceptional qualities, and therefore he is regarded as an example to be followed. They feel a great reverence and affection for him, and when they perform their daily prayers, they call God's blessings on him; when they mention his name in speech, they add: *"May the peace and blessings of God be upon him"*.

5.   The Catholic Church and the Muslims

The recent attitude of the Church towards the Muslims and the Islam has been clearly and forcefully expressed by the Second Vatican Council in the document *"Declaration on the Relation of the Church to Non-Christian Religions"*. In it the Council affirms that "the Church has a high regard for the Muslims" and then goes on to summarise succinctly the teachings of Islam: "They worship God who is one, living and subsistent, merciful and almighty, the Creator of heaven and earth, who has also spoken to men. They strive to submit themselves without reserve to the hidden decrees of God, just as Abraham submitted himself to God's plan, to whose faith Muslims eagerly link their own. Although not acknowledging him as God, they worship Jesus as a prophet, his virgin Mother they also honour, and even at times devoutly invoke. Further, they await the day of judgement and the reward of God following the resurrection of the dead. For this reason, they highly esteem an upright life and worship God, especially by way of prayer, almsgiving and fasting." (No. 3) The Council admits that "over the centuries many quarrels and dissensions have arisen between Christians and Muslims", but "now pleads with all to forget the past, and urges that a sincere effort be made to achieve mutual understanding; for the benefit of all men, let them together preserve and promote peace, liberty, social justice, and moral values." (No. 3)

Together with the Muslims we too can prayer the *Al-Fâtihah*, called the "Lord's Prayer" of the Muslims:
Praise be to God, Lord of the Worlds
The Beneficent, the Merciful,
Owner of the Day of Judgement,
Thee alone we worship; Thee alone we ask for help.
Show us the straight path,
The path of those whom Thou hast favoured;
Not the path of those who earn Thine anger nor of those who go astray.   (Sûrah I)

211

A. MUHARRAM

"Muharram" is the name of the first month of the Muslim year. The other months are: Safar, Rabia I, Rabia II, Jumada I, Jumada II, Rajab, Shaban, Ramadan, Shawwal, Zulkadah, and Zulhijah.

"Muharram" is also the name of the 10-day-long festival, somewhat similar to the Good Friday, which is observed by the Shi'ahs as days of mourning, commemorating the death of Hussain the grandson of Prophet Mohammed, and Ashura, the 10th day of the festival, is the most sacred of all the days to the Shiah community.

The Sunnis naturally look at these celebrations with a certain disapproval. They belong to the opposite camp and this sometimes creates problems. Yet the Sunnis too observe Ashura as a special day. They believe that on that day God created Adam and Eve, heaven and hell, seat of judgement, table of decrees, life and death.

1. The Historical Background

On Prophet Mohammed's death, a majority of Muslims elected his disciple Abu Bakr to be his successor. They were called the *Sunnis*. A minority, however, held that the leadership should have gone to Ali, Mohammed's cousin and husband of Fatima, the prophet's daughter. These became the *Shiites*. Following Ali's assassination by his opponents, his son, Hassan, became Imam and after him, his second son, Hussain. The conflict between the two parties continued. The Muslims of Kufa in Iraq had invited Hussain to their city. On the second day of the month of Muharram, Hussain, together with his family and his small following, encamped in Karbala on their way to Kufa. During the ensuing week of fruitless negotiations, Hussain and his family were denied access to the river Euphrates even for drinking water by the Sunnis. In the fateful battle that took place on 10th Muharram between Hussain's small band of less than one

212

hundred and the four-thousand-strong army of Caliph Yazid, under the command of Ubaydullah, governor of Kufa, Hussain and nearly all his followers were killed.

The death of Hussain produced an immediate reaction in the community. When the people of Kufa heard of the martyred Imam and of the pitiful state of the captives, they began to beat their breasts in remorse for their betrayal of the grandson of the Prophet, and son and heir of Ali. This reaction produced an important movement known as *al--Tawwabin* (the Repenters), which nurtured a spirit of revenge for the blood of Hussain and provided fertile soil for the new Ashura cult (the 10th-day cult). This thirst of Hussain, the women, and the children, and their pathetic entreaties for water in Karbala provided one of the major themes of innocent suffering and heroism for the Shiah faction to celebrate it as a **day of atonement**. Ali Zaya al Abidim, the only surviving son of Hussain, was proclaimed fourth Imam.

2. The Muharram Celebration

The ceremony varies from place to place. In India, as soon as the new moon appears, marking the beginning of the month of Muharram, people assemble either in the *"Imam Bara"* or in the makeshift *Ashurkhanah* (lit. ten-day house) and recite the *fatihah* (the first surah of the Quran) as a form of blessing over the *"sherbet"* (sweetened cool drink), in Hussain's name. This, together with some food, is subsequently distributed to the poor.

Both the Imam Bara and the Ashur Khanah are tastefully decorated with wooden structures (*ta'zian* or *tabut*) meant to represent Hussain's mausoleum in Karbala, or the Prophet's tomb at Medina, or even the Taj Mahal in Agra. There are also imitations of articles which Hussain is supposed to have used at Karbala, standards of different shapes each with its own history, especially one with the form of a human hand fixed on top of the pole representing the five members of

213

the Prophet's family: Mohammed, Fatima, Ali, Hassan and Hussain.

In some districts they then mark out a spot for the pits in which bonfires are lit at night, and the people, old and young, fence with sticks or swords, or run around calling out in grief *"Ya'Ali! Ya'Ali! Shah Hasan! Shah Hussain! Dulha! Hai Dost! Rahiyo!"* (Noble Hassan, Noble Husain, Bridegroom, Friend, Stay, Stay!)

Each evening people assemble to listen to *marsyas*, elegiac poems chanted by paid singers in honour of Hussain. Someone will mount a kind of pulpit and recite the story of the heartless ways in which the foes of Ali put him to death; they rise from their places, and with grief beat their breasts crying out *"Ali, Ali! Hussain!"* Caliph Yazid, responsible for the latter's death, is cursed. On the seventh day, processions and parades continue in the streets with standards.

On the evening before the tenth day alam and ta'zian are taken in procession. A scene of great confusion ensues with men and boys running about with masks. It is a carnival of the Muslim year.

The next day is Ashura. On this day the *ta'zian* are stripped of their trappings and carried to a large open spot near a river or pond. The water represents the plains of Karbala. It recalls the agony of thirst of Hussain before his death. Into this water the *ta'zia* frames are finally thrown. On the evening of the twelfth day people sit up all night reading the Quran and reciting *marsyas* and verses in praise of Hussain. On the thirteenth day a quantity of food is cooked and after *fatihah* has been recited over it, it is given to the poor.

3. A Reflection

The Muharram festival finds its actual focus in the ritual celebration of the passion and death of Hussain, an innocent victim, in Karbala. The "passion play" in Karbala, writes

Kenneth Cragg, is seen as epitomising innocence and suffering through all times: Jacob's anguish over Joseph, Mary's over Jesus, Mohammed's over his tiny son Ibrahim, yet transcending in the tragedy that befell Hussain. The name Karbala is traditionally explained as a compound of *Karb* ("distress") and *Balla* ("affliction"). There all human sorrows meet. Hence all who associate themselves with faith and devotion with the sufferings and death of the innocent martyr may find forgiveness for their own wrongs. This is the purpose of the intense dramatic celebrations of Muharram.

The sufferings of an innocent person having redeeming value for the sins of others was a well-accepted idea in the Judaism of Jesus' time. It is known as "vicarious atonement". The best-known expression of this idea is found in "Servant Songs" in Deutero-Isaiah, (Is 42,1-4; 49,6; 50,4-9; 52,13-35)

In the New Testament, the early Christian proclamation identified Jesus with the "Servant of the Lord" and this idea is taken up into the gospel accounts themselves (Mt 8,17; 12,18-21; Mk 10,45).

We do not intend to develop here the theology of the death and resurrection of Jesus Christ. What we would like to state is that the concept of vicarious suffering and atonement is very valid for us. Sufferings of an innocent for the redemption of others is a rich concept. It is true of Jesus Christ and of every one of us, in and through Jesus Christ, as St Paul says: "Now I rejoice in my suffering for your sake, and in my flesh I complete what is lacking in Christ's afflictions for the sake of his body, that is, the Church." (Col 1, 24).

Note that we do not seek revenge but offer our sufferings for the forgiveness of others, even our enemies, as Jesus did. God Himself is our Redeemer (Ps 78, 35). He is in no way enraged by our sins to exact a price for them (this is an idea totally alien to a Christian), but "He so loved the world that

He gave his only Son not to condemn, but to save." (Jn 3, 1-6).

With this Christian background, we can always sympathise with our Muslim brothers and sisters and look with appreciative eyes to their Muharram celebration.

B. THE RAMADAN FAST

Muslims are woken up every morning by the local *muezzin* with a loud proclamation of their faith:

Allahu Akbar, Allahu Akbar	Allah is the greatest!
Lail-ha-Illalah	No one is worthy of worship
Vallahu Akbar	except Allah.
Allahu Akbar	Allah is the greatest!
Valillahil Hamd.	All praise is for Allah alone.

Together with the faith in one God, Allah, the Muslims perform five main religious duties known as *arkanuddim* (the five "pillars of religion"), including the observance of fast (*Roza*). This observance of fast and the pilgrimage to Mecca are carried out particularly during the Muslim "holy" month of Ramadan and each ends with a special festival.

Ramadan is the ninth month of the Muslim calendar and the Muslims call it the blessed month of self-purification, re-dedication, selfmastery and discipline of the body.

It was during the hot month of Ramadan that Prophet Mohammed, distressed by the rampant idolatry among his fellow Meccans, would retire with his family to a desert cave on Mt Hira and seek to discover the way of truth. It was, then, on one such occasion that he claimed to have had a deep experience of God calling Him to become His prophet.

1. The Roza

The fasting begins each day with sunrise and lasts until sunset. It consists in abstaining from food and beverages, from inhaling of tobacco smoke, and even from swallowing of spittle, smelling of perfume, taking injection, deliberate vomiting, sexual intercourse, and intoxication. All Muslim male or female, who are adult, sound in mind and physically fit, are bound to fast throughout the month of Ramadan.

Fasting is not obligatory under certain circumstances, namely, when it causes undue hardship. Pregnant and nursing mothers, the sick, and the travellers may be exempted from fasting, but they should make up later on for the days missed. The old and infirm or those with a permanent medical condition, who are not likely ever to be able to fast again, should, if they can afford it, feed a poor person for every fasting day that they missed.

The main aim of the fast is to please God and to draw near Him. There are also other moral, spiritual and social benefits from fasting. Fasting requires self-discipline and the control of one's own desires, and thus it prepares one to face the hardships that may come along. It makes one realize that God alone is the supreme author of life, that man depends on Him and to Him alone he has to obey and submit himself. It also makes one appreciate God's generosity in giving us the gift of food, which can all too easily be taken for granted. Ramadan provides occasions to become aware of the presence of poor and needy people around. The devotee learns to give hospitality to those in need and share with them part of his earnings. Finally, as both the rich and the poor perform the fasting, it reminds one that rich or poor, male or female, all are equal before God.

Ramadan is traditionally also a time when Muslims try to devote themselves to meditation, prayer, and reading the Koran. Special, extra, night prayers are performed in the mosque. The last ten days of Ramadan are believed to be especially sacred. One of them is considered as the "Night of Power", the occasion when the first Koranic revelation came to Mohammed. Therefore during this period some Muslims will stay in the mosque in continual worship and contemplation of God.

217

2. The Id-ul-Fitr

The final breaking of the fast of Ramadan is marked by a special three-day festival, the *"Id-ul-Fitr"* (the Lesser Festival). On this day the Muslims go to the mosque to perform special prayers of thanksgiving for the successful completion of the Ramadan fasting. When prayers are completed the *Imam* (the leader) takes his place in the *mimbar* (the pulpit) and delivers the *Khutba* (sermon) and ends with a *munajat* (supplication prayer). People join this prayer for the forgiveness of their sins or for obtaining any other favour spiritual or material such as recovery from sickness, etc.. The feasting continues throughout the day. Special dishes are prepared. Friends visit and greet each other with hugs and kisses (that is why in some parts of India it is called Mithi Id, the feast of the embrace), whilst they say *"Id Mubarak"* or *"Chand Mubarak"* ("a happy moon" to you, since it begins with the sighting of the moon). The festival is also characterized by almsgiving, and offerings are made to the poor in the name of God.

A Christian Reflection

A month-long fast and self-purification, followed by a joyful celebration of breaking of the fast on Id-ul-fitr, symbolize our life in this world as a spiritual passage, a journey, a pilgrimage towards God, towards our 'home', in heaven. Seen from this point of view our great forty-day Lenten Season, traditionally characterized by fast and penance, prayers and almsgiving, followed by the Easter celebration, has for us the same meaning. In the Lenten Season the entire Church as a community, a family, purifies itself during those 40 days, and on the Easter Day rejoices in our renewed encounter with the Risen Lord. We die with Christ and rise with him, anticipating our final encounter in heaven.

This yearly cycle is again repeated in a weekly cycle. Once each week, on the day which the Church has called the Lord's day she keeps the memory of the Lord's Resurrection. In the early Church, Wednesdays, Fridays, and Saturdays, were the days of fast in several ecclesial communities. If Friday fast was in remembrance of the death of Jesus, the Saturday fast was meant as weekly recall of the great paschal or Lenten fast. Thus the following Sunday was highlighted as the day of the Lord's Resurrection on which day Christians joyfully shared in the Eucharistic Meal of the Lord; alms were collected for the poor and the day was spent with works of charity and relaxation. Thus Sunday and the Lord's Supper symbolized for the early Christians, and it does symbolize for us, the anticipation and foretaste of our eternal joy and Banquet in Heaven, after our week-long life of pilgrimage of our daily life.

Hence, in a spirit of solidarity, we too may join our Muslim brothers and sisters in their joy of Id-ul-Fitr which marks the end of the Ramadan fast.

C.   THE HAJJ AND THE BAQR-ID

It is the duty of all adult and healthy Muslims to undertake a pilgrimage to their holy city of Mecca, at least once in their lifetime, if they can afford it. This pilgrimage, that is called *Hajj*, includes a number of ceremonies that last several days. Muslims believe that one who performs the Hajj secures great religious merit. Such a person is given the honorific title of *Hajji*.

1. The Pilgrimage

The pilgrimage season begins during the month of Shawwal, soon after the Ramadan fast, and ends on the 10th day of the twelfth month, Zulhijah. The Hajji begins his/her pilgrimage by setting out from his home on the right foot, so also he will enter the Mosque in Mecca on the right foot, and depart from it on the left foot. Before entering the sacred city of Mecca, all pilgrims, rich and poor alike, put on special clothing (*Ihram*), which consists of two simple lengths of unsown white cloth, one to cover the lower half of the body and one the upper half. Women, however, wear their own clothes but may not wear face-veils, which was once considered a mark of high social ranks.

On arrival at Mecca, the pilgrims shave their hair as a symbol of entering into the consecrated state. They may not wear perfume or kill any living thing, not even a plant.

For Muslims the shrine in Mecca (Kàba) is the most sacred in the world. According to their tradition, it was built by Abraham (Ibrahim) and his son by her slave, Ishmael (Ismail), as the first house of worship. It contains the famous Black Stone, enclosed in a silver ring, which is said to have been given to Abraham by the angel Gabriel. Hence the Kàba is the focal point towards which all official prayers and mosques are physically oriented. The term 'Hajj' seems to mean "going round" or "standing" in the presence of God at the sacred mountain or shrine. The Ka'ba, therefore, is the chief goal of the pilgrimage.

The Hajj consists of a succession of rituals which include walking around the Kàba and visiting certain sacred sites, while praying and reciting verses from the Koran. On the 8th of Zulhijah, the pilgrims set out for Mount Arafat (Mount of Mercy). According to a legend, Adam and Eve first met and "knew" each other at Arafat, after the long separation following the expulsion from Paradise, and later on Ibrahim came here and performed Wukuf (standing in the presence of God). Tradition also says that on this site the final verse of the Quran was recited by Mohammed. There at Mt Arafat, the pilgrims also perform *Wukuf* at the Mount of Mercy. At sunset they assemble at Muzdalifal where they perform the official evening prayer (*Salat*).

2. The Final Rite and the Sacrifice

On the 10th of Zulhijah, which marks the end of the Hajj season, the pilgrims arrive at Mina. Here the final rite includes: (a) the casting of seven small stones at the pillars of Aquaba; (b) the main rite of major sacrifice (Id-ul-Adha or Baqr-Id); (c) the rite of deconsecration of the pilgrims; and (d) the visit back to Mecca for the *tawaf* (going round the Kàba).

a) In an account quite different from the Bible (Genesis, ch.22), it is said that, when Ibrahim founded Mecca, the Lord desired him to prepare a feast for Him and commanded him to offer up his only son Ishmael. (The Bible says it was Isaac!) As per God's direction Ibrahim took his son to a place near the Kàba to sacrifice him. Ibrahim was three times tempted by Satan to ignore God's hard command and made only ineffective attempts to cut his throat. At this stage Ishmael intervened. He said to his father: "It is through piety and compassion for me that you allow the knife to miss; blindfold yourself and then sacrifice me." Ibrahim acting on this advice, blindfolded himself, drew his knife and, as he thought, cut his son's throat; but to his surprise he found that in the meantime Gabriel had substituted a ram for his son! This event marked the end of human sacrifice for the semitic race, and made clear that the only sacrifice which God requires of man is the surrender of his will and purpose. Hence the importance of going through the experience of Ibrahim once in a lifetime and offering a sacrifice at Mecca.

Three bricks and mortar pillars stand at the centre of Mina. They remind Muslims of Satan's temptation to Ibrahim. On this day every pilgrim casts seven stones at the pillars, as a symbolic stoning of Satan.

b) The most important sacrifice of Islam, **Id-ul-Adah** (the festival of the Sacrifice or the Greater Festival) or **Baqr-Id**, is offered at the end of the Hajj, during which a lamb or a goat or even a camel, depending on the financial position of the pilgrim, is sacrificed. It is believed that it was instituted in commemoration of Ibrahim's (Abraham) willingness to sacrifice his son Ishmael. According to the popular belief, the slaughtered animal will carry its owners across the Sirat bridge to Paradise. Pilgrims are also recommended through this to express their willingness to sacrifice something dear for the sake of God. The meat is consumed by the family and friends, and a portion of it goes to the poor.

This blood sacrifice is observed simultaneously throughout the world, even by those Muslims who do not perform the Hajj. Those who perform the sacrifice at home have to follow certain rites. According to the financial situation and the number of participants, they may choose a sheep, a cow, or even a camel. The animal must be without blemish or defect of any kind. When everything is ready for sacrifice, the head of the family takes the sacrificial animal to the entrance of the house, places it facing Mecca and sacrifices it by repeating the phrase "*Bismillah Allahu Akbar*", while cutting the throat. Any other mode of slaying the victim is *haram* (forbidden, wrong).

c) After the sacrifice, the process of deconsecration (*tahallul*) of the pilgrims begins. It consists of clipping the hair. Cutting three hairs would meet this requirement. Some men, however, have their heads shaved.

d)   The pilgrims then return to Mecca and do the rite of circumambulation (*tawaf al-ifadah*), running and walking around the Kàba seven times, after which they touch the sacred Black Stone or at least try to "kiss" it from far. This marks the end of the ceremony.

When all this is over, the Hajjis put off the special garb of pilgrims and wear their normal dress. All the earlier prohibitions, such as abstention from perfumes, gold, etc., are lifted. The pilgrimage is over.

The Hajj represents the strongest symbol and expression of the unity of Muslims and their equality before God. For most Muslims it is a deep spiritual experience, bringing them closer to God.

A Christian Reflection

Sacrifice as an expression of our self-surrender is an essential element in every religion. For Jews, the sacrifice of his only son (Isaac) by Abraham was the powerful expression of Abraham's faith in God. (Gen 22,15). In the New Testament, the author of the Letter to Hebrews praises Abraham: "By faith, Abraham, when he was tested, offered up Isaac and ... was ready to offer up his only son" (11,17). Because he was `strong in his faith', he became the "Father of all who believe" (Rom 4,11).

This faith-obedience of Abraham is remembered in the Easter Night celebration and the Church prays: "Father, you promised Abraham that he would become the father of many nations; you have fulfilled your promise through the death and resurrection of Jesus..." (Easter Vigil prayer following the reading of Gen 22,1-8). The faith of Abraham and his sacrifice of his son Isaac are part and parcel of the mystery of salvation which came to fulfilment in Jesus Christ.

On the other hand, we know that it was God Himself who sacrificed His own son Jesus Christ, through whom we are forgiven and reconciled: "God so loved the world that he gave his only Son for our salvation" (Jn 3,16). Thus Abraham becomes a kind of symbol of God the Father. We have, therefore, every reason to rejoice in the Muslim festival of Baqr-Id which commemorates Abraham's sacrifice, and share in their joy.

GURU NANAK AND SIKHISM

I.   GURU NANAK

1.   Guru Nanak Dev (1469-1539) was the founder of Sikhism and the first of its Ten Gurus. Not much is known for certain about his life. According to some accounts, he was born in 1469 in a village called Talwandi near Lahore in Pakistan. He was the son of Mehta Khan, of the Bedi Khatri tribe, a village *patwari* (record-keeper.)

Nanak is said to have married at the age of 18 and had two sons. Besides fulfilling family responsibility, Nanak spent his time in discourses with the wandering fakirs and sadhus. He came under the influence of Hindu and Muslim teachers, especially Sufis like Kabir. These discussions helped him to make intimate study of comparative religion. Around 1500 he had a spiritual experience and claimed that he had a revelation from God. Thereafter he distributed all he had to the poor and whenever anyone would ask him what he had discovered, he would answer : *"Na koi Hindu, na Musalman"* (There is no Hindu here, nor a Muslim.)

The message that Nanak preached created a sensation in the town. He went about spreading this message and converting Hindus and Muslims to his views and establishing missionary centres in Punjab and wherever he went. That was the time when there was widespread dissatisfaction with Hinduism all over the sub-continent. The Puranic Hinduism had degenerated in many places into crude idolatry and ritualism, and the caste system into Brahminical supremacy and oppression of the "low castes". The arrival of Islam and conversions to it made reform even more urgent.

The challenge was taken up by many religious revivalists, especially those who promoted the Bhakti Movement — personal and loving devotion to God, expressed through prayer and service — but they remained within the fold of more or less orthodox Hinduism.

More fundamental were the reforms promoted by Kabir, a Muslim weaver who preached a universal religion based on the personal realization of God as dwelling in the heart of man, and by Guru Nanak. They both adhered to strict monotheism, complete rejection of caste distinctions, and renunciation of image worship, rituals, pilgrimages, fasts, and other outward observances that promoted disunity and intolerance.

2. The teachings of Guru Nanak were in the form of hymns, nearly a thousand, that were later collected in the Sikh holy book, the **Adi Granth** (Original Scripture). The most famous composition of Guru Nanak is the Japji which the Sikhs recite regularly. Its mool mantra is:

> "There is only one God,
> He is the supreme Truth;
> He is the Creator,
> Is without fear and without hate.
> He, the omnipresent,
> Pervades the universe;
> He is not born,
> Nor does he die to be born again."
>
> (Japji: *Mool Mantra*)

It is doubtful whether Guru Nanak wanted to start a new religion, but he declared that neither Hinduism nor Islam could guarantee salvation. He criticised their religious practices which, he said, emphasised outer forms more than inner spiritual awakening. He instructed his followers to be

225

aware of God's presence by rising early, bathing, meditating on the Divine Name, and directing each day's activities to God. In addition, a true believer should carry out his normal work properly, give what he could to the needy, and live a clean and upright life. These teachings are summed up in the famous threefold formula of nam, dan, isnan (the Name, giving, bathing).

3. The Ten Gurus

The Sikh religion, as we have it today, is the outcome of the teachings of the Ten Gurus, beginning with Guru Nanak. According to the Sikh belief, he is the one who received the Word (Shabad) directly from God, the "Wahe Guru" (the Supreme Guru), and his teachings mostly form the basic principles of Sikhism. Most of the other nine Gurus contributed something which eventually became integral to Sikhism, but nothing that added to the basic principles of Guru Nanak. The exception was the Tenth Guru, **Gobind Singh** (1675-1708), who established the "Kalsa Panth", thus giving a rather militant shape to Sikhism. Besides giving a definite shape to the Adi Granth, Guru Gobind Sing composed his own Dasam Granth (the Book of the Tenth Guru) which, though not considered sacred by some, is treated as Gurbani by some others.

II. SIKHISM TODAY

The word Sikh comes from the Sanskrit shishya (disciple). Sikhism revolves around two sacred realities: the Guru Granth Sahib and the Guru Panth. According to the Shiromani Gurdwara Parbandhak Committee (SGPC), the supreme authority on the Sikh religious affairs, "Any man or woman, who believes in one Almighty God, the Ten Gurus, Sri Guru Granth Sahib, Gurbani (prayer), and Teachings of the Ten Gurus and the "Amrit" of the Tenth Guru, and does not accept any other religion, is a Sikh." (See: Sikh Raihit Maryada, the Code of Conduct for the Sikhs.)

226

1. The Guru Granth Sahib

The fundamental beliefs and principles of Sikhism are to be found in the 6,000 hymns that make up the *Adi Granth*. After he had given it its final form in 1704, Gobind Singh, declared that after his death the Adi Granth would be the only Guru of the Sikhs, the mystic presence among them of the "Wahe Guru" and the Ten Gurus. They would have no more human gurus. "The Guru is the Word and the Word is the Guru," he said.

The Guru Granth Sahib, therefore, is central to Sikhism. A Sikh's worship consists mainly in reciting or singing hymns from the Granth (*Gurbani*). Votive recitation of the Granth by special Granthis is often sought by devotees for a stipend. Children are given names according to the first letter on the page appearing when the Granth is opened at random, and the recitation of the Granth is the main part of important ceremonies like initiation, marriage, and funeral.

There is, however, some uneasiness among the more learned Sikhs that the Grant Sahib has attracted very little scholarly attention, with the result that the many problems that it raises still remain unanswered.

The Granth Sahib occupies the central place in the Sikh temple, the *Gurudwara* (Guru's gate). The gurudwara itself is distinguished by its tall yellow flagpole flying a triangular yellow flag with the Sikh symbol consisting of two curved swords, a double-edged dagger, and a discus. The symbol stands for bravery and spiritual power. Besides being places of worship, the gurudwaras serve as schools, meeting places, and shelter for travellers.

The Granth Sahib is enthroned in the sanctuary of the Gurudwara, being placed on a low platform covered with precious cloth strewn with flowers, with a fan being waved over it. Worshippers approach it with covered heads and bare feet, rubbing their foreheads on the ground in obeisance. The veneration shown by the Sikhs to their holy book far surpasses that shown to the Vedas, the Koran, and the Bible, by their respective followers.

The main teachings of the Granth Sahib promote, not violence and bloodshed, but serenity, purification, and yearning for the Transcendent. "Sikhism," writes L. Pereira S.J., of St Xavier's College, Bombay, "is a religion of praise of the One God whose Name is True and whose Word enlightens those who receive it through the Ädi Granth of the ten gurus. Its monotheism is very pure and does away with all intermediaries, whether prophets, avatäras or godly images. The Will of God takes account of the karma of his creatures but transcends and may bypass it through his mercy. The Granth inculcates doctrine and moral norms with a concreteness and simplicity mingled with the persuasive charm of poetical beauty."(See: L. Pereira: "Sikhism", in RELIGIOUS HINDUISM, ed. by R. De Smet and J.Neuner, St Paul, Bombay, 1997, pp. 340-1. Much of the information given here is taken from this article. A reading of the entire book is highly recommended.)

2. The Guru Panth

Initially, the disciples of Guru Nanak were not a religious group apart from Hinduism. The distinctiveness, however, began with his successor. It was under the tenth guru, Gobind Singh (1675-1708), that Sikhism underwent a radical change and became militant. The Sikhs had to defend themselves against Muslim and Hindu persecution. So in April 1699, at a special ceremony on the Baisakhi (Hindu New Year) Day, Sikh men and women were called upon to take "*amrit*", a ritual drink made of a mixture of water and sugar stirred by a double-edged dagger (*khanda*). It symbolised sweetness as well as strength.

Those who accepted the invitation and underwent the initiation ceremony were constituted into the militant brotherhood "the Khalsa Panth" (community of the pure

Sikh). The first five to be initiated were drawn from different castes and constituted into the "panchayat". These have been traditionally called "the Five Beloved". These and the others who were then initiated into the Khalsa had to wear the five K's: *kesh* (long hair and beard), *kangh* (comb), *karā* (iron bangle), *kacch* (underwear), and *kirpän* (sword), and follow a certain code of conduct. They had to refrain from cutting the hair and beard, from tobacco, and alcoholic drinks, from adulterous relations with Muslim women, and from meat obtained by certain forbidden slaughter methods.

Once initiated through the partaking of the *"amrit"*, the males would add the suffix *"Singh"* (lion) to their names, and the females *"Kaur"* (princess). The others, the *Sahajdhäris* (easy-goers), who did not undergo the *"amrit"* initiation, though they followed the teachings of the Adi Granth, would not enjoy the special rights, privileges, and obligations of the *Keshdhäris* (hair-wearers).

The Khalsa ideal is that of the soldier-saint. The Sikh is to follow the peaceful (*shanti*) and devotional (*bhakti*) religion of the Adi Granth, but at the same time be ready to fight for it (*shakti*) like lions. "When all other means have failed," wrote Guru Gobind Singh in his Dasam Granth, "it is righteous to draw the sword." Practice of non-violence beyond certain limits results in more evil than good for the society.

Guru Gobind proclaimed that the authority of the Guru would reside in the *Khalsa Panth* (community): "The Khalsa is my other self; in it I live and have my being." In the ultimate analysis, the Guru resides in the collective will of the Khalsa — the *"Guru Panth"* who are infused with the spirit of the Guru through the Great Words of the Guru Granth Sahib. As a result, a majority decision of the Panth's representatives becomes binding on all as a *Gurumata* (verdict of the Guru).

3. Later Developments

As it happens in every religious movement, not all the Sikhs remained faithful to the Granth Sahib. Image worship, caste considerations, the rite of satí, etc., began to make inroads. There also arose reform groups like the Nirankäris of Dyal Das (1783-1855), the Namdhäris of Satguru Ram Singh (d. 1862), the missionary Singh Sabha, and the Khalsa Tract Society.

In order to ensure some coordination and control in faith and morals, the Shiromani Gurudwara Prabandhak Committee (SGPC) was formed with the blessing of the British in 1920, and a political party subject to the SGPC, the Akali Dal in 1925, which was responsible for the passing of the Sikh Gurudwara Bill in the same year. Promises made periodically by those in power and then broken with equal regularity began to foster resentment and fundamentalism among many Sikhs. The All India Sikh Student Federation sowed the seeds of militant separatism that from 1980 began to demand an independent Khalistan (Country of the Pure).

A Christian Reflection

Guru Nanak and Sikhism are a noteworthy example of that characteristic of our country, which Pope Paul VI eulogized during his visit to India in 1964: "Yours is a land of ancient culture," he said, "the cradle of great religions, the home of a nation that has sought God with a relentless desire, in deep meditation and silence, and in hymns of fervent prayer." As Fr L. Pereira wrote in the book quoted above, "all monotheists — Muslims, Jews, Christians as well as Upanishadic ones or Brähmo-Samajis — can recognise and appreciate the quality of this faith and the attraction of the hope it conveys."

Unlike most of the other monotheistic religions, Sikhism does not possess a well-systematized doctrine. Yet, we may notice a number of features that are common to Sikhism and

Christianity. We both believe in One Omnipotent, Omnipresent, and Omniscient God. Like them, we too believe that this God has manifested Himself through a Guru — Jesus Christ; but for us, Jesus Christ is more than just a Guru: He is the Son of God, God Himself. Like the Sikhs, we too worship God, singly and jointly, by singing hymns and psalms to His Holy Name; we too meet God and our Guru in His Holy Word — the Bible — and we too believe that God through our Guru is present also in our "Panth", the Church, in which the "Panch" (hierarchy) has a special role to play. But even more than the hierarchy, we believe that there is in the Church the Holy Spirit who continues to teach and sanctify the Church. It is He who helps the Church to understand God's Word in the Bible, so that individuals are not led astray on their own.

3

MAHAVIR AND JAINISM

1. Vardhamana Mahavir

Mahavir was a Kshatriya of Vaishali, born around 599 B.C., to the leader of one of the wealthy tribes living in the region north of the Ganges. His father belonged to a religious sect which strongly opposed the idea of Vedic revelation. The sect advocated the belief that one could escape the cycle of rebirth by means of suicide, which was committed by starving oneself to death. They argued that in this way, the life-force was reduced to a degree of extinction which made it incapable of further transmigration. Mahavir's parents undertook upon themselves this form of "martyrdom".

Mahavir at first rejected the ideals and method followed by his parents. But gradually he reconciled himself to the basic principle that liberation is possible only through self-renunciation. Hence, in his late twenties, he left home to become an ascetic in search of a means of deliverance from the cycle of deaths and rebirth. The religious system of his time did not provide the answer.

Mahavir undertook the challenge upon himself and after twelve years of meditation and mortification and renunciation of all worldly possessions, including clothing, he received full enlightenment and became a "perfected soul" (*Kevalin*) or "conqueror" (*jina*). He had a following mainly from the merchant classes. After more than thirty years of preaching and directing, he underwent the rite of voluntary self-starvation (*sellekhana*) at the age of seventy-two. The place of his death is localized at Pava (a village not far from modern Patna). He is supposed to have died in 527

B.C., but some scholars hold that he died in 468 B.C., at the age of one hundred and thirty-one years. He is considered the 24th *Tirthankar* or guide of Jainism.

2. Jain Philosophy

Jainism teaches that in the world there are only eternal souls (*jivas*) and eternal non-living material element (*a-jivas*). The jivas and the a-jivas exist in close contact with one another. In human beings, the jiva is in bondage of the a--jivas, namely, false knowledge and evil deeds. The human being has to free itself from the a-jivas by means of Right Faith, Right Knowledge, and Right Conduct, the three spiritual gems of Jainism.

The state of deliverance (*mukta*) is a state enjoyed by "perfected souls" who are endowed with rare qualities: they can avert famine in a broad area, about eight miles in radius, by a simple act of the will; they remain raised above the ground while sitting, standing, or walking; they are able to face everyone simultaneously in all directions; they can destroy all destructive impulses in persons around them; they are completely immune from all possibility of pain and disturbance; they live without food, possess mastery of all sciences and arts; and their bodies do not cast a shadow. In addition, the "perfect souls" acquire the attributes of perfect knowledge, power, perception, and happiness.

3. Jain Theology

There is no place for God in Jainism, but it presents a complicated theory of **Karma**. Karma is understood as the general energy of the soul which causes its attachment to matter and its subsequent defilement, a kind of link between matter and spirit. The process of liberation should be directed towards controlling karma and each person must work out his/her own deliverance. Divine grace is considered evading the problem of sin, suffering, and redemption. Jainism has

eight kinds of karma and about **148 sub-divisions**. Knowledge of these categories is a great help to know what stage in the process of deliverance one has reached.

4. Jain Ethics

The main ethical principal of Jainism is "non-hurting" of life (*ahimsa*). "Hurt no one" is a sacred mandate which enjoins love and compassion for all living beings. Because of this, Jains have asylums and rest homes for aged and diseased animals where they are fed and lodged. A Jain is not supposed to kill anything, even an ant, intentionally or unintentionally, because one who kills is punished with the accumulation of Karmic matter. Even disrespect and waste of things in nature, like water and fire, can bring increase to one's karma. To stop the growth of Karmic matter in the soul, one needs to have preservation, carefulness, observances, meditation, conquest of sufferings, and good conduct. Preservation means proper control over mind, speech, and body; Carefulness requires taking proper care in walking, speaking, eating, lifting, and lying down; Observances means forgiveness, humility, straight-forwardness, contentment, truth, restraint, austerities, renunciation, non-attachment, chastity; Meditation should be on themes like transitoriness, unprotectedness, the cycle of life and death, loneliness; Right conduct consists of equanimity, absolute non-injury, freedom from subtle passion, and a passionless conduct.

A faithful Jain also undergoes certain austerities which are external and internal. External include fasting, eating less than one's fill, daily renunciation of delicacies, sleeping in a lonely place, mortification of the body. Internal include expiation, reverence, service, study, detachment towards the body, concentration. A Jain is called upon to avoid wicked concentration, keep off delighting in hurtfulness, falsehood, theft.

To insure that the right conduct is followed in life, the

Jain takes vows or solemn pledges. They are never to take life intentionally; never to lie or exaggerate; never to steal or take what is not given; never to be unchaste by marital infidelity or unclean thoughts; they are to curb desire; avoid occasions of sins; limit the number of things used; guard against unnecessary evils; keep fixed periods of sinless meditation; observe special times of limitation; spend some days as a monk; and give alms to support the ascetic community. As the Jain approaches death, he/she takes the vow of "non-attachment" in which he/she disposes all possessions and refrains from taking food.

These pledges are a prelude to ascetic life. An ascetic (*arhat*) binds himself to the strictest self-denial. He takes another five vows: to forbid any injury to anyone or anything: to forbid anyone from stealing; to be absolutely sincere in speech; to be chaste even from sexual thoughts; and renunciation of attachment for any person or things.

The Jain ethical standards are considered the most glorious part of Jainism. It is noted that the Jains have a very low rate of civil and criminal charges against them in India.

5. Jain Monastic Life

Mahavir is said to have organized an order of monks with various Superiors. About 300 B.C., the Superiors were reduced to two who jointly governed the whole community. By the end of the first century A.D., there were two chief branches of Jains: the *"Swetambaras"* (white-clad), and *"Digambaras"* (skyclad). The white-clad allow their members to own property and permit clothing. They also admit women as full members of the monastic order. The sky-clad insist that a true Jain owns nothing, not even clothes and hence goes naked. They hold that fasting is absolutely necessary for deliverance. They claim that women cannot attain salvation, because they are the greatest temptation in the world and the cause of all sinful acts, and therefore are never admitted as saints (arhats) and cannot become nuns.

6. Jain Scriptures

The Jains in general are known as *Nirgranthas* "people having no books". However, the Swetambaras have a Scripture canon which was systematized by the Council of Patali-Putra around the end of the fourth century B.C., This canon consists of the reputed teaching of Mahavir in three divisions. The Digambaras hold that all Jain literature was destroyed by Sankara, a Hindu protagonist of Vedanta philosophy around 789 A.D.

7. Jainism Today

Jainism has never been a popular religion but its influence on Hinduism has been tremendous. There are more than three million Indian Jains. As a wealthy community, Jains have had a powerful influence on the life and history of the Indian subcontinent. The followers of Jainism can be grouped in four: monks (*muni*), nuns (*sadhvi*), laymen (*shravaka*) and laywomen (*shravika*).

Jains vow not to kill any living creature. They keep a vegetarian diet and monks and nuns carry brooms to sweep all surfaces to avoid crushing insects accidentally. Ahimsa for Jains requires positive acts of kindness, compassion, and charity. Jains use their wealth to set up and run hospitals and clinics for both humans and animals. They have made major contributions to education and the arts in India. Jain temples are among some of the most beautiful in India. They are found mostly on the western coast.

Mahavir Jayanti, the birthday of Vardhamana, is celebrated on the 13th day of the bright fortnight of Chaitra, but the holiest feast of the Jains is the 10-day Dasha-lakshana Parva, which is celebrated from the 5th to the 14th of the bright half of Bhadrapad. During these days, after taking a bath in the morning, they go to the temple for worship. Each day there is a lecture on the ten chapters of the holy book *"Shritatvarth Sutra"*. These ten chapters dwell on the ten "dharmas" (duties): *Kshama* (forgiveness), *Mardava* (humility), *Arjava* (simplicity and frankness), *Shaucha* (cleanliness), *Satya* (truthfulness) *Samyama* (self-control), *Tap* (austerity), *Tyag* (renunciation), *Akimchanya* (detachment) and *Bramhacharya* (celibacy). On the day dedicated to "tyag", gifts are offered to social-service institutions. On the first day of the dark half of Ashvin, at the end of the celebration, all men embrace one another as a sign of reconciliation for the sins committed during the past year. The 14th day of the bright half of Bhadrapad is known as Anant Chaturdasi (endless fourteenth). This is the last day of the feast and observing a vow on this day, a Jain can gain much merit.

8. A Reflection

Although Jains do not believe in God, yet their ethical standards of respect for life and creation can be considered as a great worship rendered to the Creator. The Bible explains creation by God as "good" and creation of human beings as "very good". Hence, what is good and very good needs to be preserved and not destroyed. The other Jain principles like non-violence, respect for life, charity, etc., are very much in tune with Christian gospel values.

4

THE BUDDHA AND HIS RELIGION

I. GAUTAMA BUDDHA

Buddha is the title given to the founder of Buddhism, one of the world's great religions. It means the Enlightened or the *Awakened One*. Another of his titles is *Shakyamuni*, which means "the wise man of the Shakya clan". Buddha's real name was Siddhartha Gautama and he is considered by Hindus the ninth avatar of Vishnu, though not many show him the same devotion as they do to Krishna or Rama.

Scholars agree that Siddhartha Gautama lived in northern India over 2,000 years ago, but there is still some debate about his exact birth and death dates. His birthday, however, is celebrated in the month of Vaishakh.

1. Birth and Early Life

Buddhists believe in rebirth, and many tales are told about Gautama's previous births. The tales describe how, through human and animal forms, Gautama attained the moral perfection needed for a final birth. These moral perfections are qualities such as generosity, patience, and loving kindness. The stories are part of the folklore of India.

The accounts of Gautama's last birth are set in the upper Ganges Valley of northern India, in the foothills of the Himalayas. Siddhartha Gautama was born near the town of Kapilavastu, in what is now Nepal. Gautama was from the warrior Kshatrya caste and his father was Suddhodhana, a local ruler and prince of the Shakya people, while his mother's name was Maya. She is often referred to as Mahamaya, or Great Maya.

As the stories go, Maya dreamed that a white elephant entered her womb when Gautama was conceived. White elephants are very rare, so Buddhists take this as a sign of the child's future greatness. When the time came for her child to be born, Maya was on her way to her parents' home. She stopped near Kapilavastu in a grove of trees called the Lumbini grove. This site now attracts many Buddhist pilgrims. The story describes how Gautama was born, without pain, from Maya's side. This may have been a way of describing an early Caesarian section, or an emphasis on the miraculous. Maya died quite soon afterward and the future Buddha was brought up by his aunt, Prajapati.

At the traditional naming ceremony of the new child, one of the court astrologers, or wise men, predicted that the baby would become either a great world ruler or a great religious teacher. The astrologer said that if Gautama became a religious teacher, it would be as a result of seeing great suffering. Gautama's father tried to prevent his son from seeing suffering. He kept the child within the royal palace and its park.

When Gautama reached marrying age, about 20, he won an archery competition and the right to marry a princess called Yasodhara. They had a son, Rahula, and lived a pleasant life within the royal palace.

2. The Four Signs

When he was about 29, Gautama persuaded his charioteer, Channa, to drive him outside the palace grounds, and into the neighbouring villages. There he saw an old man, a sick man, a corpse being carried in a funeral procession, and a holy man. In some accounts these four signs appear as visions, or dreams, rather than actual encounters. Whatever their origin, they had a profound effect on Gautama. For the first time he faced the reality of old age, sickness, and death. Gautama could not forget these experiences. he became restless and dissatisfied, and decided to leave home to seek religious enlightenment.

3. The Great Renunciation

In the middle of the night, the prince left his sleeping wife and baby son in the protection of his family. He crept out of the palace, accompanied by Channa. He cut off his long black hair, took off his fine clothes, and put on the clothes of a wandering monk. He sent Channa back to the palace with his horse, to tell his family what he had done.

Gautama went into the forest. For six years he learnt about meditation from some of the famous teachers of the time, such as Alara Kalama and Ukkaka Ramaputta. Gautama tried to learn about the true nature of life, and how to be freed from suffering. He practised strict physical asceticism (self-denial), but soon found that self-denial brought him no closer to the end of his search than had the life of luxury in the palace. He began to eat moderately, and some of the other ascetics thought he had given up his quest for enlightenment. In fact, Gautama had found that the middle way, between luxury and self-indulgence as a prince and extreme self-denial as a hermit, was the most helpful for his spiritual quest.

4. The Enlightenment

One day, Gautama came to the outskirts of a village called Gaya. He sat down to meditate under a sacred tree. He accepted food from a village girl, and decided he would stay under that tree until he had found the answer to his quest.

Gautama meditated throughout the night, using the methods he had been taught. He overcame various obstacles and temptations, and finally obtained "enlightenment": an understanding of how everything changes all the time. Gautama believed that the root of all suffering caused by change is desire and ignorance. Knowing this is what it means to be enlightened.

The tree under which Gautama was sitting when this happened came to be known as the bodhi or enlightenment tree, or Bo-tree. Buddhists call the place of his enlightenment "Bodh Gaya". It is in Bihar and has become a centre of Buddhist pilgrimage since the Buddha's death. From the time of this enlightenment, Gautama came to be called the Buddha.

5. Teaching

Gautama knew that other people would find it difficult to make the disciplined search he had made, and experience the truths he had experienced. Therefore, he did not immediately think of teaching others. Finally, he went into a deer park at Sarnath, near the city of Varanasi (Benares). There he met five holy men whom he had known before his enlightenment. The holy men realised there was something different about the Buddha and were prepared to listen to what he had to say. At the deer park, the Buddha preached his first sermon. Buddhists often call this the "turning of the wheel of the law." The English word law here is a translation of dharma, which also means teaching the truth. The contents of the sermon are the basis of all Buddhist teaching. They are called the Four Noble Truths and the Noble Eightfold Path.

6. Followers of the Buddha

The five holy men became the Buddha's first followers. The Buddha was then 35. He spent the next 45 years travelling round northeast India, teaching all kinds of people, and debating with many other religious teachers. The main body of sacred writings, called the **Tripitaka** or

241

Pali Canon, is concerned with the teachings of the Buddha. Buddhists believe these teachings are more important than the life story of the Buddha. The Buddha always based his teachings on what people already understood and on what was good in their lives. Many people became his followers, but stayed with their jobs, homes, and families. These lay followers provided food and shelter for others who decided, like the Buddha, to give up ordinary life and become wandering monks wearing saffron robes. The community of monks and nuns became known as the sangha.

7. Buddha's Death

At the age of 80, the Buddha became ill and died. His death took place at Kusinara (modern Uttar Pradesh), and is called *pari* or final nirvana. Buddhists believe that the Buddha attained eternal peace and happiness at his enlightenment, when all greed, hatred, and ignorance, were overcome in his life. But they believe that he had to wait until the natural death of his body for his state of nirvana to be fully realised.

The Buddha told his followers not to be sad. He had taught them that he was only human, and would die like everyone else. His followers gave him a ceremonial cremation, and buried his bones as relics in burial mounds called stupas. These mounds are the characteristic monuments of Buddhism all over the Buddhist world.

The place where the Buddha died, as well as the places of his birth, enlightenment, and first sermon, have become important places of pilgrimage for Buddhists. Such places generally have two kinds of statues. One shows the Buddha in his enlightenment, sitting in a lotus posture. The other shows him death, lying peacefully on his side.

II. BUDDHISM

The Buddha had seen old age, illness, and death. This experience made him realize that nothing in the world is permanent. Buddhists believe that a person is a chain of life, a continuity from baby to child, to young adult, to old adult. Every part of each individual changes physically and mentally in one lifetime. The realization led the Buddha to teach anatman (not-self). This is the belief that there is no ultimate, unchanging essence in anyone or anything.

According to anatman, human beings are part of an ever--changing pattern that runs through all life. When a person no longer clings to a sense of self, there is no feeling of separateness from others, no fear of the self, no fear of dying. People become selfless persons. They experience a mental state of loving kindness, compassion, sympathetic joy and equanimity (calmness of mind).

1. The Three Jewels of Buddhism

People become or are counted as Buddhists if they "take refuge" in (1) the Buddha, (2) the dharma (the teaching), and (3) the sangha (the community). These three refuges are also called the "three jewels" or precious things of Buddhism. In the Sanskrit language the word for the three jewels is triratna. At the beginning of most Buddhist gatherings and on special occasions, people say three times: "I go to Buddha for refuge, I go to the dharma for refuge, I go to the sangha for refuge."

a) Buddhists believe that taking refuge in the **Buddha** means more than just following him. It also means that a person has confidence in the nature of enlightenment, whether it is manifest in one's own life or in other beings.

b) **Dharma** means teaching, especially the teaching of the Buddha and his followers. Dharma also involves the wider idea of truth, especially the truth about the way things are. This idea is taught in various summaries, such as the

Four Noble Truths, the Noble Eightfold Path, the Three Marks of Existence, and the Twelve-Linked Chain of Dependent Origination.

c) **The sangha** is the Buddhist religious community. It consists of four groups of people: laymen, laywomen, bhikshus (monks), and bhikshunis (nuns). These people are called the sons and daughters of the Buddha. The lay people support monks and nuns with gifts of food, shelter, and clothing. In return the monks and nuns give to the lay people the example of lives lived close to the example of the Buddha. Monks and nuns also have a special task to preserve and pass on the dharma. Often the word sangha is used to mean just the monastic community. In most Buddhist countries, monks are expected to live a life of poverty, meditation, and study. Some Buddhists become monks for life. Others serve in the sangha for short periods of time. The monks wear special orange or red robes, and are a common sight in Buddhist countries.

2. The Four Noble Truths

a) The starting point for the Buddhist is *dukkha*, the realization that life is unsatisfactory, that everything is changing all the time, that all that we experience here in the world is impermanent (*anitya* in Sanskrit). This is summarized in the first of the Four Noble Truths — that **all is suffering**. Gautama's encounter with old age, sickness, and death, started his quest for enlightenment.

b) He then discovered the teaching that is expressed in the second Noble Truth — that suffering originates in people's desire, greed, or attachment to things. Greed, hatred, and ignorance, are like three fires which must be put out.

c) Buddhism is not, however, pessimistic. Having stated the problem of suffering and its cause, the third Noble Truth says that suffering can be stopped. The Buddhist greeting

"May all things be happy" is optimistic. Happiness, in this sense, is a permanent state of peace and calm, which Buddhists say is too profound to be described. It is usually called nirvana, a Sanskrit word that conveys the image of stopping, or "blowing out". What needs to be blown out in this case are the flames of greed, hatred, and ignorance. A Buddhist believes that trying to describe this state to anyone is as difficult as describing to a fish what it is to live on dry land, or describing the colours of the rainbow to someone who is colour-blind.

d) The fourth Noble Truth is that there is a path to the happiness of nirvana. This path involves morality, meditation, and wisdom. The eight stages on the path are spelled out in more detail in the "Noble Eightfold Path", which starts with two stages of wisdom, goes on to four essential types of morality, and ends with two stages of meditation.

3. The Noble Eightfold Path

A person can start anywhere on the Noble Eightfold Path, and progress to different stages at different times. The eight stages of the Noble Eightfold Path are:

(1) right knowledge and understanding, seeing the world and life as it really is;

(2) right intention and thoughts, resisting evil, thinking with kindness and compassion;

(3) right speech, saying nothing to others;

(4) right action, not harming living things, not taking what is not given, not having harmful sexual relationships, not taking drugs or drink which cloud the mind;

(5) right livelihood, earning a living in a fair and honest way that does not injure others;

(6) right effort, using what energy you have in the right way;

(7) right mindfulness, being attentive to what is going on inside you and around you;

245

(8) right concentration, applying the mind to meditation and concentrating on what you are doing. The word right means what is appropriate to help a person progress toward enlightenment.

4. Buddhist Sects

There are two main schools of Buddhism: the Theravada and the Mahayana. The **Theravada Buddhism**, more ancient, is found in southern Asian countries such as Sri Lanka, Thailand, and Myanmar (Burma). It is also known as Pali Buddhism, because its scriptures are in the Pali language. Theravada Buddhists believe that Gautama Buddha was only a human being, whose example and teachings help his followers become enlightened.

The **Mahayana Buddhism**, sometimes called the northern Buddhism because it is found in countries like Tibet, China, Korea, and Japan. Its original key texts are in Sanskrit, hence is also called Sanskrit Buddhism. The Mahayana Buddhists claim to be more liberal and more enlightened. According to them, people do not have to rely on their own efforts to become enlightened, nor do they have to become monks and nuns. They can be helped toward nirvana by "cosmic" Buddhas (from the other world) and by *"bodhisattvas"*, holy persons who vow to help others to attain nirvana, and may even postpone their own nirvana for this purpose. Mahayana Buddhism introduced the idea of a deity in the religion and for the purposes of popular religion, Buddha became the supreme deity. The bodhisattvas also use many kinds of practices including idols, mantras, and rituals, for the purpose of helping others to attain nirvana. Zen of Japan, Tantra of Tibet, and the Vajrayana of the Dalai Lama are branches of the Mahayana Buddhism.

5. A Reflection

The Hinduism of his days, like the Judaism in the days

of Jesus Christ, was characterised by excessive ritualism and Brahminic supremacy, making it a matter of rites and practices, and social control by the religious leaders, rather than a relationship with God which led to service of his children. Both the Buddha and Jesus Christ reacted against such a religion by their teachings and actions.

Whilst agreeing with Buddhism that mere external acts do not achieve "*moksha*" (salvation), Christians will see an essential difference between their understanding of "salvation" and the Buddhist understanding of "nirvana", particularly in the role of human effort in achieving it. As St Paul insisted, "No one is put right in God's sight by doing what the Law requires... But by the free gift of God's grace all are put right with him through Jesus Christ, who sets them free." (Rom. 3:20,24). Even when it comes to prayer, there is a vast difference between the Buddhist "vipasana" and the Christian understanding of "prayer".

On the other hand, the Christians will find in the teachings of Jesus echoes of some of the Buddhist teachings about and value of suffering, renunciation, selflessness, service, etc., and will be much benefited by the practice of the Noble Eightfold Path.

5

THE RELIGION OF THE PARSIS

Yathä Ahü vairyo athä ratush, ashät chit hachä,
Vangheush dazdä manangho shyaothnanäm angheush Mazdäi;
Khshathremchä Ahuräi ä yim dregubyo dadat västärem.

Just as God is to be admired
so the prophet on account of his righteousness;
the benefit of good mind is for those who work
in the name of God, that is, selflessly;
that man develops the moral courage of Ahura Mazda
who helps the poor fellow beings.

The Parsis in India number about 76,500 and are based mainly in Bombay and Pune. Their numbers are decreasing, both because many remain unmarried or marry late, either because they do not normally marry outside their community — as they do not want to mix their blood with non-Parsis — and find it difficult to get suitable partners within their own community; or because many have become career-minded and have no time or inclination for family life. As a result, there are more aged people who will die soon, and less number of births. Further, they do not believe in conversion, even when on a rare occasion a Parsi does marry a non-Parsi. Thus, a Parsi boy marrying a non-Parsi girl will remain a Parsi and his children too will be Parsis, but not their mother, who may not even enter the Fire Temple (the Agiary). Similarly, should a Parsi girl marry a non-Parsi boy, she ceases to be a Parsi and neither her husband nor their children are considered to be Parsis and may not enter the Agiary!

As the name suggests, the Parsis are descendants of the emigrants that came to Gujarat from the territory of Paras or Persis (modern Fars) in south Iran. The emigration had started from the 10th century, following a persecution by the Moslem who had conquered that country in 635 A.D.

Under British rule, the Parsis, who were previously engaged in agriculture and animal husbandry, started to enrich themselves through commerce, then through industry. They became a most prosperous and "modern" community. Formerly they had adopted the language (Gujarati) and the dress of their Hindu milieu. Later they adopted British customs, British dress, the education of girls, and the abolition of child marriage.

Our country can be proud of a freedom fighter like Sir Pherozshah Mehta, and other eminent Parsis like Dadabhai Naorojee, Bhikaji Cama, and Jamshedji Tata. The industrial houses of the Tatas, Godrejs, Damanias, and Wadias, have contributed much to the economy of the country; whilst others have shone in sports, travel, defence of the country, and many other fields. They are well known for charities, not only to the members of their own community but to the public in general.

1. The Founder

The religion of the Parsis is Zoroastrianism, named after its founder, Zoroaster or Zarathushtra Spitaman. Hardly anything is known about him for certain. Even his date of birth is placed anywhere between 600 B.C., and 6000 B.C.! From circumstantial evidence, however, it may be safely said that Zoroaster was born before Iran became unified under Cyrus II the Great (590-529 B.C.), around 628 B.C. He belonged to a modestly-situated family of knights, the Spitama, probably at Rhages (now Rayy, a suburb of Tehran), a town in Media. The area in which he lived was not yet urban, its economy being based on animal husbandry and pastoral occupations.

Aryans by origin, the Iranians initially worshipped the same deities as the people of the Vedas. There were daivas and ahuras in Iran, as there were devas and asuras in India; but whereas here the devas were "good spirits" and the asuras were demonic, in Iran the ahuras were extolled, to the exclusion of the devas who were reduced to the rank of demons.

Zoroaster had become a priest of a certain Ahura called "Mazdāh" (wise) and was dissatisfied with the polytheistic concepts of his contemporaries. It is said that at the age of 30, he had a vision of Ahura Mazda who appointed him to teach the truth about himself. Under his inspiration and in his honour, Zoroaster composed innumerable hymns, the Gāthās, in what was called the Ghatic language. A legend has it that he had composed more than 2,000,000 verses dealing with religion, philosophy, ethics, medicine, astronomy, astrology, and other sciences. However, much of what he wrote is said to have been destroyed when Alexander the Great burnt down the royal palace at Persipolis. What has finally come down to us are a mere 83,000 words that form the core of the collection of scriptures referred to collectively as **Avesta**. Zoroaster is said to have lived for 77 years, thus indicating that he died in about 551 B.C..

2. His Teaching

According to Rabindranath Tagore, Zoroaster is perhaps the first prophet in human history to preach that God is one — the Ahura Mazda, the Lord of Wisdom, a God of spirit and truth, of righteousness and justice, of love and compassion. He desires all his creatures to come to him of their own free will. Hence, freedom of choice is a cardinal doctrine in Zoroaster's teaching. Every man and woman has a choice to make between good and evil. This choice gives rise to the two categories of people in the world: the

Ashavants or Followers of the Truth (*Asha*) and the Dregvants, Followers of the Lie (*Druj*).

The nature of the human mind and the origin of evil are explained by the parable of Twin Spirits (*Mainyu*): In the beginning, according to Zoroaster, there was a meeting of the Twin Spirits created by Ahura Mazda, who were free to choose "life (*gaya*) or not-life (*ajyait*). This original choice gave birth to a good and an evil principle. Corresponding to the former is a Kingdom of Justice and Truth (*Asha*); to the latter, the Kingdom of the Lie (*Druj*), populated by the daevas, the evil spirits. Even now, the Twin Spirits mingle in the mind of man to form his dual nature. When man exercises hi Better Mind, he creates Life, and draws Ahura and His Divine Powers towards himself; when he exercises his Evil Mind, he enters the state of Not-life, that is, spiritual death. Confusion descends upon him and he rushes towards Aeshma, wrath and bloodlust, by whose actions human existence is poisoned.

To protect his true believers from the onslaughts of Aeshma, Ahura Mazda sends forth his Divine Powers (comparable to the Archangels?): *Spenta Mainyu* (Bounteous Spirit), *Asha Vahishta* (Truth, Justice), *Vohu Mana* (Righteous Thinking), *Armaiti* (Divine Devotion), and *Khshathra Vairya* (Desirable Dominion).

How does Zoroaster explain the dualism of good and evil? The Wise Lord, Ahura Mazda, has an opponent, Ahriman, who embodies the principle of evil, and whose followers, having freely chosen him, also are evil. The Divine Powers, therefore, were from the very beginning in array against the forces of evil, in the conflict between Truth and Falsehood. The Bounteous Spirit (*Spenta Mainyu*) headed the army of Ashavants, the partisans of Asha, and entered into a conflict with the host of the Dregvants, the partisans of the Druj, who were headed by the Destructive Spirit (*Angra Mainyu*). Each combatant faced his exact counterpart: the Good Mind opposing the Bad Mind, and Aramati being

251

opposed by Taromati. The entire world is even now engaged in this struggle, each opposing entity soliciting the support of the various material elements.

In spite of this apparent dualism, monotheism prevails because Ahura Mazda is Father of both spirits, who were divided into the two opposed principles only through their choice and decision. Further, the Wise Lord will at last vanquish the spirit of evil: this message, implying the end of the cosmic and ethical dualism, seems to constitute Zoroaster's main religious reform. His teachings seem to have influenced the development of Judaism, especially from the time of the Babylonian exile, and early Christians, following a Jewish tradition, identified him with Ezekiel, Nimrod, Seth, Balaam, and Baruch.

3. The Avesta

Also called Zend-Avesta (interpretation of the Avesta), the Avesta is the sacred book of Zoroastrianism, containing its cosmogony, law and liturgy, and the teachings of Zoroaster. The extant Avesta is all that remains of a much larger body of scripture. The voluminous manuscripts of the original are said to have been destroyed when Alexander the Great conquered Persia. The present Avesta was assembled from remnants and standardised under the Sassanian kings (3rd-7th cent. A.D.) and rendered into Pahlavi language that had replaced the Ghatic language during this period.

The Avesta is in various parts. Its religious core is a collection of songs or hymns by Zoroaster, the Gathas. They form a middle section of the chief liturgical part of the canon, Yasna, which contains ritual formulas that are recited by the priests during the ceremony of the same name, meaning "sacrifice". The *Visp-rat* ("All the Judges") is a lesser liturgical scripture, containing homages to a number of Zoroastrian spiritual lords (ratus) belonging to the different classes of beings. The *Vendidad* or *Vidëvdät* ("Law Exposed to the Daevas") consists of two introductory sections recounting how the law was given to man, followed by 18 sections of ritual and civil rules. It also gives an account of creation and the first man, *Yima*. The Siroza enumerates the deities presiding over the 30 days of the month. The *Yashts* are 21 hymns, rich in myth, to various yazatas (angels) and ancient heroes such as Mithra, Anahita, or Verethraghana. The Hadhoxt Nask ("Section Containing Sayings") describes the fate of the soul after death. The **Khurda Avesta** (or Little Avesta) is a group of minor texts, hymns, and prayers for specific occasions. The Avesta is, therefore, a collection of texts compiled in sucessive stages until it was completed under the Sassanians kings.

4. After the Prophet

Zoroaster had tried to promote monotheism during his lifetime. In a later period, the dualist principle reappeared in an acute form. It was reflected in the Pahlavi scriptures, especially in Bundahishn ("Primal Creation"), a book of cosmology. Here, Ahura Mazda, now called Ormazd, is brought down to the level of his opponent, Ahriman.

a. The New Cosmology. According to this cosmology, the history of the world is conceived as a vast drama divided into four periods of 3,000 years each. In the Beginning (Infinite Time) there existed **Ormazd**, who dwelt in the light, and **Ahriman**, who dwelt below him in the darkness. At the end of the first 3,000 years, Ahriman crossed the Void that separated them and attacked Ormazd who, perceiving that their struggle would last forever unless realised in finite terms, made a pact with Ahriman limiting the duration of their struggle. He then recited the *Ahuna Vairya*, the most sacred prayer of the Zoroastrians, which is believed to contain the germ of their whole religion. Ahriman, aghast, fell back into the abyss where he lay for another 3,000 years.

During this time Ormazd called creation into being, first the spiritual creation including the Beneficent Immortals (*amesha spentas*), then a corresponding material creation —

sky, water, earth, plants, the Primeval Ox, and the Primeval Man (*Gayōmart*). Next, to the *fravashis* (preexistent souls) of men Ormazd offered a choice between staying forever in their embryonic state or becoming incarnate in the physical world in order to secure his triumph over Ahriman; they chose birth and combat. Meanwhile, Ahriman generated six demons and an opposing material creation.

At the end of the second period of 3,000 years, Ahriman, instigated by Primeval Woman, the Whore, burst through the sky and corrupted the creation of Ormazd. He killed Gayōmart, from whose body mankind and the metals were generated, and the Primeval Ox, from which arose animals and plants.

In the third period Ahriman triumphed in the material world, but was unable to escape from it; trapped by Ormazd, he was doomed to generate his own destruction. The beginning of the last period witnesses the coming of religion on earth, namely the birth of Zoroaster.

The end of each of its millennia is to be marked by the coming of a new saviour, successor and posthumous son of Zoroaster. The third and the last is to be Astvat-ereta (justice-incarnate), called simply "*Saoshyans*" (Saviour), who will bring about the final judgement, dispense the drink of immortality, and usher in the new world. The first human couple had at first fed on water, then on plants, on milk, and at last on meat. The people in the last millennia will, at the advent of the three successive saviours, abstain in the reverse order from meat, milk, and plants, to keep finally only water.

The primeval combatants will have their counterparts at the end of time. The dragon that was killed in order to liberate the imprisoned waters will appear again at the resurrection to be killed by another hero. In a last great struggle, the host of good and the host of evil will vie with each other, and each soldier of Ormazd will defeat and kill his special adversary. This will restore the state of peace that

254

had prevailed initially. The wicked will then submit to an ordeal of molten metal and fire. Fire and Ahriman will cause the metals of the mountains to melt and to flow down as a river of fire. The whole resuscitated mankind must traverse it; it will burn only the wicked, whereas to the just it will be as sweet as warm milk. But the suffering of the wicked will only last three days, after which all mankind will enjoy happiness. Hell will be sealed forever, and Ahriman will be either powerless or annihilated. Thus, Finite Time, which had come forth from Infinite Time, will merge with it again after the interval of 12,000 years.

b. Human Responsibility. B. J. Khodaiji writes in his article on Zoroastrianism in WAY TO PEACE (Lucknow: The Lucknow Publishing House, 1981) that according to the Zoroastrian religion, each human act, speech, and thought, is as being related to an existence in the afterlife. With every decision man makes, he is walking over *Chinvatoperetu* (the Bridge of the Separator), which separates the Ashvant from the Dregvant. Hence, the motto: *Humata-hukta-huvarashta* or *Manashni-Gavashni-Kunashni* (good thoughts, good words, good deeds).

In the Pahlavi texts, it is said that good thoughts dwell in the starry heavens, for if thought is not translated into act, its influence is as remote as that of the stars. Good words dwell in the moonlit heavens, for if sweet speech does not lead to right action, it is as ineffectual as the silvery light of the waxing and waning moon. Good deeds, however, dwell in the Mansions of the Sun, for good deeds shine with their own lustre and do not need any one to proclaim their existence.

c. The Afterlife. The earthly state is connected with a state beyond, in which the Wise Lord will reward the good act, speech, and thought, and punish the bad. So, after death too the soul of man must pass over the "Bridge of Judgement" (*Chinvat*), which every one looks upon with fear and anxiety. After judgement is passed by Ahura

Mazda, the good enter the kingdom of everlasting joy and light (*Garo Demana*), and the bad are consigned to the regions of horror and darkness (*Drujo Demana*). Zoroaster however goes beyond this, announcing an end phase for the visible world, "the last of creation". In this last phase, Ahriman will be destroyed, and the word will be wonderfully renewed and be inhabited by the good who will live is paradisiacal joy.

5. Rites and Institutions

The two great emblems of Zoroastrianism are *Hvare kshaeta*, the Glorious Sun, and *Atar khvareh*, the Radiant Fire. The Sun is the symbol of Ahura Mazda who is clothed with it. It is also called "son of Ahura Mazda". Just as the physical fire burns up any filth flung into it, itself remaining pure, even so must the Lie be burnt up in heart and mind so that thought, word, and deed, may be dedicated to the Truth (*Asha*). The sacred fire must be kept burning continually and has to be fed at least five times a day with sandalwood and incense. Prayers also are recited five times a day. The founding of a new fire involves a very elaborate ceremony. There are also rites for purification and for regeneration of a fire.

Initiation. All young Parsis must be initiated when they reach the age of seven. They receive the shirt (*sadre*), and the girdle (*kashti*), which they are to wear their whole life.

There are three types of purification, in order of increasing importance: the *padyab*, or ablution; the *nahn*, or bath; and the *baresnum*, a complicated ritual performed at special places with the participation of a dog —whose left ear is touched by the candidate and whose gaze puts the evil spirits to flight— and lasting several days.

The chief ceremony, the *Yasna*, essentially a sacrifice of *haoma* (the sacred liquor), is celebrated before the sacred fire with recitation of large parts of the Avesta. There also are offerings of bread and milk, and formerly, of meat or animal fat.

Penance entails reciting the *patet*, the firm resolve not to sin again, and the confession of sins to a *dastoor* (the high priest) or to an ordinary priest (*mobed* or *herbad*) if a dastoor is not obtainable.

Burial Rites. After death, a dog is brought before the corpse; it should preferably be a "four-eyed" dog (i.e., it should have a spot above each eye, as this is said to increase the efficacy of its look). The rite is repeated five times a day. After the first one, fire is brought into the room where it is kept burning until three days after the removal of the corpse to the Tower of Silence. The removal must be done during daytime.

The interior of the **Tower of Silence** is built in concentric circles, like Dante's hell, except that there are only three circles, one each for men, women, and children. The corpses are exposed there naked. The vultures do not take long to strip the flesh off the bones, and these, dried by the sun, are later swept into the central well.

No less interesting are the rites performed after the funeral. The morning of the fourth day is the most solemn occasion, for it is then that the departed soul reaches the next world and appears before the deities who are to pass judgement over it.

Festivals. Festivals, in which worship is an essential part, are characteristic aspects of Zoroastrianism. The principal festivals are the six seasonal festivals (*Gahanbars*), and the days in memory of the dead at year's end. Also, each day of the month and each of the 12 months of the year is dedicated to a deity. The day named after the month is the greatest feastday of that particular deity.

The New Year (**Noruz**), is the most joyous and beautiful of Zoroastrian feasts, a spring festival in honour of

Rapithwin, the personification of noonday and summer. The festival of Mithra or Mehragan, was traditionally an autumn one, as honoured as the spring feast of Noruz.

6. Zoroastrianism and Christianity

A lengthy entry in the Encyclopedia Britannica on Zoroastrianism, points out that many similarities can be noticed between the Christian and the Zoroastrian beliefs, mainly in dualism, angelology, and eschatology. It is said that chapters 40-48 of Isaiah offer striking parallels with the Gatha 44:3-5. Besides the common procedure of rhetorical questions, there is the notion of a god who has created the world and notably, light and darkness. The idea of a creator god, even if almost absolutely new in Isaiah, may, however, be common to all of the western part of the Semitic world. But the notion that god created light and darkness appears in both prophets. It is true that Zoroaster associates light and darkness only to waking and sleep, and that no Zoroastrian text says that God created good and evil. Nevertheless, the juxtaposition, in Isaiah, of light-darkness with good-evil sounds remarkably close to Zoroastrian belief.

At the time of the Exile of the Jews in Babylonia, their traditional hope in a messiah-king of the House of David who would re-establish Israel as an independent nation and make it triumph over all enemies gave way gradually to a concept at once more universal and more moral. The salvation of Israel was still essential, but it had to come about in the framework of a general renewal; the appearance of a saviour would mean the end of this world and the birth of a new creation; his judgement of Israel would become a general judgement, dividing mankind into good and evil. This new concept, at once universal and ethical, recalls Zoroastrianism so strongly that many scholars attribute it to the influence of that religion. This influence is seen especially in the saviour's defeat of the demons, his gathering of men for the judgement scene, his raising of the dead, and his administration of the judgement. The occasion of this influence may be found in the contacts between the Jews and the Parthians that were initiated in the 2nd cent. B.C., but that reached a climax in the middle of the 1st cent.

7. Conclusion

Zoroastrianism is first of all an ethical religion that encourages a lifelong battle against evil. Often a Zoroastrian is so constantly involved in a meticulous struggle against the contamination of death and the thousand causes of defilement, and against the threat, even in his sleep, of ever-present demons, that he does not often believe that he is leading his life freely and morally. He prays for a long life with "health of the body and strength of the body" so that he can fight the evil to the last. Man's duty in this life is to play his part in the great cosmic drama of the conquest of death and evil by Life and Truth.

> *Ashem Vohü Vahishtem astí;*
> *Ushtä astí; Ushtä ahmäi*
> *Hyat Ashäi Vahishtäi Ashem*
> Blest is Asha, the highest good
> It is the highest happiness.
> He who follows Asha for its own sake
> is happy forever.

> *Khshnaothra Ahurate Mazdaö*
> *Nemase-të, Atarsh Mazdaö,*
> *Ahurahë hudhaö mazishta Yazata!*
> Propitiation unto Ahura Mazda,
> Homage unto thee, O Fire of Ahura Mazda,
> Thou beneficent and supreme spirit.

Ushtā astī, Ushtā ahmāi

is happy forever.

PART V

SUGGESTIONS FOR PRAYER MEETINGS

In many schools and prayer groups, prayer meetings are often conducted on the occasion of important festivals, including festivals celebrated mainly by the Hindus but which have not only religious but also social and cultural origins. Hints are given here for some such meetings. The selected festivals are arranged as follows:

I. Celebration of union with God

1. Longing for the saviour — Mahashivratra
2. Presence of God with us — Janma Ashtami

II. Celebration of God's loving providence through

1. the animal world — Nag Panchmi
2. the daily bread — Narali Poornima
3. the produce of the land — Ganesh Chaturti
4. the entire creation — Holi

III. Celebration of God's victory as

1. Good vs. evil — Dasrah
2. Light vs. darkness — Divali
3. Life vs. death — Makar Sankrant

IV. Prayer for God's family

1. Love and friendship — Raksha Bandan
2. Dignity of women — Navratra
3. Family values — Rama Navami

It is hoped that both Christians and others will participate in these prayer meetings. With this in view, readings from both Christian and other Scriptures are suggested. Alternate readings may surely be used if desired. The pattern followed here is the following:

1. Begin with a religious song from any familiar hymn book.

2. By way of introduction, read some passages from this book that describe and explain the respective festival.
3. The prayer theme is mentioned and elaborated if required.
4. A couple of scripture passages are read, with suitable introduction/explanation.
5. Time for silent reflection, followed by sharing of reflections by a limited number of participants.
6. Song of praise and thanksgiving for the message of God given through the readings and sharing of reflections.
7. Intercessory prayers, first previously prepared, then ex tempore.
8. Concluding prayer and song.

APPENDIX

SELECTED RELIGIOUS TEXTS

Suitable for Inter-Faith Prayer Services

I. THE VEDAS

A. Rig Veda

1. The Creation

In the beginning the Prajapati (alias Golden Embryo)
Stirred and evolved:
Once born he became the one and only Lord of the universe,
Comprising the heaven and the earth.
Who is the god we revere with sacrifice and oblation?
He who is the giver of life, giver of strength,
Whose will all must obey, Whose will the gods obey;
Whose shadow is immortality, Whose shadow is death....
Who is the god we revere with sacrifice and oblation?
He who by his own might has ever been
the one king of all the living.
He who rules all creatures that have two feet or four...
Who is the god we revere with sacrifice and oblation?
He by whose might exist the snowy peaks,
the sea, the earth-encircling stream;
By whose might, exist the cardinal directions which are his
    arms...
Who is the god we revere with sacrifice and oblation?
He by whom the mighty heaven and earth are held in place,
By whom the sun is given a firm support,
By whom the firmament, by whom the ether
Is measured out within the atmosphere...
Who is the god we revere with sacrifice and oblation?
He who looked upon the waters, looked on them with
    power,
As they conceived insight, brought forth the sacrifice;
He, among all the gods, was the One god above...
This god we revere with sacrifice and oblation.
May he not harm us, father of the earth,
Who generated heaven — for truth is his law —,
Who gave birth to the waters, — shimmering, strong....
This god we revere with sacrifice and oblation.

Prajapati! None other than thou hath comprehended
All these creatures brought to birth.
Whatever desires be ours in offering up
The oblation to thee, may they be fulfilled!

(X, 121)

2. In the beginning...

...there was neither Being nor Not-being,
neither air nor the sky which is beyond it;
There was neither death nor immortality,
nor any sign of night or day.
There breathed the One airless, by self-impulse.
Apart from That was nothing whatsoever.
Darkness was concealed in darkness then,
and all this was indiscriminate chaos.
Then the ONE who was covered by the void
was manifested through the light of tapas.
That One is Lord of all that moves and that is fixed,
of what walks, what flies — this multiform creation.
The loving sage beholds That Reality
which lies hidden in mystery,
where the universe finds one single home.
In That all this unites, from That all this emerges.
The all-pervading One is wrap and woof in created things.

(X, 129, 1-3)

(See Genesis 1)

3. The Sacrifice of the Purusha

A thousand heads had the Purusha
A thousand eyes, a thousand feet:
Encompassing the earth on every side,
He exceeded it by ten fingers.
That Purusha is this whole universe:
What was and what is yet to be,

The Lord of immortality
Which he outgrows by food.
When the gods performed the sacrifice
With Purusha as their oblation,
Spring was the melted butter,
Summer the fuel, and autumn the oblation.
From this sacrifice completely offered
The clotted ghee was gathered up:
From this He fashioned beasts and birds,
Creatures of the woods and creatures of the village.
When the gods, performing sacrifice,
Bound the Purusha, their sacrificial beast,
With sacrifice the gods
Made sacrifice to sacrifice:
These were the first religious rites (dharma),
To the firmament these powers went up
Where dwell the ancient Sadhya gods.

(X.90,1-2,6,8,15-16)

(Isaiah 52,13-53,12; Ps 22)

4. The charitable man

The gods inflict not hunger as a means to kill;
Death frequently befalls even satiated men.
The charitable giver's wealth melts not away;
The niggard never finds a man to pity him.
Who, of abundant food possessed, makes hard his heart
Towards a needy and decrepit suppliant;
Whom once he courted, come to pray to him for bread;
A man like this as well finds none to pity him.
He is the liberal man who helps the beggar
That, craving food, emaciated wanders,
And coming to his aid, when asked to succour,
Immediately makes him a friend hereafter.
He is no friend who gives not of his substance
To his devoted, intimate companion:
This friend should turn from him — here is no haven —

269

And seek a stranger elsewhere as a helper.
The wealthier man should give unto the needy,
Considering the course of life hereafter;
For riches are like chariot wheels revolving;
Now to one man they come, now to another.

(X, 117)

B. Yajur Veda

5. I bow to Thee

O Lord, Thou art beyond the sea of relative existence;
Thou art also in the midst of it: I bow to Thee.
Thou enablest one go beyond sin by means of holy chants...
Thou art present in sacred flowing streams
as well as on the coast: I bow to Thee.
Thou art in the tender grass, on the sea-shore,
as well as in the foaming waves: I bow to thee.
O Lord, Thou art on the sandbanks,
as well as in the midst of the current: I bow to Thee.
Thou art in the little pebbles
as well as in the calm expanse of the sea: I bow to Thee.
O all-pervading Lord, Thou art in the barren soil
and in crowded places: I bow to Thee.

C. Atharva Veda

6. God knows all

The great guardian among these gods, (sees all) as if from
   near.

He that thinks he is moving stealthily: all this God knows.

If a man stands, walks, or sneaks about, if he goes to his
   hiding place; if two persons sit together and scheme: King
   Varuna (the god of the wind) is there as a third, and
   knows it...

He that should flee beyond the heaven far away would not

be free — from King Varuna. His spies come hither from heaven, with a thousand eyes do they watch over the earth;

May all thy hurtful snares which seven by seven threefold lie spread out, catch him that speaks a lie. But he that tells the truth, they shall let go free.

King Varuna sees through all that is between heaven and earth and through all that is beyond. He has numbered the winkings of man's eyes. As the gamester casts the dice, so does he arrange all things.

(IV,vi,1,2,4,6,5)
(See Psalm 39; Mt 10,30)

II. THE UPANISHADS

A. Brihadāranyaka Upanishad

7. From death to immortality

Now we come to the recital of the formulas of purification. The priest whose function is to praise begins his praises with the Saman chant. When he begins his praises he should mutter these words:

From the unreal lead me to the real!
From darkness lead me to the light!
From death lead me to immortality!

When he says, 'From the unreal lead me to the real', by the unreal he means death, by the real immortality. When he says, 'From death lead me to immortality', he means, 'Make me immortal'; and when he says, 'From darkness lead me to the light', by darkness he means death, and by light immortality. When he says, 'From death lead me to immortality', he means 'Make me immortal'.

(I.iii, 28)
(Ps 43,3-4; Mk 12,24-27; Jn 11,25; 14,1-4; IJn 1,5;
Jas 1, 16-18)

8. Only One God

Then Vidagdha Shäkalya questioned him, saying: 'How many gods are there, Yajnavalkya?'

He answered by reciting this invocatory mantra (formula):

'As many as are mentioned in the invocatory formula in the hymn to the All-gods, — three hundred and three and three thousand and three (=3306).'

'Yes,' said he, 'but how many gods are there really, Yajnavalkya?' — 'Thirty-three.'

'Yes,' he said, 'but how many gods are there really, Yajnavalkya?' — 'Six.'

'Yes,' he said, 'but how many gods are there really, Yajnavalkya?' — 'Three.'

'Yes,' he said, 'but how many gods are there really, Yajnavalkya?' — 'Two.'

'Yes,' he said, 'but how many gods are there really, Yajnavalkya?' — 'One and a half.'

'Yes,' he said, 'but how many gods are there really, Yajnavalkya?' — 'One.'

'Yes,' he said, 'but who are those three hundred and three and those three thousand and three?'

Yajnavalkya said: 'These are only their attributes of majesty'

(III.ix, 1)
(Deut 4,33-40; 1Jn: 4,13-116)

B.   Khata Upanishad

9.   The two paths

The better *(sreyas)* is one thing, and the pleasanter (preyas) quite another. Both these, of different aim, bind a person.

Of these two, well is for him who takes the better;

He fails of his aim who chooses the pleasanter.

Both the better and the pleasanter come to man.

Going all around the two, the wise man discriminates.

The wise man chooses the better, indeed, rather than the pleasanter.

The stupid man, from getting-and-keeping (yoga-ksema)
   chooses the pleasanter.

(I,2,1)

10. Docility to the Spirit

More subtle than the subtle, greater than the great,
The Spirit is hidden in the heart of creatures here:
The man without desire, all sorrow spent, beholds It —
The majesty of the Spirit—, by the grace of the Ordainer.
Seated he strides afar,
Lying down he ranges everywhere:
This God is joy and joylessness, —
Who but I can understand Him?
In bodies bodiless,
In things unstable still, abiding,
The Spirit, the great Lord all pervading,-
Thinking on Him the wise man knows no grief.
This Spirit cannot be won by preaching Him,
Not by sacrifice or much lore heard;
By him alone can He be won whom He elects:
To him this Self reveals his own true form.
Not he who has not ceased from doing wrong,
Nor he who knows no peace, no concentration,
Nor he whose mind is filled with restlessness,
Can grasp Him, wise and clever though he be.

(II, 20-24)

(Ps 139,1-10; Is 57,15-16; Wis 7,25-27; Mt 13,1-9; 18-23;
Jn 6,60-65; Rom 8,9-17)

C.   Mundaka Upanishad

11. In the cave of the heart

He abides, manifest, quite near, the dweller in the cave
   (guha), the great Goal, the centre of all;
on him are settled all the worlds, all the inhabitants of the
   worlds,

273

everything that moves and winks and breathes.
He, the shining One, is the object of all desire,
tinier than the atom, beyond the reach of all knowing...
That One is Brahman, the Supreme, the Unchanging,
He is life; he is speech; he is spirit; He is the Real; he is
  Immortality.
It is He who is the mark to aim at.
My dear, aim straight for that mark.
Take into your hands the shining bow of the Upanishads;
on it set your arrow sharpened by meditation.
With your mind stretched towards the unity, bend that bow.
My dear, aim at this mark. It is he, the Unchanging.
OM, the pranava, is the bow; the arrow is the self, it is you
  yourself.
The mark is Brahman.
Aim at it without allowing any distraction.
Fix yourself there, like the arrow in the mark.
He on whom all this world is woven, heavens and earth,
  breath and spirit, ...
Let go all other words; this is the bridge that leads to non-
  death.
Greetings to you who pass to the other shore, beyond the
  darkness.
Truly Brahman is all this, Brahman before! Brahman behind!
Brahman on the right, Brahman on the left! Brahman above,
  Brahman below!
Only Brahman indeed in everything and everywhere!

(II,ii)
(Jn. 15)

D.   Shvestāshvatara Upanishad

12.   Once God is known, all fetters fall away

Once God is known, all fetters fall away,
All cares dissolve,
Birth and death are left behind;

274

And, thirdly, by meditating on Him
At the time of the body's breaking up,
There is mastery supreme: his desires fulfilled
A man is then absolute, alone (kevala).
This must be known, — the Eternal Self-subsistent:
For there's nothing higher than That to be known.
The enjoyer of experience — the thing experienced —
The one who provides the impulse, —
Know these and there is nothing more!
This is the triple Brahman.
As oil in sesame, as butter in cream,
As water in river-beds, as fire between the fire-sticks,
So is that Self to be grasped within the self
Of him who by austerity beholds Him in very truth,-
The Self who all pervades
As butter inheres in cream,
Root of self-knowledge, root of ascetic practice, —
That is Brahman, that the highest teaching (upanishad).

(I, 11-16)

(Ex 19,16-20; 24,9-11;33,17-23; Ps 63,1-4; Acts 17,22-28;
Rom 11,33-36; 1Cor 3,16; Eph 1,15-23; Phil 2,5-13;
Col 1,15-19; 2/1-10)

E. Maitri Upanishad

13. Food and Bread of Life

Food is indeed the highest form of the Spirit:
for the breath of life is made up of food.
Now, if one does not eat, one cannot think,
hear, feel, speak, smell or taste,
and so one loses one's vital breaths, he dies.
So Maitri said: "From food do creatures come to birth,
Once born by food they grow:
Eaten it eats all beings,
Hence it is known as food (an-na)."
Now, this too has been said elsewhere:

"The form of the Lord Vishnu known as 'supporter of all'
is nothing less than food.
The breath of life is the sap of food, mind, of life;
the understanding, of mind; bliss, of the understanding.
The man who knows this will come to possess food,
the breath of life, mind, understanding and bliss;
knowing this, he will eat the food of as many beings as eat
    food here on earth, for he will indwell them:
Food overcomes decay, is full of charm, they say:
Food is the breath of life in beasts;
Food is the foremost, food the healer:
Such is the tradition handed down.

(VI, 11-13)
(Jn 6,27-35, 47-59)

III.   THE BHAGVAD GITA

14.   The Revelation

To you, who are eligible, I'll now reveal
This profound secret lore, illumined with
Wisdom, which shall help you to outsoar all evil.
This is the sovereign knowledge, sovereign secret,
To be known by direct experience, beneficent,
Attended with felicity and eternal.
Those who have no faith in this gospel of mine
Shall not attain me and must time and again
Tread the circling track of this death-bound universe.

(IX, 1-3)
(Mt 13,10-17; Rev 1,1-3; 22,18-21)

15.   God's Omnipresence

My unmanifested Being pervades this
Universe. All creatures reside in me:
But I do not indwell any of them.

276

As the vast, ubiquitous, untrammelled air
Abides in the sky — even so, know this,
That every creature does abide in me.

(IX, 4,6)
(Jer 23,23-24; Ps 139,7-12; Jn 14,116-17; 15,5; 17,22ff.)

16.   The Unbelievers and the Believers

The fools look down on me when I assume
The human body, because they do not know
My highest status as the Lord of all.
Their actions, hopes and knowledge come to naught
For they feel a kinship with the demonic nature
Which deludes their fool intelligence and will.
But the great-souled who dwell in the divine nature,
Knowing me as the eternal source of the world,
Worship me with a single-minded love,
And, pledged to me, bow before me in devotion,
Singing of me day after resonant day.

(IX, 11-14)
(Ps 14; Mt 13,53-58; Jn 6,35; 8,12-23; 10,14-15; 11,25-26;
14,5-7)

17.   Blessings of the Believers

To those who worship me, meditating on
My utter Self, and who are in constant touch
With me — I grant the boons they have not won
And security in all that they have garnered.
Even the devotees of other gods —
Who worship in faith — are, in reality,
Worshipping me, though not in the right way.
'Tis I who am the Lord and the enjoyer
Of all sacrifices. But these ignorant men,
Not knowing me, in my essence, stumble and fall.
Those who worship the gods wend to the gods,
Who worship the ancestors repair to them,

277

Who worship the elemental spirit go
To their abode and my own priests come to me.

(IX,22-25)

(Mt 25,31ff.)

18. The Love Offerings

Whatever you offer me in simple love —
A leaf, fruit, flower or even a drop of water —
I accept in love as your heart's dedication.
Whatever you do enjoy or sacrifice,
Whatever you give away in charity,
Whatever asceticism you undertake
All offer to me in complete surrender.
For only then shall you shake off the bondage
Of works with their good or evil consequences
And through renunciation of all attachment,
Achieving liberation, shall commune
With me and finally repose in me.

(IX, 26-28)

(Mt 6,1-18; 18,4-6, 9-12, 45-47, 56-57; 1Cor 3,5-13; 10,31-33)

19. You cannot see Him with human eyes

Behold, my friend, my multitudinous forms
In manifold celestial hues and shapes.
Behold the Vasus, Rudras and Adityas
And a myriad wonders you have never glimpsed
In my body now behold the whole universe
Moving and moveless and all else you would o see.
But you cannot see me with these human eyes,
So I will endow you with the sight divine:
Behold now my celestial Yoga's power.

(XI, 5-8)

(Ex 20,18-21; Mt 17,1-13)

20. The Benevolent

I promptly save from the death-bound ocean of life
Those who dedicate all their works to me
And with an unfaltering ardour meditate
And worship me with their hearts affianced to me.
Centre your mind on me alone and let
Your intellect abide in me — thereafter
You shall ever in my Self dwell, rest assured.
But if, my friend, you fail to rivet your thoughts
On me, then seek to win me by the practice
Of concentration and mental discipline.
If, however, you cannot discipline
Your mind, then do your works all for my sake
For, doing all your works for me alone,
You shall attain the ultimate self-fulfilment.

(XII, 9-13)

21. The near and dear to Him

Who bears ill-will to none and forgives all,
Who, emancipated from the ego-sense
Of "I and mine", is compassionate and kind,
Who reacts nor to pain nor to joy, who's ever
Contented, resolute and master of self,
His mind and intellect focused on me alone —
Such a devotee is near and dear to me.
Who do not ruffle another, nor is ever
Ruffled by others, who is unaffected
By happiness or pain, anxiety or fear, —
Such a devotee is near and dear to me.
He who is pure and has no expectations,
Who is unconcerned, untroubled and serene,
Who never presumes to take on things on his own,
Such a devotee is near and dear to me.
Who neither grieves nor hankers, neither hates
Nor exults, and who is beyond good and evil,
Such a devotee is near and dear to me.

279

Who sees with an equal eye a friend or foe,
Who stays unmoved by insults or applause,
Suffers from cold nor heat, whom pain nor joy
Can ever effect, who is attached to nothing,
To whom dispraise and eulogy are one,
Who's homeless and yet feels allwhere at home,
Contented with whatever comes his way —
Such a devotee is near and dear to me.
Those who are faithful votaries of this
My immortal gospel and live but for me
I cherish as my beloved devotees.

(XII, 13-20)

22. The divine and the demonic

A man born with the divine nature is
Fearless, simple and pure, a votary
Of the Yoga of knowledge, generous, master of self,
A student of the scriptures. He practises
Strict asceticism and offers sacrifices.
He is ingenuous, truthful, free from anger,
Tranquil in mind, serene, unmarred by malice,
Gentle, forgiving, peaceful, strong, not fractious,
Greedy, haughty or hypersensitive.
A man born with demonic nature is
Conceited, arrogant, choleric and harsh.
The divine endowments lead to liberation
And demonic proclivities will lead to bondage.
Arrogant braggarts, inflated by their wealth's
Purblind intoxication, they sacrifice
To the gods only in name, not in the way
Approved of saints but bound by shackles of pride
And lust and wrath they castigate me, the Lord,
Indwelling in themselves even as in others.

(XVI, 1-20)
(Rom 8,13; Gal 5,16-26; 1Jn 2,29-3,1; 3,7-10)

280

23. The gates to perdition

Three are the gates to this perdition, the death
Of the soul: the gate of lust, the gate of wrath
And the gate of greed. Therefore beware of these.
When a man bypasses these three gates of darkness,
He does what leads in the end to the soul's salvation
And enters the path of the supreme fulfilment.
But he who flouts the commandments of the scriptures
And is driven by his lusts, can never attain
Happiness or the soul's summit perfection.
So be guided by the scriptures' findings when
You want to know what's right and what is wrong :
Aye, you must follow their lead whenever you act.

(XVI, 21-24)
(Mt 7,13-14)

IV.   RELIGIOUS POETS AND MYSTICS

A.   CHAITANYA

24.   I only ask: Reveal Thyself to me

O Lord, I do not beg for a kingdom,
nor for gold and jewels.
Nor do I ask for a beautiful bride,
so eagerly desired by men:
Do Thou reveal Thyself unto me,
O mighty Lord of the universe,
Whose glory is always sung
even by the greatest of gods.
O God of gods, pray,
remove forthwith from my mind all fascination
for this vain and fleeting world.
Lord, take away the heaps of heinous sins from me.
O God, Thou ever bestoweth Thy unfailing mercy
upon the miserable and the hopeless.

O mighty Lord of the universe,
do Thou reveal Thyself unto me.

B. DINKAR

25. I am a sinful man

I am Thy loving one, poor and altogether sinful,
Hold me responsible for all my sins,
So that henceforth I may do so no more, Merciful One!
Forgive Thy Dinkar all his sins.
Thou who seest the inner desires, knowest everything.
Who aside from Thee is able to see all this?
Such are Thy profound and wonderful deeds,
Forgive Thy Divakar all his sins...
I am a sinner, Thou, Almighty One, art the Purifier.
The needy have no other saviour but Thee.
All this Thou knowest through the working of Thy soul.
Forgive Thy Divakar all his sins...

C. DÑYANESHVAR

26. God is beyond words

It is no praise to Thee to call Thee Father and Mother,
because it implies the defiling assumption of my being a
    child.
O Lord, what is the good of praising Thee as the Lord
when the lordship depends on another one's being a slave?
The praise of thy greatness is defiled by dependence.
If I call Thee pure spirit, O giver,
it would be as if driving Thee out who abides within.
Therefore, I see no way of truthfully praising Thee;
for except silence Thou dost not put on any other ornament.

D. KABIR

27. God is one

He is one : there is no second.

Rama, Khuda, Shakti, Shiva, are one;
tell me pray, how will you distinguish them?
By the One name I hold fast; this Kabir proclaims aloud.
In heaven, the realms below, in earth and waters,
one alone, Rama, watches over all.
Saith Kabir, I have searched in heaven,
And have seen none equal to God.
The one Name, like the trees of life, saveth mankind.
Then shall man know that one God is everywhere contained,
     and there is no second.

28. Where is God?

If God be within the mosque, then to whom does this world
     belong?
If Ram be within the image which you find upon your
     pilgrimage,
then who is there to know what happens without?
Hari is in the East: Allah in the West: Look within your heart,
for there you will find both Karim and Ram.
All men and women of the world are His living forms.

E. MIRABAI

29. Longing for God

Dear One, come and bestow Thy vision on me:
Without Thee, O Love! I cannot be.
As the lotus without the water, as the night without the
     moon,
So do I, Thy maid, feel without Thee.
Troubled and distracted, I move about night and day long,
While the pangs of separation gnaw at the heart.
The days pass without hunger and the nights go without
     sleep.
When the words do not come out of the lips,
What can then complain about, without speech?
Except Ye, O Lord, what other hope can I cherish?

Come, soothe this burning heart.
Come, be kind and meet me, O my Master.
Mira, Thy maid of Ages,
In supplication falls at Thy feet.

F. TAGORE

30. The following songs from *Gitanjali* may be found in the
    hymn book WITH JOYFUL LIPS (Bombay: St Paul's, 1999)

There are numerous strings (C4)
Accept me, my Lord (G5)
Where the mind is without fear (O1)
This is my prayer to thee, my Lord (P3)
Let thy love play upon my voice (P4)
I have come to thee (P5)

G. TIRUKURAL

31. True charity

To give to the destitute is true charity. All other gifts have
the nature of what is done for a measured return.

Even in a low state not to adopt the mean expedient of
saying: "I have nothing", but to give — is the characteristic
of the man of noble birth.

The power of those who perform penance is the power of
enduring hunger. It is inferior to the power of those who
remove the hunger of others.

The fiery disease of hunger shall never touch him who
habitually distributes his food to others.

Do the hard-eyed who lay up and lose their possessions not
know the happiness which springs from the pleasure of
giving?

Solitary and unshared eating for the sake of fullness of riches
is certainly much more joyless than begging.

H. TUKARAM

32. Why worry!

Birds and beasts gather up no store
yet the Infinite one protects them.
My poor weak mind, why are you always dejected?
Your only solicitude is about your food,
better than you are the blessed birds.
Mark certain animals in flood and field:
what food do they find!

(Luke 12,22-24; Mathew 6/26)

33. Wherefore fast?

Ah, wherefore fast or wherefore go
To solitude apart?
Whether thou joy or sorrow know,
Have God within thy heart.
If in his mother's arms he be,
The child knows nought amiss.
Cast out, yes, cast out utterly,
All other thought than this.
Love not the world nor yet forsake
Its gifts in fear and hate.
Thy life to God an offering make,
And to Him dedicate.
May, Tuka says, ask not again,
Waking old doubts anew.
Whatever else is taught by men,
No other word is true.

I. TULSIDAS

34. I am yours

I do not know the chants of the Vedas or Puranas.
I am ignorant of science or learning,

And unskilled in the techniques of meditation,
concentration and ecstasy.
Neither yoga, nor dispassion,
nor sacrifice are in Tulsi's faith,
In mercy and alms-giving am I wanting,
in iniquities alone replete;
Who is such a treasury of faults
and greed, infatuation, lust and anger?
The Dark Age has taught me all this filthiness.
I have but one faith, O Ram, that I am called yours;
Yours, O friend of the wretched, is the compassion,
and mine the wretchedness.
I call myself yours, O Ram, and sing of your virtues,
So that from respect of you I may gather a scrap or two of
     bread,
Ram, the world knows, and to my mind
it is my great cause for pride.
That I have acknowledged no other,
nor do I acknowledge, nor ever will.
I put no confidence in the elders,
nor trust in my own self;
You have made me your own
— this shall I fully know.

J.   THE LAWS OF MANU

35.   Almsgiving

A twice-born householder gains, by giving alms, the reward
   his meritorious act which a student obtains for presenting,
   in according with the rule, a cow to his teacher.

Both he who respectfully receives a gift and he who
   respectfully bestows it, go to heaven; in the contrary case
   they both fall into hell.

V. THE HOLY KORAN

36. God is One

Your God is One God; there is no God save Him, the Beneficent, the Merciful.

Lo! in the creation of the heavens and the earth, and the difference of night and day, and the ships which run upon the sea with that which is of use to men, and the water which Allah sendeth down from the sky, thereby reviving the earth after its death, and dispersing all kinds of beasts therein, and (in) the ordinance of the winds, and the clouds obedient between heaven and earth: are signs (of Allah's sovereignty) for people who have sense.

Yet of mankind are some who take unto themselves (objects of worship which they set as) rivals to Allah, loving them with a love like (that which is the due) of Allah (only) — Those who believe are stauncher in their love for Allah — Oh, that those who do evil had but known, (on the day) when they behold the doom, that power belongeth wholly to Allah, and that Allah is severe in punishment!

(Sûrah II, 163-165)

37. The All-powerful God

Allah! There is no God save Him, the Alive, the Eternal. Neither slumber nor sleep overtaken Him. Unto Him belongeth whatsoever is in the heavens and whatsoever is in the earth. Who is he that intercedeth with Him save by His leave? He knoweth that which is in front of them and that which is behind them, while they encompass nothing of His knowledge save what He will. His throne includeth the heavens and the earth, and He is never weary of preserving them. He is the Sublime, the Tremendous.

There is no compulsion in religion. The right direction is

henceforth distinct from error. And he who rejecteth false deities and believeth in Allah hath grasped a firm handhold which will never break. Allah is Hearer, Knower.

Allah is the Protecting Friend of those who believe. He bringeth them out of darkness into light. As for those who disbelieve, their patrons are false deities. They bring them out of light into darkness. Such are rightful owners of the Fire. They will abide therein.

(Sûrah II, 255-257)

38. The Annunciation to Mary

And when the angels said: O Mary! Lo! Allah hath chosen thee and made thee pure, and hath preferred thee above (all) the women of creation.

O Mary! Be obedient to the Lord, prostrate thyself and bow with those who bow (in worship). ...

(And remember) when the angels said: O Mary! Lo! Allah giveth thee glad tidings of a word from Him, whose name is the Messiah, Jesus, son of Mary, illustrious in the world and the Hereafter, and one of those brought near (unto Allah).

He will speak unto mankind in his cradle and in his manhood, and he is of the righteous.

She said: My Lord! How can I have a child when no mortal hath touched me? He said: So (it will be). Allah createth what He will. If He decreeth a thing, He saith unto it only: Be! and it is.

And He will teach him the Scripture and wisdom, and the Torah and the Gospel.

And will make him a messenger unto the children of Israel, (saying): Lo! I come unto you with a sign from your Lord. Lo! I fashion for you out of clay and likeness of a bird, and

I breathe into it and it is a bird, by Allah's leave. I heal him who was born blind, and the leper, and I raise the dead, by Allah's leave. And I announce unto you what ye eat and what ye store up in your houses. Lo! herein verily is a portent for you, if ye are to be believers.

And (I come) confirming that which was before me of the Torah, and to make lawful some of that which was forbidden unto you. I come unto you with a sign from your Lord, so keep your duty to Allah and obey me.

(Sûrah III, 42-50)

39. The Moslems and the Christians

Lo! We did reveal the Torah, wherein is quidance and a light, by which the Prophets who surrendered (unto Allah) judged the Jews, and the rabbis and the priests (judged) by such of Allah's Scripture as they were bidden to observe, and thereunto were they witnesses. .... And We caused Jesus, son of Mary, to follow in their footsteps, confirming that which was (revealed) before him, and We bestowed on him the Gospel wherein is guidance and a light, confirming that which was (revealed) before it in the Torah — a guidance and an admonition unto those who ward off (evil).

Let the People of the Gospel judge by that which Allah hath revealed therein. Whoso judgeth not by that which Allah hath revealed; such are evil-livers.

And unto thee have We revealed the Scripture with the truth, confirming whatever Scripture was before it, and a watcher over it. So judge between them by that which Allah hath revealed, and follow not their desires away from the truth which hath come unto thee. For each We have appointed a divine law and a traced-out way. Had Allah willed He could have made you one community. But that He may try you by that which He had given you (He hath made you as ye are). So vie one with another in good

289

works. Unto Allah ye will all return, and He will then inform you of that wherein ye differ.

(Sûrah V, 44,46-48)

VI. THE WISDOM OF THE BUDDHA

40. The Three Warnings

Did you never see in the world a man or a woman, eighty, ninety, or a hundred years old, frail, crooked as a gable--roof, bent down resting on crutches, with tottering steps, infirm, youth long since fled, with broken teeth, grey and scanty hair or bald-headed wrinkled with blotched limbs?

And did the thought never come to you that you are also subject to decay, that you also cannot escape it?

Did you never see in the world a man or a woman, who being sick, afflicted and grievously ill, and wallowing in his or her own filth, was lifted up by some people, and put to bed by others? And did the thought never come to you, that you also are subject to disease, that you also cannot escape it?

Did you never see in the world the corpse of a man or a woman, one or two or three days after death, swollen up, blue-black in colour, and full of corruption? And did the thought never come to you that you also are subject to death, that you also cannot escape it?

41. The Middle Path

Neither abstinence from fish nor flesh, nor going naked, nor shaving the head, nor wearing matted hair, nor dressing in a rough garment, nor covering oneself with dirt, nor sacrificing to Agni, will cleanse a man who is not free from delusions.

Reading the Vedas, making offering to priests or sacrifices to the gods, self-mortification by heat or cold, and many such penances performed for the sake of immortality, these do not cleanse the man who is not free from delusions.

Anger, drunkenness, obstinacy, bigotry, deception, envy, self--praise, disparaging others, superciliousness, and evil intentions constitutions uncleanness; not verily the eating of flesh.

Let me teach you, O bhikshus, the middle path, which keeps aloof from both the extremes. By suffering, the emaciated devotee produces confusion and sickly thoughts in his mind. Mortification is not conducive even to worldly knowledge; how much less to a triumph over the senses! He who fills his lamp with water will not dispel the darkness, and he who tries to light a fire with rotten wood will fail.

Mortifications are painful, vain, and profitless. And how can anyone be free from self by leading a wretched life if he does not succeed in quenching the fires of lust? All mortification is vain so long as self remains, so long as self continues to lust after either worldly or heavenly pleasures. But he in whom self has become extinct, is free from lust; he will desire neither worldly nor heavenly pleasures, and the satisfaction of his natural wants will not defile him. Let him eat and drink according to the needs of his body.

To satisfy the necessities of life is not evil. To keep the body in good health is a duty, for otherwise we shall not be able to trim the lamp of wisdom, and keep our mind strong and clear.

This is the "Middle Path", O bhikshus, that keeps aloof from both extremes.

The Blessed One spoke so kindly to his disciples, pitying them for their errors, and pointing out the uselessness of their endeavour, and the ice of ill-will that chilled their hearts melted away under the gentle warmth of the Master's persuasion.

42. Compassion

Whatsoever may be the cause of your suffering, do not wound another.

Follow the path of duty; show kindness to thy brothers and free them from suffering.

Whosoever hurts and harms living creatures, destitute of sympathy for any living thing, let him be known as an outcast.

Goodwill toward all beings is the true religion; cherish in your hearts boundless goodwill to all that lives.

The distinctive signs of true religion are goodwill, love, truthfulness, purity, nobility of feeling and kindness.

All beings long for happiness; therefore extend thy compassion to all. Hatreds never cease by hatreds in this world. By love alone they cease. This is an ancient law.

By inflicting pain on others, he who wishes his own happiness is not released from hatred, being himself entangled in the tangles of hatred.

Let him cultivate goodwill towards all the world, a boundless (friendly) mind, above and below and across, unobstructed, without hatred, without enmity.

VII. THE WISDOM OF ZOROASTER

43. Good and Evil

Ahura Mazda alone has created pairs of opposite characteristics in every walk of life in the entire creation. Ahura Mazda is capable of exercising and one of the two features depending on what He thinks fit to fulfil His eternal plan. Ahura Mazda made human beings in His own image. He has conferred upon them the power of choosing and exercising any one of the pairs of opposite characteristics.

Never be dispirited if your efforts to achieve something positive are thwarted by the forces of reaction. The greater your efforts, equally great will be the resistance thereto.

Life is one eternal struggle between the forces of good and evil. The true Mazdayasni is he who harnesses evil to subserve and furtherance of that which is good.

Ahura Mazda recognizes only two classes among mankind, the righteous, and the wicked. One who wishes ill of others achieves nothing worthwhile. No sooner he does one evil than one hundred evils recoil upon his own self.

44. The purpose of temptation

Just as gold needs to be put in a crucible before it can be freed from its dross, so a man needs to be put in a large crucible of the world's rough and seductive ways before he can rightly consider himself to be free of earthly dross.

No one can call himself pure until he has met and subdued the evils and temptations that beset his path, and tuned to nobler channels the passions with which he is born.

Seek not the innocence of a child, but seek the purity of a saint by casting off unrighteous thoughts, unrighteous words, and unrighteous deeds and holding fast to Righteous Thought, Righteous Words and Righteous Deeds.

What an ineffable loveliness comes over the face of an earthly creature when its spirit is attuned to the Highest, so that even a celestial being looks coarse and vulgar. Therefore, have a conscience finer than the finest hair, that would guide the mind and soul to abstain from evil and warn that crookedness never pays.

45. Spirit of Thanksgiving

Offer thanks to Ahura Mazda with every breath that you take in and with every breath that you let out, for, one never knows which will be the last breath.

Ahura Mazda requires only two things of the sons of men; first, they should not sin; second, they should be grateful for the many blessings He is continually bestowing on them.

Our thoughts fail to grasp the abundance of Ahura Mazda's unbounded bounty. Our words fail to give adequate expression to our feelings of gratitude. We owe Him a debt which we can never discharge.

I cannot rest in peace without Thee, O Ahura Mazda! I cannot enumerate Thy obligations. Even if every hair on my body becomes a tongue, I cannot express one out of the thousand thanks that are Thy due.

BIBLIOGRAPHY

Abhishiktananda, *Hindu-Christian Meeting Point* (Delhi: ISPCK, 1976)

Abbot Justin E., *Stotramala: A Garland of Hindu Prayers* (Pune: Scottish Mission Industries Co. Ltd., 1929)

Anand Subhash, *Major Hindu Festivals* (Bombay: St Paul Publications, 1991)

Bahadur Om Lata, *The Book of Hindu Festivals and Ceremonies* (New Delhi: UBS Publishers' Distributors Ltd., 1997)

CBCI Commission for Dialogue and Ecumenism, *Guidelines for Inter-Religious Dialogue* (New Delhi: CBCI Centre, 1989)

Chopra P.N. (ed.), *Religions and Communities of India* (New Delhi: Vision Books, 1998)

De Smet R, Neuner J. (ed.), *Religious Hinduism* (Bombay: St Paul's, 1996)

Pereira Theodore OFM (Cap), *Towards an Indian Christian Funeral Rite* (Bangalore: Asian Trading Corporation, 1980)

Pickthall Md. Marmaduke (ed.), *The Meaning of the Glorious Koran* (New York: The New American Library, Mentor Books, 1961)

Prabhavananda Swami, Manchester Frederick (transl.), *The Upanishads: Breath of the Eternal* (New York: The Vedanta Society of Southern California, Mentor Books, 1957)

Prajapita Brahma Kumaris, *One Week Course — for Attainment of Complete Purity, Peace and Prosperity* (Mt Abu: Ishwariya Vishwa Vidyalaya, 1996)

Prajapita Brahma Kumaris, *A Brief Biography of Brahma Baba* (Mt Abu: Ishwariya Vishwa Vidyalaya, 1984)

Rajagopalachari C., *Ramayana* (Bombay: Bharatya Vidya Bhavan, 1979)

Roy Dilip Kumar (ed.) *The Bhagavadgita* (Delhi: Hind Pocket Books (P) Ltd., 1976

Sarva Dharma Milan, *Way to Peace: A Compedium of Spiritual and Moral Principles of Various World Religions* (Lucknow: Sarva Dharma Milan, 1981)

Shilananda Swami, *A Rainbow of Feasts: An Inter-religious Appreciation* (Bombay: Better Yourself Books, 1994)

Suddhasatwananda Swami (ed.), *Thus Spake the Buddha* (Madras: Sri Ramakrishna Matth, 1995)

Surti B.S. (ed.) *Thus Spake Zarathushtra* (Madras: Sri Ramakrishna Matth, 1996)

Thomas P., *Hindu Religion: Customs and Manners* (Bombay: D.B. Taraporevala & Sons, 1960)

Vempeny Ishanand, *Inspiration in the Non-Biblical Scriptures* (Bangalore: Theological Publications of India, 1973)

Zacharias OCD, *Studies on Hinduism* (Alwaye: St Joseph's Apostolic Seminary, 1951)

Zaehner R.C., (ed.) *Hindu Scriptures* (London: J.M. Dent & Sons Ltd. Everyman's Library, 1966)